AF323817

THE GIFT AND ITS PARADOXES

Classical and Contemporary Social Theory

Series Editor: Stjepan G. Mestrovic, Texas A&M University, USA

Classical and Contemporary Social Theory publishes rigorous scholarly work that re-discovers the relevance of social theory for contemporary times, demonstrating the enduring importance of theory for modern social issues. The series covers social theory in a broad sense, inviting contributions on both 'classical' and modern theory, thus encompassing sociology, without being confined to a single discipline. As such, work from across the social sciences is welcome, provided that volumes address the social context of particular issues, subjects, or figures and offer new understandings of social reality and the contribution of a theorist or school to our understanding of it. The series considers significant new appraisals of established thinkers or schools, comparative works or contributions that discuss a particular social issue or phenomenon in relation to the work of specific theorists or theoretical approaches. Contributions are welcome that assess broad strands of thought within certain schools or across the work of a number of thinkers, but always with an eye toward contributing to contemporary understandings of social issues and contexts.

Also in the series

The Puritan Culture of America's Military
U.S. Army War Crimes in Iraq and Afghanistan
Ronald Lorenzo
ISBN 978-1-4724-1982-8

A Genealogy of Social Violence
Founding Murder, Rawlsian Fairness, and the Future of the Family
Clint Jones
ISBN 978-1-4724-1722-0

Liquid Sociology
Metaphor in Zygmunt Bauman's Analysis of Modernity
Edited by Mark Davis
ISBN 978-1-4094-3887-8

The Gift and its Paradoxes

Beyond Mauss

OLLI PYYHTINEN
University of Turku, Finland

ASHGATE

Published by
Ashgate Publishing Limited
Wey Court East
Union Road
Farnham
Surrey, GU9 7PT
England

Ashgate Publishing Company
110 Cherry Street
Suite 3-1
Burlington, VT 05401-3818
USA

www.ashgate.com

British Library Cataloguing in Publication Data
A catalogue record for this book is available from the British Library

The Library of Congress has cataloged the printed edition as follows:
Pyyhtinen, Olli, 1976-
The Gift and its paradoxes : beyond Mauss / by Olli Pyyhtinen.
   pages cm. – (Classical and contemporary social theory)
  Includes bibliographical references and index.
  ISBN 978-1-4094-5097-9 (hardback) – ISBN 978-1-4094-5098-6 (ebook) – ISBN 978-
  1-4724-0474-9 (ebook) 1. Gifts. 2. Mauss, Marcel, 1872-1950. Essai sur le don. 3.
  Critical theory. 4. Social sciences–Philosophy. I. Title.
  GT3040.P99 2014
  394–dc23

                                                                                    2013032357

ISBN 9781409450979 (hbk)
ISBN 9781409450986 (ebk – PDF)
ISBN 9781472404749 (ePUB – PDF)

Printed in the United Kingdom by Henry Ling Limited,
at the Dorset Press, Dorchester, DT1 1HD

Contents

Series Editor's Preface

Marcel Mauss—who was Durkheim's nephew, collaborator, and disciple—first published *The Gift* in 1925, but the book did not gain traction until the 1950s. Its insights are profound: that the social (not private) obligations to give, receive, and reciprocate are the fundamental building blocks of social solidarity. Mauss's ideas have been discussed primarily by philosophers, anthropologists, and intellectuals ranging from Jacques Derrida to Jean Baudrillard and his concept of the counter-gift. Ironically, Mauss's sociological theory of the gift was never taken seriously by sociology. For the most part, the discipline of sociology has thrown out Mauss and Durkheim with the bathwater of Talcott Parsons and structural-functionalism since the 1970s. This is the historical and cultural context for the publication of Olli Pyyhtinen's book on the gift in the year 2014.

Given this context, Pyyhtinen's approach to the gift necessarily begins with reactions by anthropologists, philosophers, and intellectuals to Mauss and gift-giving. Pyyhtinen admits that he is more of a critic of Mauss's theory than its promulgator. He questions—in the manner of philosophers—the meaning of the "object" in gift-exchange. He seeks out and finds paradoxes and ironies in gift-giving. For example, he analyzes the social type of "the parasite" as one who takes but does not reciprocate the gift. He points out, correctly, that there is a tendency for gifts to be regarded as gratuitous—with no obligation to repay or form social bonds. He discusses how gifts can be destructive and dangerous as well as good and as promoting social bonds. Pyyhtinen illustrates these and many other points by analyzing films, novels, and popular culture vis-à-vis the gift.

The outcome of his analysis is thought-provoking. For example, Mauss wrote that the "object" that the worker gave to the boss, corporation, and nation was ultimately his or her life. Therefore, Mauss reasoned that the boss, corporation, and nation owed a debt to workers that could never be fully repaid, but certainly included security, health care, and other provisions that are characterized today by some politicians as a socialist agenda. On the other hand, as Pyyhtinen observes, the so-called welfare state is regarded by many today as parasitic. Who is right? Pyyhtinen does not come down on one side or the other, and neither do I. The more important point is that this socio-political issue should be framed in the context of the social theory of "the gift."

Similarly, Pyyhtinen makes Mauss and Durkheim seem somewhat naïve in their arguments that the gift is never gratuitous, and always makes the recipient indebted to the giver—regardless of the "object" in question, and of the identity of the giver and recipient (ranging from nations and corporations to family members and individuals). Nowadays, gifts are often gratuitous, with no thought given to the effects on social structure. This is where Baudrillard's concept of the counter-gift is illuminating: the act of taking the gift as a form of sabotage to the social system which is perceived to disregard the individual totally. When neither side in the gift-exchange relationship feels an obligation to the other, the result is the sabotage of the counter-gift. For example, the Internet revolution has opened up the sphere of "sharing" films, music, and games that are the copyrighted works of artists and corporations. This "sharing" is labeled as piracy by those who believe that the objects in question are gifts to the larger community that obligate some sort of payment. But those who "share" gratuitously seem to believe that it is the artists and corporations who are the parasites and pirates. Again, discussions of this sort are typically not framed in the context of the theory of gift-giving, and perhaps they ought to be.

As I write this preface, much of the Western media is discussing the unprecedented spying by governments of individual phone records, emails, and other records that used to be considered "private." In the context of the theory of the gift, this unprecedented, neo-Orwellian spying is made possible not only by technology, but by the erosion of the idea of the gift. Phone records are considered to be the property of telephone companies, not of the individuals who made the calls, and various "contracts" with email providers have created the subversive reality that one's thoughts and messages expressed in emails belong to Internet providers, not their authors. One "gives" one's phone calls and emails to corporations and governments, with no clear idea of the obligations that corporations and governments owe to the authors of these "gifts." Of course, Mauss and Durkheim could not have foreseen our Internet, electronic, and nano revolutions. But one should perform the thought-experiment of asking what they would have thought of these developments vis-à-vis the gift.

What a wide gulf exists between the almost idyllic vision of the social universe envisioned by Mauss and Durkheim and our postmodern reality! Mauss and Durkheim idealized cooperation, reciprocity, solidarity, and other qualities that they understood to belong to the concept of society. These beneficial aspects of society were possible, according to them, because of social coercion, obligations, and innumerable reciprocal relationships. Today, their ideas have been deconstructed by many intellectuals as promoting dangerous and oppressive obligations and bonds. Far from viewing their theories as "gifts" to the community, they are perceived as dangerous, backward, and oppressive. On the other extreme, Baudrillard offers us a disturbing vision of a "society" of self-absorbed narcissists, plugged into their laptops, iPhones, and other electronic gadgets that feed us simulacra without origin or referent—and therefore, without obligation to anyone or anything. Other writers, such as Zygmunt Bauman, celebrate this vision as the freedom of "liquid modernity." The time is right for Pyyhtinen's book, which examines the idea of the gift critically, and urges us to re-examine past as well as contemporary theories of gift-giving, and, thereby, of the very idea of society.

Stjepan Mestrovic
Texas A&M University

Acknowledgements

I would like to acknowledge my debt of gratitude to the numerous friends and colleagues who have read either the whole manuscript or some parts of it. I wish to make mention especially of Jari Aro, Tiina Arppe, Dave Elder-Vass, Kai Eriksson, Kaisa Ketokivi, Kim Kullman, Turo-Kimmo Lehtonen, Seppo Poutanen, Teemu Taira, Jarno Valkonen and Soile Veijola. During its final stages the book greatly benefited from their careful reading, feedback, criticism and insightful comments.

In spring term 2013, I organised two reading groups around the first draft of the manuscript at the Sociology unit of the Department of Social Research, University of Turku. I am grateful to the students who took part. Their relentless questioning and the inspiring discussions we had were of inestimable worth for the editing process.

Sections from a version of Chapter 4 were presented to the Theory stream at the British Sociological Association conference in London, April 2013. The questions and comments received from the participants and audience members gave some good ideas for the fine-tuning of the chapter.

Neil Jordan, Jude Chillman and Matthew Irving at Ashgate are to be praised for tending to this project and for making things advance so smoothly. I also thank Claire Bell for the copy-editing and Ville Savolainen for compiling the index.

I wrote the book during my sabbatical year in 2012–13. The sabbatical was made possible by a research grant from The Emil Aaltonen Foundation, for which I am grateful. I also thank the Department of Social Research at the University of Turku for granting me the leave and for all the support.

For my son Eliel

Chapter 1

Genesis

In the beginning was the apple.

In the mythical origin of humankind, the birth of human collectivity is closely woven with a gift. The gift in question was an apple, a small, random, minimum cause, which nevertheless had the enormous effect: as the very first object and the very first gift, the apple created the very first human relation. In the myth of Genesis, on the arche scene of all the scenes of the Western world, a pome fruit growing in trees causes human collectivity to emerge, for the very first time in world history. The myth places the apple, the fruit of 'the tree of the knowledge of good and evil', in the green boughs of the family tree of humankind or, better perhaps, at its roots. The fruit[1] passed over from Eve to Adam, as the French philosopher Michel Serres (in Serres with Latour 1995: 200) notes, brings about the first 'relation of love, of disobedience, of knowledge, of risk, and of mad prophecy'. It was because of the apple passed around between them that Adam and Eve discovered themselves not only as sinful and mortal, but also as lovers. And they did not even commit gluttony, later specified as one of the seven deadly sins. A single bite was all that was needed, one for each, and Adam and Eve were banished from the joys of the Garden of Eden. Ultimately, by sinking their teeth into the juicy fruit and circulating it via their mouths and hands, they found themselves standing before a tribunal at once 'divine, moral, civil, penal', deciding about good and evil (ibid.: 201).

We can see the *pomum donum* surfacing across our cultural imagery. One of its manifestations is the teacher-gift. We know the cliché all too well: the obedient student bringing an apple to one's teacher. The apple is at once the archetypical teacher-gift and its symbol.To be sure, compared to the forbidden fruit, the teacher-gift involves a very different kind of apple, and a very different kind of relation, too. A token of love as in the case of Adam and Eve, perhaps, yet of a very different kind of love: platonic and unequal instead of carnal and equal. And not a relation of joint disobedience, but one of submissive obedience on the part of the giver. The offered apple appears here as an expression of complaisance rather than as that of rebellion: the student wishes to become the apple of the teacher's eye. No tree of knowledge to be seen here, either, nor any expectation to become as wise as one's master: but reminiscent of a believer, who, full of joy, bursts into praise in servitude to God, the student offers the apple as a token of pure gratitude to the admired omniscient donor, to a tribunal deciding about good and evil, for sure, yet not a sovereign one, no; rather a mediocre, almost impersonal

---

1   The etymological root of pome, like that of the French word *pomme*, is the Latin word *pomum* which means fruit.

disciplinary authority entangled in the vast network of the educational apparatus, with few formal powers of one's own.

The apple has travelled to fables, too. In a fairy tale collected by the brothers Grimm, Snow White, gifted by her beauty, is under three successive murder attempts by her evil stepmother, wedded by her father the King after Snow White's mother had deceased. (Or four in fact, if one counts the Queen's orders to a huntsman to take Snow White into the woods and kill her.) The stepmother Queen, jealous of Snow White for her beauty, wants to be the fairest of all and therefore Snow White must go. Three times the Queen disguises herself and three times she approaches Snow White, each time with different items. First, disguised as a pedlar, she goes over seven mountains to the seven dwarfs, knocks on the door and cries: 'Pretty things to sell, very cheap, very cheap'. Little Snow White, home alone, lets her in and buys pretty stay-laces. However, the disguised Queen laces so tightly that Snow White falls down as if dead. Assuming her to be dead, the evil stepmother flees the scene. When the dwarfs come home from delving in the mountains they nevertheless manage to revive Snow White by loosening the laces.

In the murder attempt number two, the Queen dresses as another old woman and again goes over the seven mountains and knocks on the door, this time pretending to be peddling good things, 'cheap, cheap!' But Snow White has learnt by now. She has grown suspicious about strangers, especially those claiming to sell good or pretty things on the cheap. So she puts her head out of the window and replies: 'Go away; I cannot let any one come in'. But the old woman does not give up. 'But surely you can look', persuades the old woman and offers to comb Snow White's hair. Of course, the comb is poisoned, and so again Snow White loses consciousness and the Queen quickly takes flight. However, also this time Snow White is saved by the dwarfs.

Finally, as her preparations for the murder attempt number three, the Queen prepares a poisoned apple. The apple is so pretty that anyone who would see it would lust for it, though so poisonous that whoever takes a bite dies. And, in the disguise of a country woman, she goes over the seven mountains to the seven dwarfs again and knocks on the door. Snow White looks out and says: 'I cannot let any one in; the seven dwarfs have forbidden me'. But unlike the previous women, this one isn't selling anything – she has come bearing gifts: 'It is all the same to me', she answers, 'I shall soon get rid of my apples. There, I will give you one'. However, being uncertain whether the *pomum* is a *donum* or a *dosis* of poison, in other words, whether the apple is a gift-present or a gift-poison,[2] Snow White rejects the offer. 'No', she says, 'I dare not take anything'. In order to convince Snow White of her bona fides, the evil stepmother, aka the Queen, cuts the apple in half, eats herself one half, white, and offers the poisoned red part to Snow White. This gesture finally wins over the trust of Snow White. She accepts the gift and

---

2   In the piece 'Gift, Gift' (1997 [1924]) Marcel Mauss famously draws attention to the two meanings into which the word 'gift' has diverged in various Germanic languages: *present* and *poison*.

takes a bite eagerly – and immediately falls into a deep dormancy, a slumber so deep that when the dwarfs arrive they cannot revive her, and thus assume that she must be dead. It ultimately takes a gratuitous gift of kiss from a charming prince – who, given that he has not developed an erotic attraction to corpses, cannot expect to receive anything from the assumedly dead beauty – to resurrect Snow White from her glass coffin in which the dwarfs have placed her.

What do these different apples have in common? As an 'object', the gift-apple is vague and ambiguous. Though it appears to be one and the same object – an apple – that is given in each of the above cases, each time the apple appears as something different. It alters its meaning in each relationship. The three apples provide us with three different kinds of objects: first, a forbidden fruit; second, a symbol or sign of admiring affection; and third, a dose of poison. So, what is it about the apples that permits us to designate all of them with the same word: 'gift'? While all the apples are no doubt given, they seem to involve three different kinds of relations of giving: in the first case, a relation of love mixed in with rebellious disobedience (where the gift simultaneously accomplishes togetherness between two and cuts their unit from others); in the second, one of subordination and superordination (where the gift marks submission to an authority); and, in the third, a relation of rivalry and betrayal (where the donor intends to defeat one's rival by giving her, literally, a poisoned gift).

The present book takes particular interest in this peculiar object. The concept of the 'object' is intended here in an open-ended manner, the notion of the gift being understood, to quote an apt formulation by Kieran Healy (2006: 15), as 'something much more general than a present wrapped up and given on a special occasion'. With regard to this, the book asks, what kind of things pass as gifts? What is the 'object' that we pass over from one to the other as a gift, give and accept as one? In other words, what is it that we actually give in giving; what is *the given* of the giving? At the same time, the book also asks what it is to *give* a gift. In several languages, there is a close semantic link between 'giving' and 'gift'. In French, for example, the noun *le don* ('the gift') is derivative of the verb *donner* ('to give'), and the German counterparts *die Gabe* and *geben* share the same root *geb-*.[3] Of course, the two terms do not collide in each and every use. When one gives one's word, when an army officer gives orders, a parent gives one's children into custody, a buyer gives as much money for something as it is worth, or when

---

3   Mauss remarks in *The Gift* (2008 [1924]: 78) the true abundance of derivates of the words *geben* and *gaben* in German. These include such words, many of them in themselves remarkably rich in meanings, as *Aufgabe* (for example, task, mission, assignment, job, duty, task, surrender, abandonment), *Ausgabe* (for example, issue, cost, expense, release, output) *Hingabe* (for example, commitment, dedication, devotement), *Trostgabe* (consolation prize), *Morgengabe* (morning gift), *Liebesgabe* (alms), *vorgeben* (for example, to pretend, to pass forward, to predefine, to give something, to stimulate), *vergeben* (for example to award (a prize), to throw away, to assign, to forgive) and *wiedergeben* (for example, to return, to pay back, to re-give, to portray, to reintroduce).

someone is given a beating, we usually do not think that what is 'given' in these instances is a gift. The book asks, what kind of giving does gift-giving involve? What kind of practices of giving pass as giving of gifts? When does the giving of some-thing amount to the giving of a gift?

With regard to the unavoidable link of giving to a given, Jacques Derrida has outlined the necessary conditions for every gift in a manner that I find instructive and substantially draw from in the book. According to Derrida, 'In order for there to be gift, gift event, some "one" has to give some "thing" to someone other, without which "giving" would be meaningless' (Derrida 1994: 11). In the book, I commence from the idea that the compound structure of someone giving something to someone else is indispensable for the gift. The following three chapters explicitly explore this threefold structure, with each chapter focusing on one of its components: while Chapter 2 asks, what kind of 'giving' the gift entails, Chapter 3 discusses the given 'thing' and Chapter 4 pays special attention to the recipient and the act of receiving. The subsequent three remaining chapters before the conclusion deepen and extend the question of the gift in relation to specific themes.

While the book takes a very straightforward interest in the gift itself by asking what it is and how it is conditioned, it also stresses the relevance and importance of the subject matter to broader issues. The gift is not just an anthropological curiosity, but it is crucial for the understanding of human life in general and, with particular interest for sociology, of social relations. We have not seized our life by our own effort, nor have we asked to be born, but our life is a gift, given to us by our parents (according to Judeo-Christian belief, ultimately by God), who themselves, in the same event, are *given* children. Giving birth is the proto-gift. It designates the beginning of the 'chain of gifts' in everyone's life (Godbout and Caillé 1998: 39). What is more, as beings we are thrown into the world, which in many respects precedes our own existence. Thus the past, as the 'already there' that conditions my being, who and what I am, is at once a *gift* and a *debt* (Stiegler 1998: 140). It is always inherited, it becomes *my* past only via inheritance, for 'my past is not my past; it is first that of my ancestors' (ibid.: 5). I have not lived it myself, but it is mine only as a given, as something passed over and down to me in the chain of generational succession.

In addition, as already suggested by the example of Adam, Eve and the apple, by looking at the gift we can get a hold of the birth of human relations and the constitution of human community or collectivity. And, against the disbelief in the existence of the gift today – because of the widely spread assumption that contemporary society is driven by production, economic exchange and accumulation of wealth – the gift constitutes still the very foundation of our relations and togetherness. The gift is part of the substance of social relations; it is something of which our relations are made. Various sociological studies have emphasised that giving, receiving and returning are deeply seated in the organisation of social life.[4] As Jacques T. Godbout

---

4   See for example Otnes and Beltrami (1996); Mortelmans and Sinardet (2004); Komter (2007).

and Alain Caillé (1998: 11) grandly put it, the gift 'does not affect only isolated and discontinuous incidents in social life but social life in its entirety. Today, still, nothing can be initiated or undertaken, can thrive or function, if it is not nourished by the gift'. In other words, the gift is much more than a specific form of relation – it is a precondition for the social or community as such. Interestingly, also the etymology of the word 'community' points to this direction. As Roberto Esposito (2010: 4) has shown, the term, derived from the Latin *communitas*, is traceable to the word *munus*, which consists of the root *mei-* and the suffix *-nes*. According to Esposito, the term *munus* oscillates among three meanings: *onus*, *officium* and *donum*, with the first two referring to the conceptual area of 'duty' and 'obligation', while the third denotes 'gift'. *Munus* designates a very specific, particular kind of gift, distinguished from the voluntary and spontaneous general meaning of *donum*. It means a gift that one cannot *not* give. Thus, in etymology at least, at the heart of community lies the obligatory gift. The constitution of community is intrinsically tied to the obligation to give.

House Guests

The book at the same time significantly draws from the work of Marcel Mauss and is in dispute with it. Mauss's *Essai sur le don*, originally published in 1923–24 in *L'Année Sociologique* and translated into English as *The Gift* in 1954, is without doubt the one single most influential work authored on the gift. It set the stage for basically all subsequent studies on the gift, from the field of anthropology to sociology, philosophy and literary criticism.[5] In the essay, Mauss takes an interest primarily in archaic societies and their forms of gift-exchange and examines both economic and contractual institutions. In its explorations of economic institutions, *The Gift* focuses geographically mainly on Polynesian, Melanesian and American Northwest systems of exchange, whereas the contractual institutions are studied by Mauss by taking the ancient Roman, Indian and Germanic legal systems as his object. Mauss was by no means the first one to study the exchange institutions of archaic societies. In fact, Mauss did no empirical work himself for the essay. On the contrary, *The Gift* draws entirely upon materials gathered by ethnographers, such as Bronislaw Malinowski, Franz Boas, John R. Swanton and Eldon Best. However, the novelty of *The Gift* was in what Mauss did with these materials. Firstly, none of the previous studies had attempted a comprehensive theory of the gift based on a careful comparison of the various forms and modalities of gift-exchange across the different regions. Alongside providing a detailed account the archaic institutions of exchange, Mauss reaches beyond the empirical to sketch a model of relations based on reciprocity. Secondly, Mauss approaches the archaic forms of exchange with a specific 'archaeological' aim in mind. He is set to find

---

5   See for example Lévi-Strauss (1987 [1950]); Firth (1959); Sahlins (2004 [1974]); Davis (1996); Godelier (1999); Godbout and Caillé (1998); Hyde (2007 [1983]).

the origin of economy, and he is convinced that it is in the gift that we discover it. Thirdly, by drawing on the archaic ethics of donation and generosity, and conforming to his social-democratic ideals of solidarity, Mauss tries to rework the basis of contemporary morality. From the archaic gift-exchange he aspires to find an alternative moral to the contemporary commercialised moral dominated by economic calculation. This is the political aim of *The Gift*.

In its focus on the gift-object, the book at hand is greatly informed by Mauss's work. For Mauss, gifts are all about objects that circulate. On the opening pages of his seminal and classical essay, he formulates his twofold question as follows: '*What rule of legality and self-interest, in societies of a backward type, compels the gift that has been received to be obligatorily reciprocated? What power lies in the object given that causes its recipient to pay it back?*' (Mauss 2008: 4) What Mauss is saying here is that no gift is devoid of obligations, but on the contrary any gift, no matter how voluntary it appears, is given and reciprocated obligatorily. What is more, he thinks that it is a certain property in '*the object given*' that forces the gift to be reciprocated. I claim that the importance of Mauss's essay lies significantly here, in the fact that he *takes seriously the gift-object*. However, paradoxically, it is precisely this dimension of Mauss's theorising that has been left in the dark over the years. Several anthropologists and sociologists after Mauss have stressed how the gift plays an important part in the organisation of social life. More often than not, this emphasis on the constitutive role of the gift to relations is, however, accompanied by an ignorance of the gift-object. It is typical of the studies of the gift to reduce the gift to a relation. For instance, John Frow writes in *Time and Commodity Culture* (1997: 124): 'Gifts are precisely not *objects* at all, but transactions and social relations'. To pick another example, Godbout and Caillé note in *The World of the Gift* (1998: 7) that 'the gift is not a thing but a social connection. It is perhaps the social connection *par excellence*' (ibid.: 7).[6] To me, these authors and several others are too hasty in substituting the logic of relation for that of the object or the thing. They take as a given what I think is precisely the problem, namely: *is the gift a thing or a relation*? Or, to put it slightly differently, I assume that the gift presents, in a manner perhaps more visible and explicit than any other phenomenon, how relation is transformed into thing, and thing into relation.

Mauss's account of the gift-object is supplemented in the book by using Serres's notion of the 'quasi-object'. I will examine the gift as a quasi-object in the Serresian sense, that is, as an object that is not independent of the collective but constitutes itself in the relations of the latter. For us, objects are always quasi-objects. As argued by Bruno Latour (1999a: 193) in a manner reminiscent of what Serres intends, objects can exist independently of humans only provided that they are completely 'detached from a collective life […] unknown, buried

---

6   For the sake of fairness, let it be noted, however, that in their book Godbout and Caillé also note, for example, that 'a present is an object that is linked to social ties' (1998: 8), and somewhat later remind that 'what is exchanged cannot be ignored' (ibid.: 24).

in the ground'. The gift is tied to social relationships so intimately that it cannot be grasped *as* gift completely in itself, without paying attention to the ties that accompany it. To do so would mean to miss the 'phenomenon of the gift', as also Godbout and Caillé (1998: 24) note. The gift-object is only there to be given and received. It gains its meaning, value and force in and through relations, based on who has given it and with what intentions, through whose hands it has passed (one can think of a heirloom, for instance) and what is the relation between the giver and the givee like – all these shape the gift in what it is and becomes. In fact, in many cases what are usually called the 'social' properties of a gift may matter more than its 'material' properties (even though the social and the material appear nowhere as such, as pure, but are everywhere muddled; all in all, the elements of each thing do not come from only two resources, but are much more heterogeneous). And yet, there is no gift-relation without some-thing being given and received. It is the movement of the gift which creates the bond between the donor and the donee. While being a relation, perhaps, the gift is thus also the origin of that relation. There is no gift collective, no community of gifts, without an object circulating through the collective. There must be some-*thing* that is given and passed on. Any community becomes visible in the objects circulating between its members. Accordingly, the gift is treated in the book as a 'luminous tracer' of social relations (cf. Serres 1995b: 87). It affords a view on the unravelling of the social.

While drawing on Mauss, the book is also essentially in dispute with him. The fact that Mauss takes reciprocity as his point of departure in his thinking of the gift, as I will argue in more detail in Chapter 2, underestimates the sacrifice and loss necessarily involved in the gift, in order for it to constitute itself a gift. I will claim that, as Mauss models the gift according to exchange,[7] in the last instance his account proves incapable of distinguishing the gift from loan and debt. Ultimately, for Mauss, the gift is 'given' by debt. He sees gifts as means of repaying debts: we give because we owe. In contrast to this, I will suggest that it is precisely in debt that the gift gets annulled. One of my main points in the book is that gift-giving is more elementary than, and even incompatible with exchange. One gives and the other takes; exchange, in itself always suspect to interruptions, is built on that, and thus comes only second.

In going against Mauss, my key interlocutors and accomplishes are Derrida and Serres. The publication of Derrida's *Donner le temps. 1. Le fausse monnaie* in 1991, which was translated into English as *Given Time: 1. Counterfeit Money* the following year, can be said to have sparked the growing philosophical in the

---

7 Drawing on Georg Simmel's conceptualisation of exchange in *The Philosophy of Money*, I consider the notions of reciprocity and exchange as interchangeable with one another. Simmel (2004: 82) proposes that 'most relationships between people can be interpreted as forms of exchange'. In the broad sense of the term, the notion of 'exchange' (*Tausch*) is for Simmel synonymous with that of *Wechselwirkung*, which translates as 'reciprocal causation', 'reciprocal effect', 'reciprocity of effects' and occasionally as 'interaction'.

gift as a theme (Schrift 1997: 1).[8] While *Given Time* offers Derrida's perhaps most extensive explorations of the gift, he varies the theme in a whole series of other writings. Among them is *The Gift of Death*, originally published as *Donner la mort* in 1992. Together with *Given Time*, it appears as an important source of information and inspiration for the present book. *The Gift of Death* significantly continues and complements Derrida's musings on the possibility and impossibility of the gift that appear in *Given Time*. However, as it weaves the problem of the gift to the thinking of responsibility and religion, the book is no volume 2 of the latter, but an independent study that adopts a perspective somewhat different from that adopted in *Given Time*.

Unlike Derrida, Serres has not authored a single book in his voluminous oeuvre that would take the gift as its primary object of study. However, as I will suggest in Chapter 4, his notion of the 'parasite' can be fruitfully employed in relation with that of the gift, especially to the end of undermining the exchangist perspective on gift-giving. Importantly, Serres's theorem of the parasite 'complements' the Derridean approach in that whereas Derrida focuses on the conceptual preconditions of the gift irrespective of its empirical actualisations, parasitism provides a perspective on the dynamics of actual social relations initiated by the gift. I hold that it is not enough to pay attention solely to the conceptual conditions of possibility and impossibility if we wish to understand the gift, but one has to consider the *real logics* of the social as well, for in social relations the gift hardly ever appears as pure. In addition, as already mentioned, I hold that when thinking the thingness of the gift, Serres's concept of the quasi-object offers itself as a highly useful tool that significantly complements Mauss's account.

Mappings

Almost all of the anthropological and sociological theories of the gift begin from the archaic, non-Western forms of exchange and circulate the compulsory examples of the *potlatch* and the *kula*, for example. While they are perfectly legitimate to do so, one may also ask whether one could not find the same features just by looking at the modern forms of the gift. This is precisely what Serres laments in Mauss:

> Now open *The Gift* and you will undoubtedly be disappointed. There you will
> find match and counter-match, alms and banquet, the supreme law which directs

---

8   Of course, in philosophy giving and givenness had already made appearance for instance in Martin Heidegger's explorations of the givenness (*Gegebenheit*) of being. According to Heidegger (1972), being is no thing, but an event: *es gibt*, 'there is' being or, verbatim, 'it gives' being. Even before that, Friedrich Nietzsche had written on the virtues and dangers of gift-giving in *Thus Spoke Zarathustra* (1999), where there is even one chapter entitled 'On the Gift-Giving Virtue'. However, it was to a great extent due to Derrida's reading of these authors that the theme of the gift in Heidegger and Nietzsche began to draw substantial attention.

> the circulation of goods in the same way as that of women and of promises;
> of feasts, rituals, dances, and ceremonies; of representations, insults, and *jests*.
> There you will find law and religion, esthetics and economics, magic and death,
> the fairground and the marketplace – in sum, *comedy*. Was it necessary to wander
> three centuries over the glaucous eye of the Pacific to learn slowly from others
> what we already knew ourselves, to attend overseas the same archaic spectacles
> we stage every day on the banks of the Seine, at the Théâtre Français, or at a
> brasserie across the street? (Serres 1982: 13)

In the following two chapters, I myself will make the – ritualistic – literary journey over the Pacific. This is simply for the reason that I honestly think it was only after reading Mauss that we were able to know that we 'already knew'. Nevertheless, instead of taking colonized others as its object, the present book places the contemporary, Western forms and practices of giving and receiving gifts under a critical magnifying lens. By so doing, it attempts something of an anthropology of ourselves and our present. However, what the book is primarily concerned with are *not* the particular, heterogeneous gifts given by people in their complex and messy relations in the reality 'out there' that is often elusive, indefinite and irregular, and not even with the more general systems of gift-relations (which were Mauss's primary object of study), but it takes interest above all in the *philosophical idea* of the gift. To be sure, these three referents to the term 'gift' are not completely apart from each other, but in practice they are often intermeshed. That holds true also for the explorations presented over the course of this book, as the notion of the gift will be explored and exemplified by discussing gift institutions and the gifts that people give to one another. Nevertheless, I will make an analytical distinction between them, that is, between the gift as a system or institution, the actual gifts intertwined with empirical relations and the abstract philosophical notion. Although the philosophical concept is, in principle, an adequate account of every gift ever given, it may nevertheless be inapplicable to this or that specific case of gift-giving. Thus, by focusing on the philosophical concept of the gift, the book to a large extent brackets the messiness of actual empirical relations, in which diverse gifts are placed in the ordinary everyday world.

Accordingly, instead of being based on empirical research – for example by reporting the results of interviews of people on why they give, who gives, what, when and to whom[9] – the book aspires to provide a theoretical account of the gift by engaging with existing anthropological, sociological and philosophical literature. However, in almost each of the chapters theoretical matters will be elucidated through stories, narratives, fairy tales, myths and fables drawn from the Western cultural heritage and modern art and popular culture, mainly movies and novels. My use of these materials is motivated by a belief that sometimes fiction may enrich and intensify concepts. That is to say, I feel that occasionally certain

---

9 For empirical studies of this kind, see for example Caplow (1982a and b); Mortelmans and Sinardet (2004); Komter (2005).

matters and phenomena may have been dealt with in stories in a manner that is subtler and more profound than philosophy or social scientific research can ever accomplish. However, I also believe that we still need philosophy or scholarship to tell us what it is exactly that is so profound in fiction.[10]

The materials used are thus meant to serve as much more than mere 'illustrations'. To a certain extent, the book is also *about* the movies, novels, myths and fairy tales discussed – they are interpreted from the perspective of the gift. However, rather than presenting a systematic 'analysis' of the chosen materials, I think with them. To me they contain important insights, ideas, narratives and impressions about what the gift is. And, it is because of trying to let them speak – and, literally, give – for themselves that I try to avoid the use of meta-language as far as possible. Consequently, instead of testifying to a pure voice of one's own, to a being-one, the book is populated by a multiplicity of voices; it is a being-multiple. It is not always perfectly clear, who/what *gives*: that is, is it the author, who provides the explanation, or the theories commented and/or the stories told? Thereby, theorising becomes woven together with storytelling. The act of weaving belongs to geography: the book maps the connections between ideas and narratives, concepts and myths, forges passages between people, places and times, as well as between different discourses. Just as any act of exploratory mapping, it simultaneously seeks to find and found, expose and relate, uncover what has remained hidden so far and tell us how is it that we are able to travel from place to place.[11] By being fixed in a position one is unable to trace what a gift does, unfold its effectivity. One has to follow, perhaps even emulate, its movements. Therefore, knowledge necessitates a journey:[12] paths, routes, planes, territories, maps, being on the move and getting lost.[13] True, getting lost is a prerequisite of finding. At times, in the hope of gaining new insights, I consciously allow the territories on which I travel to (mis)lead me to sidetracks, off the beaten track. All in all, instead of moving on fully ordered territories, here and there I plunge myself into the stories and write about them extravagantly and even excessively, without sparing my words and calculating how much I give. I am aware that this may give the literary journey an eclectic and disordered feeling, but I've tried to render the disorder somewhat rigorous, at least.

---

10   The idea significantly owes to my reading of the works of Serres. Besides the fact that his writings exhibit a liking for the use of stories, he has also explicated his reasons for making use of them for instance as follows: 'In some respects a well-told story seems to me to contain at least as much philosophy as a philosophy expressed with all this technical voluptuousness' (in Serres with Latour 1995: 24). Serres also remarks that, 'Blindly understood, narrative gets through where philosophy repeats and stagnates. *But only philosophy can go deep enough to show that literature goes still deeper than philosophy*' (Serres 1997: 65).

11   For mapping, see Abbas (2005); Olsson (2007).

12   See Serres (1997).

13   For cartographic reason as the map of human thought and action, see Olsson (2007).

In Chapter 2, which discusses the conditions of possibility and impossibility of the gift, I engage with the film *The Sacrifice* by Andrei Tarkovsky in order to elucidate the way the gift must always involve a sacrifice. Before advancing this thesis, the chapter introduces first the Maussian perspective on the gift. Mauss lays stress on obligations that pertain to the gift. According to Mauss, there are no voluntary and free gifts, but the gift is always marked by three obligations: the obligation to give, the obligation to receive and the obligation to reciprocate. For Mauss, these obligations always render the gift a form of exchange. After criticising Mauss for failing to acknowledge the crucial distinction or opposition, even, between the gift and exchange, I will turn to Pierre Bourdieu and his effort to reconcile the arrow of giving and the circle of exchange. Bourdieu argues that there is a way to bring the gift and exchange into unison. However, the chapter will note that, despite its merits, Bourdieu's analysis nevertheless regards the gift only as an element of exchange.

Chapter 3 focuses on the gift-object. It insists that each act of giving requires a given thing. Without some-thing that is given the act of giving becomes meaningless and impossible, for there is no giving without such a thing. The chapter begins with an explication of Mauss's interpretation of the *hau*, the spirit of things in the archaic societies studied by him. That will be followed by the criticism levelled by Claude Lévi-Strauss at Mauss's rendering of the *hau*. Lévi-Strauss accuses Mauss of being naïve and falling victim to indigenous beliefs. However, I will argue in the chapter that the problem with Lévi-Strauss's criticism is not only that he believes that others naïvely believe, but it also reproduces a total, sharp-cut separation of humans and objects. I will suggest that, with his account of the *hau*, Mauss avoided this separation and paid attention to how the collective existence of the people he studied was thoroughly mixed in with objects. Nevertheless, in spite of its merits, Mauss's conception of the active powers of objects ultimately remains unsatisfactory, because he sees their animating principle as something additional to the objects themselves. And, therefore, I see it necessary to complement Mauss's account with insights drawn from the work of Serres and the so-called new materialist philosophies. I will examine the gift as a 'quasi-object' in the Serresian sense: as an object that is not only a thing in the world out there but that also concerns the collective. Towards the end of the chapter, I will also discuss how the gift is connected to the problem of violence and claim that one of the contributions of Mauss's *The Gift* is that it ties the gift to the problem of the conditions of peaceful alliance and co-existence.

Chapter 4 explores the relation of the notion of the gift to that of the 'parasite' by Serres through the film *The Beach* by Danny Boyle. The parasite is a reverse of the gift and the communal duty and obligation to give. The parasite always takes, never gives. Nevertheless, the chapter suggests that the gift is anything but annulled by the parasite. The parasite does not contradict the gift, but is at once a condition of possibility and impossibility of the gift, in a sense perhaps even the system of the gift itself, or the kula ring reversed. The discussion of the problem of the gift and the parasite ties itself to three main points of the book. The first is the irreducibility of the gift to exchange. The notion of the parasite helps us conceptualise the interruption, disturbance and uncertainty pertaining to exchange. Second, while I emphasise the primacy of giving over exchange, I nevertheless hold that it is not enough to focus on giving alone, but it is crucial to pay attention to taking and receiving as well. The possession that I abandon must be accepted by the other for there to be a gift. Third, the gift-relation is not about equality and balanced exchange, but it is in perpetual difference from equality. We cannot avoid being placed in the position of the parasite through receiving.

Chapter 5 enriches the notion of the gift developed in the preceding chapters by drawing attention to how the gift is inclusive and exclusive at the same time. What is more, it will be discussed in the chapter how gifts not only create and nourish relations but may also threaten them. The focus on the dynamics of inclusion and exclusion complicates the image of the elementary gift-relation developed in the previous chapters. While the initial schema was triangular – consisting of someone giving some-thing to someone other – the chapter argues that the elementary gift-relation is more like a square or a cross, with four elements always involved. To every relation between a donor and a donee, there is an element excluded from the relation. The chapter explores the interplay of inclusion and exclusion mainly by way of two examples: blood donation and alms for the poor. The gift of blood is examined in the chapter as a quintessentially modern gift, for it is a gift to strangers. The other case, alms for the poor, is discussed by engaging with Georg Simmel's analysis of 'the poor'. Like the stranger, a more famous social type analysed by Simmel, the poor makes visible the boundary between the inside and the outside of the community. Towards the end of the chapter, I will also present a criticism of Mauss's view on social security as being essentially about gifts and generosity. My main point is that the welfare system and the system of the gift need to be conceived of as two different systems, for while the first is based on rights, the system of the gift is to be distinguished from any system of rights.

Chapter 6 addresses the complex relations of the gift to gender and economy. Through a reading of the novel *Story of O* authored by Anne Desclos under the pseudonym Pauline Réage, the chapter examines how economies are articulated in relation to the problematic of the gendered gift. Allegedly exhibiting misogyny and the objectification of women, the novel has evoked negative sentiments in readers. However, instead of repeating – not to speak of feasting on – the sexed violence of the novel, in the chapter I approach the book in conjunction with feminist authors Luce Irigaray and Hélène Cixous, together with Serres. I will argue that the novel is ultimately a book about economy: by its depiction of the obscene sexual relations that the main heroine is embedded in, the novel displays the law (circle) and basis (appropriation) of economy. In addition, the chapter sketches the particular form of property that the gift presents. The gift is a form of property that is not to be kept to oneself, but given away; gift property is not static, but on the move, in motion. Instead of accumulation of capital, the gift economy, if there is one, is about reversibility and recurrent annulment; instead of exchange value about bonding value; instead of neutral, impersonal objects about objects closely intertwined with the persons of the giver and the givee; and instead of the exchange of exact equivalences about reciprocal alternation in inequality.

Chapter 7 ties the possibility of the unconditional, gratuitous gift to death or, more precisely, to the *giving* of death. The chapter discusses two gifts of death, very different from one another. The first takes the form of self-sacrifice, that is, dying for the other. This will be discussed in the chapter through the children's book *The Brothers Lionheart* by Astrid Lindgren together with short novel *The Death of Ivan Ilyich* by Leo Tolstoy. The other form of the gift of death discussed in the chapter is euthanasia. It will be examined mainly through the film *The Sea Inside* by Alejandro Aménabar. In the chapter, the gift of death is tied to the question of care and responsibility for the other. It is suggested that the gift of death is a gift placed outside the economy, as it suspends exchange.

Ultimately, I propose in the book that the gift can only be understood through various paradoxes. Chapter 8 marks the end of the exploration by summing up the paradoxes of the gift that have come up in the preceding chapters. In addition, the chapter suggests that while the gift is any object and no object, it is possible to think of three more general forms that the gift may take as an object: token of exchange, sacred object and weapon.

Chapter 2
The (Im)possible Gift

The gift cannot be what it is, and it is what it cannot be.

We will have to begin again all over and ask: what is a gift? First of all, the gift only ever appears on the horizon of *the other*. The gift is either given to the other or received from the other. 'Gifts' to one*self* are nothing but a euphemism for self-reward, though this does not exclude the possibility of myself giving a gift to me (as an other to an other). For instance, one can think of gifts – such as frozen gametes – made to one's future self, who to some extent is indeed other than one's present self. In addition, the division of the psychic apparatus into different parts – ego, superego and id – as specified by Sigmund Freud could also allow, hypothetically speaking, for the possibility of the giver and the recipient being one and the same person.[1]

Furthermore, besides necessitating a givee, an other, let us tentatively state that a gift is anything given gratuitously, without guarantee and expectation of repayment. And for that reason the gift is deemed as being imbued with goodwill and generosity, even grace. As regards the gift, there is no price set on what is given, but the thing given is given unconditionally, for free, without explicit consideration or demand of recompense. We are not dealing with a gift whenever an explicit payment, especially a monetary one, is required for the given thing. When what is given is given only in exchange and thus for a certain price, the relation in question is not a gift-relation. Furthermore, in the gift, the giving is assumed to be free also in another sense, in being voluntary and spontaneous. Whenever the giving is obligatory, a duty, in other words, whenever one cannot not give, what we have on our hands is no longer a gift in the strict, absolute sense of the term.

However, at the same time we are all perfectly aware of several rules and norms that apply to the giving and receiving of gifts – and thus we know painfully well the care and skill required by the art of giving (and receiving). The most important of the rules and expectations involved in gifts is the *reciprocity rule* observed by several anthropologists and sociologists.[2] It is captured well by the Latin phrases *quid pro quo*, 'this for that' or 'a favour for a favour', and *do ut des*, 'I give you so that you will give'. While the gift is always given without setting a price on it, usually the recipient is nevertheless expected to give back, either an actual counter-gift that will compensate the giver his/her due or its symbolic equivalent by expressing gratitude, for instance.

---

1 On gifts to oneself, see also Schwartz (1967: 3).
2 See for example Mauss (2008); Gouldner (1960); Caplow (1984).

So, if this holds, the gift seems to demand at least a minimum of reciprocity. Mauss's *The Gift* is the most famous rendering of the gift along these terms. In the essay, Mauss shows how common wisdom is mistaken in assuming gifts to be free, disinterested and voluntary. He argues that no gift is given completely without self-interest. On the contrary, according to him, gifts always involve a wish or expectation of compensation: 'A gift is received "with a burden attached"' (Mauss 2008 [1924]: 53). Therefore, Mauss writes that although 'in theory, [gifts] are voluntary, in reality they are given and reciprocated obligatorily' (ibid.: 3). According to him, there is no gift without a bond, no gift that would not bind the donor and the donee. On this account, a gift that bears no obligation to be reciprocated would therefore be a contradiction in terms (Douglas 2008). Mauss remarks that not even the gifts given by Trobriand men to their wives, which Malinowski assumed to make an exception to the rule, were without ulterior motives. Not at all. They too were part of a system of exchange, as they can be regarded as a 'payment made by the man to his wife, as a kind of salary for sexual services rendered' (Mauss 2008: 93).[3]

From the predominance of expectations of reciprocity, some authors have concluded that the voluntary, disinterested gift is nothing but a deceit, an illusion (for example Blau 1964). While it appears on the surface that people are acting out of generosity and altruism, they nevertheless expect some kind of compensation for their effort and the sacrifices they've made. According to the utilitarian approach, the denial of self-interest in the gift amounts thus to a ritualistic masquerade.[4] If not for direct profit, in the act of giving one nonetheless wishes to gain something, be it power over others or social acceptance.

What are we to make of this? Is the gift, what, non-existent? Is gratuitous giving impossible, nothing but an illusion, either self-deception or a way of deceiving the other? Throughout the book, I will claim the contrary. I have mainly two reasons for this. The first is that the subjective experience of people may really be that they give out of generosity. They may perceive the gifts they give as being gratuitous and voluntary instead of being ruled by calculation. I hold that this experience is not a delusion to be dispelled. Instead of denouncing the views and beliefs of the so-called 'ordinary people', like the so-called 'critical thinking' has been prone to do over the years (see Chapter 3), it is important to take them very seriously. Second, thinking of the gift solely on the basis of exchange results in a conceptual confusion. While it may be empirically true that basically no gift can – totally and

---

3   Of course, as he makes such a point, Mauss seems to assume, rather problematically, that in sexual intercourse with their husbands the women only gave, without getting anything themselves, and the men only got some, without giving anything. For if the wives, too, took (equal) pleasure in sex, no extra-sexual 'salary' would be needed. Accordingly, it is as if the women possessed no sexual desire nor received any satisfaction in sex. Mauss's account of the relations of the Trobriand men with their wives thus renders the latter prostitutes of some kind.

4   The utilitarian approach has been discussed for instance by Caillé (2005), Godbout and Caillé (1998) and Komter (2007).

absolutely – exempt itself from reciprocity and return (insofar as giving involves reciprocity already by the very recognition and acceptance of the gift as gift by the recipient (Simmel 1992 [1908]: 663 n), in order to remain a gift, the gift must nevertheless to some extent free itself from exchange. Otherwise nothing would have been truly given (up) at all. In this chapter, I will focus on the conceptual distinction between the gift and exchange. But before we get to the gap between the gift and exchange as well as to that between the subjective and objective truth of the gift stressed by Bourdieu, let us begin by exploring Mauss's rendering of the gift as a form of exchange.

The Threefold Obligations of Gifts

In his study of the gift, Mauss emphasises the obligations involved in the gift. According to him, as was noted above, any gift entails the obligation to give, to receive and to return. Usually, our obligations attain their meaning only in relation to the rights of others. In the chapter titled 'Der Arme' in *Soziologie* and later translated into English as 'The Poor', Simmel writes that, 'Insofar as man [sic] is a social being, to each of his obligations there corresponds a right on the part of others' (Simmel 1965: 118). What is more, according to Simmel obligations are essentially derivative of rights: 'right is always the primary element that sets the tone, and obligation is nothing more than its correlate in the same act'. He suggests that it would even be possible to imagine a society without obligations. Interestingly, gift-exchange, however, seems to reverse this order. The three obligations pertaining to it – the obligation to give, the obligation to receive and the obligation to return – do not derive from any more originary or fundamental rights. On the contrary, in gift-exchange it is obligations that are primary. Gifts know of no rights of getting them. In principle gifts are unmerited: we cannot acquire a gift by our own efforts. Nobody is entitled to a gift, nor can we earn or deserve one. (We may become worthy of a gift only retroactively, due to the gift given to us, or on the basis of preceding gifts.) No matter how much we might arrogate, demand or wish for a gift, we may still remain without it. The gift is always '*bestowed upon* us' (Hyde 2007 [1983]: xiv; italics added). And, because of this, there is always also something intrusive in the gift. I would dare to claim that it is by no means an uncommon experience to feel – even despite immediate delight – that something unpleasant is being forced upon us when we are unexpectedly presented with a gift.

The only right acknowledged by the gift is that of bestowal, the *right to give*, to give away.[5] The individualism involved in the gift is thus of a very unusual

---

5   This is not to say that anyone is automatically considered eligible to give. Blood donation provides one example of this. Potential donors are screened by those who collect and process the blood, and such groups as drug addicts, alcoholics, carriers of HIV, hepatitis, malaria and some other diseases are excluded from donors (Titmuss 1970).

kind: instead of benefiting the one who has a right, the right involved in the gift is beneficial to the other(s). It concerns the flow of property away from the individual, not towards him/her (ibid.: 81 note). However, from the right to give it does not necessarily follow that gift-giving would automatically be voluntary or free. According to Mauss, in archaic societies gift-giving is obligated by certain rules and norms. A chief can only reproduce his authority of tribe and village by way of expenditure; he is thus obligated to give. He 'can only prove his good fortune by spending it and sharing it out, humiliating others by placing them "in the shadow of his name"' (Mauss 2008: 50). In the same way we who are working within academia are expected to share with our colleagues the good fortune that has been bestowed upon us for example in the form of a permanent post or a research grant by throwing a party or at least by serving cake and coffee.

Let us now look more closely at the nature of archaic gift-exchange explored by Mauss. Mauss calls the non-Western societies that he studies *systems of total prestations*,[6] for in them the *presetation* is linked to everyone and everything. In the societies in question the gift is a total prestation or a total social fact, meaning that all aspects of the life of the clans, from moral to economic, legal, religious, aesthetic and morphological, for instance, are organised in relation to and in accordance with gift-exchange (Mauss 2008).[7] They all come together in the phenomenon of the gift. Gifts permeate equally the life of community, the significant rites of passage in each individual's life course (for example birth, marriage, death), physiological phenomena, subconscious categories, as well as individual and collective representations alike (Lévi-Strauss 1987 [1950]: 27). The life of the societies is saturated by the exchange of gifts. The collectives exchange as much with each other as with past generations, nature and gods. It is characteristic of the pacts that they are not made by individuals but groups: by clans, tribes and families, which take part in the exchange either as represented by their chiefs, as whole groups or in both ways simultaneously. It is noteworthy that what is exchanged is not restricted to wealth or property alone. On the contrary, according to Mauss (2008: 6–7) valuables or economically useful things form only a portion of the things exchanged. The groups exchange with each other anything from tributes to entertainment and military assistance, and from rituals to ceremonies and dances. As Mauss puts it, 'everything – food, women, children, property, talismans, land, labour services, priestly functions, and ranks – is there for passing on, and for balancing accounts' (ibid.: 18). In the last resort, everything belongs to the 'inextricable network' (ibid.: 8) of exchanges:

---

6   In the English translation of *The Gift* by W.D. Halls, *prestation* is translated as 'service'. However, I will use the term 'prestation', which is not completely foreign to Anglo-American and Anglo-Saxon anthropological vocabulary. The main reason for using the technical term is that 'service' does not exhaust all the relevant meanings of the original French word. Besides 'service', *prestation* also means 'benefit', 'cover' and 'performance'.

7   Mauss took up the notion of 'social fact' from his uncle, Émile Durkheim, who discusses it notably in *The Rules of Sociological Method* (1982 [1894]).

> The circulation of goods follows that of men, women, and children, of feasts,
> rituals, ceremonies, and dances, even that of jokes and insults. All in all, it is one
> and the same. If one gives things and returns them, it is because one is giving and
> returning 'respects' – we still say 'courtesies'. (ibid.: 58–9)

What is crucial in the systems of total prestations examined by Mauss is the obligation to *reciprocate*. He also pays much more attention to it than to the other two obligations, the obligation to give and the obligation to accept. One must always respond to a gift one has received under the threat of private or public warfare, or at the expense of losing one's 'face' – one's honour, prestige or authority (ibid.: 7). A gift once received always needs to be repaid, debts have to be settled, scales must be balanced. If not, the chain of reciprocity threatens to be cut. According to Mauss, a gift creates a bond, a relation of reciprocity between the parties; they are bound to one another by the gift.[8]

From the Maussian perspective, the free gift is therefore a paradox. As the anthropologist Mary Douglas (2008: ix) puts it, 'the free gift entails no further claims from the recipient'. Insofar as the gift is always burdened with obligations, however implicit they be, a gift that refuses requital shoves the gift given 'outside any mutual ties' (ibid.), ultimately outside the gift process itself.

In the archaic societies, the reciprocity of prestations and counter-prestations is visible as a manifest circulation of gifts. This can be observed especially well among the inhabitants of the Trobriand Islands in the West Pacific. They have a system of circulating gifts called the *kula*. The *kula* is an extensive and complex form of ceremonial gift-exchange between different tribes, which has an immediate or mediate affect on the life of every tribe in the region. Mauss's discussion of the *kula* draws essentially from Malinowski's ethnographic studies. Malinowski leaves the term *kula* untranslated, but Mauss is confident that is means 'circle' (Mauss 2008: 27). All the tribes in the area participate in the *kula*. Mauss notes that it is as if all the tribes, their valuables, utility articles, food, festivals, services, even men and women, were travelling in a circle, 'following [...] a regular movement in time and space' (ibid.: 27–8). The circulation of the gifts is strictly regulated down to their course: while bracelets, for example, move regularly from West to East, necklaces go from East to West. In principle the gifts are in continuous circulation. One should not hang onto what one has received for too long a time, but one must pass them on within a reasonable time (ibid.: 30). The Trobriand people also distinguish the *kula* clearly from the plain 'economic exchange of useful goods' termed *gimwali*. Bargain is regarded as something completely inappropriate for the *kula*: of bargainers it is said that they conduct the *kula* like a gimwali (ibid.: 28).

Within two tribes of the American Northwest, the Tlingit and the Haïda, there appears a highly developed though rare type of total prestations, which Mauss

---

8   However, besides establishing a bond between the giver and the recipient, a gift may also, as we will see in Chapter 5, increase the distance between them and even cause their relation to disrupt.

names *potlatch* ('to feed', 'to consume') by employing the Chinook word (ibid.: 7). Besides, among Tlingit and the Haïda, examples of the potlatch have also been perceived in Melanesia and Papua. In addition, some intermediate forms have been met elsewhere, though everywhere else the basis of exchanges has seemed to be of a more rudimentary kind. In the potlatch institutions, everything is based on the obligation to reciprocity. One must always redistribute a potlatch in which one has been beneficiary (ibid.: 50). No one is allowed to get rich by the potlatch.

The salient feature of potlatch institutions is the rivalry and the hostility between clans. Accordingly, Mauss defines potlatch as '*total services of an agonistic type*' (ibid.: 8; italics in the original). The clans compete with one another by means of expenditure or dissipation for *mana*, honour. One is obliged to reciprocate on pain of losing one's *mana* (ibid.: 11). Potlatches are given in order to acquire honour and promote 'not only [...] oneself, but one's family, up the social scale' (ibid.: 48). The rivals aspire to humiliate others 'by placing them "in the shadow of his name"' (ibid.: 50).

It is as if something of the rivalry of the archaic potlatch had survived in the rap battle,[9] for instance, where two rappers compete with one another by using their verbal gifts in order to defeat the other, to 'freeze' their contestant. The improvised rhymes contain witty, bad-mouth punchlines that put down one's rival. And, much like in the potlatch, what is salient is not just the flattening of one's rivals, but the manner in which this is done. One proves one's superiority by consuming verbal and musical riches, by spending it out. The rappers try to beat one another by dropping rhymes better than those spoken or chanted by their contestants. This is analogous to how in the potlatch each party in its turn throws a festival that is more extravagant than the ones given before. The potlatch one has received always needs to be repaid with interest (ibid.: 53). Accordingly, Mauss describes the potlatch as 'a kind of monstrous product of the system of presents' (ibid.: 54), and, much along the same lines, Georges Bataille (1984 [1933]: 122) has famously called it a 'deliriously formed ritual poker'. The stakes are raised beyond all bounds. The rivals are ready to consume as much as it takes to 'flatten' one another. Mauss remarks that, '[i]n certain kinds of potlatch one must expend all that one has, keeping nothing back' (Mauss 2008: 47). At times the rivalry escalates into sheer destruction. In order to outdo their rivals, the parties may dispose of large amounts of property, for instance burn boxes of fish, whale oil, blankets, houses or even entire villages, kill slaves, nobles, or chiefs, break valuable copper objects and throw them into the sea (ibid.: 47).

The potlatch is at once a war and a game, a mixture of both. Mauss calls it for example a 'war of property' (ibid.: 47) and a 'game of gifts' (ibid.: 50). The Tlingit have a name for it that brings the two sides in unison: 'War Dance' (ibid.:

---

9   Another good example of contemporary forms of potlatch is to be found in cracker culture. Alf Rehn has shown in his book, *Electronic Potlatch* (2001), how cracker groups compete with each other in who will be the first to crack a software and consequently distribute the 'warez'.

142 note 141).[10] The potlatch is a war in that the desolation is indeed real, not only figurative or symbolic. People who lose in the potlatch, lose as they lose in war (ibid.: 47). Yet, the potlatch is also a game in that all obligations and debts derive from the rules of the exchange itself and nowhere else. A gift is at once a token of generosity and a *challenge*. The recipient takes up the gauntlet. The moment one has accepted a gift, 'one has accepted a challenge, and has been able to do so because of being certain to be able to reciprocate, to prove one is not unequal' (ibid.: 53).

Stressing the obligations pertaining to the gift against the altruistic notion has unquestionably been one of the most original and enduring contributions of Mauss's *The Gift*. According to Mauss, as we saw, every gift is governed by the principle of reciprocity: I give so that ultimately, at some point, someone will give me in return. Hence, the gift establishes a relation, a bond between the giver and the givee. While now I am the giver and the person I give to the recipient, at some point that person will become the giver and I the recipient. And, when that happens, then I will be obliged to repay what I receive, just as the person to whom I gave was obliged to pay me back earlier. As long as we wish to retain the relationship, the exchange will never come to a halt. There will never come a point when we will call it quits, but it is in principle a never-ending circle.

Gift Versus Exchange

To me, the major problem with Mauss's account of the gift is that he never comes to problematise the connection between the gift and exchange. He pays no attention, nay, gives no chance to the possible gap, incompatibility or opposition, even, between gift and exchange. Mauss never comes to ask, as Derrida (1994: 37) notes, 'whether gifts remain gifts once they are exchanged'. On the contrary, Mauss automatically assumes that there are gifts only in exchange – this is already betrayed by the subtitle of *The Gift*: 'The form and reason for exchange in archaic societies'. Or at least he takes an interest in the gift only as an element of a system of exchange. Besides serving him in his bid to trace the origin of modern economic exchange, the gift also offers him a form of prestation through which to delineate the foundation of social relations in terms of a general model of reciprocity.

Symptomatic of the permeability of exchange in Mauss's conception of the gift is the emphasis he places on the figure of the *circle* in his analysis. For Mauss, circulation is a self-evident part of the nature of gifts *as gifts*: 'Gifts circulate [...] with the certainty that they will be reciprocated' (Mauss 2008: 45).[11] Gifts tend

---

10   Mauss is citing Swanton here.

11   The circulation of gifts is taken as a given among others by Lewis Hyde. In *The Gift: How the Creative Spirit Transforms the World* (2007), Hyde discusses the matter at length under the section *The Circle*. In it, he remarks without hesitation: 'The gift moves in a circle' (Hyde 2007: 16).

to return to their origin, or at least be compensated by a material or symbolic equivalent, as one is always expected to pay back for what one has received. In any case, exchange implies circularity. In the potlatch, at least, as we saw, the exchange is *de jure* a never-ending process. But circularity applies to exchange also more generally. The 'metaphor of the circle', as Rodolphe Gasché (1997: 107) suggests, is even 'the very figure of reciprocity'. The participants condition each other and shift places: the former donor, now the creditor, puts in debt the donee, who will discharge the debt only by becoming a donor him/herself (and thus making the previous donor a donee and placing him/her in debt, respectively).[12]

By subsuming the gift within the order of exchange, Mauss ultimately subjects the gift to the logic of the debt.[13] For him, every gift is a means of paying and discharging a debt imposed on the subject. When discussing the notion of 'money' in an endnote, it is revealing how Mauss suggests that the gifts given in archaic societies 'served as a means of exchange and payment' and as 'instruments for discharging debts'. And, because of this, so Mauss argues, the archaic gifts can therefore reasonably be conceived of as first forms of money (Mauss 2008: 127 note 29). While admitting that their values were 'unstable' and thus could not serve as a 'standard or measure' of value, Mauss nonetheless concludes that 'these precious objects have the same function as money in our societies and consequently deserve at least to be placed in the same category' (ibid.: 127–8).

Therefore, the gift is always an economic phenomenon for Mauss.[14] Nowhere does he come to ask whether and how the gift might free itself from and stand in opposition to economy, but he always interprets it in the framework of exchange.[15] With regard to this, it is symptomatic that in *The Gift* Mauss for example notes of the potlatch that, 'If one so wishes, one may term these transfers acts of exchange or even of trade and sale' (ibid.: 48). So, Mauss seems to regard the generosity of gift-exchange as something simply *added to* trade. This is revealed by the sentence following up the one just cited. It reads: 'Yet such trade is noble, replete with etiquette and generosity' (ibid.). This does not seem to leave any place for generosity, expenditure and disinterestedness as nothing but a supplement for the mechanism of exchange; even the noblest of trades is still trade, only pursued by slightly other means. Consequently, it is as if the gift-relation became in *The Gift* a continuation of trade with other means.

---

12   Here I depart from Hyde (2007: 16), who states that 'two people do not make much of a circle'. This notwithstanding their exchange may nevertheless be *circular*. For more on the circularity of exchange, see Simmel (2004: esp. pp. 115, 119).

13   More for debt, see Graeber (2012).

14   This is not to say that the gift is nothing but economic for Mauss. As we remember, he examines the archaic gift as a total social fact at once economic, juridical and religious, for example. In relation to this, Baudrillard (1993 [1976]: 1–2) has argued that Mauss's essay to some extent nonetheless exhibits an economistic understanding of the gift.

15   I will discuss the relation of the gift to economy in more detail in Chapter 6.

For this reason, as paradoxical as it seems, there is ultimately no place for the gift – in the pure, absolute sense of the term – in *The Gift*. As Derrida notes in his famous criticism of Mauss: 'One could go so far as to say that a work as monumental as Marcel Mauss's *The Gift* speaks of everything but the gift: It deals with economy, exchange, contract (*do ut des*), it speaks of raising the stakes, sacrifice, gift *and* countergift – in short, everything that in the thing impels the gift *and* the annulment of the gift' (Derrida, 1994: 24). Mauss only ever speaks of the counter-gift, never of the gift itself, in itself. Every gift is *always already a counter-gift* for him.[16] I give because I have already received: 'by giving one is giving *oneself*, and if one gives *oneself*, it is because one "owes" *oneself* – one's person and one's goods – to others', Mauss (2008: 59) writes. Mauss himself emphasises the term *oneself* here, but it is the term 'owes' that is revealing in the passage. Mauss fails to distinguish the gift from debt and exchange. According to him, one gives because one owes; because someone else has given first. Hence, 'the donor is always already a *donee*' (Gasché 1997: 115); s/he is 'already in the game at the start of the game' (ibid.: 111).

However, it is important to draw a conceptual distinction between the gift and the counter-gift, for there's a deep asymmetry between giving and compensation. While the absolute, pure gift is voluntary, as one is *free not to give*, the same cannot be said of the counter-gift. The recipient is obligated to reciprocate; s/he *cannot not give*, without facing consequences, at least. This makes the counter-gift not only compulsory but also reactive with respect to the initiatory gift, which according to Simmel (1950: 392) 'has a freedom without any duty'. Following Esposito (2010: 10–11), one could therefore even say that the moment we receive a gift in a relationship, the possibility of the gift – the possibility of giving one ourselves – is withdrawn from us.

So, what I argue, basically, is that as he takes reciprocation as his point of departure in thinking the gift, Mauss ends up annulling the gratuitousness in and of the gift. This is not to say that his observation of the immanence of the social obligations to the gift in the natural societies were not valid. While it may indeed be empirically true that hardly anywhere is the gift not accompanied by moral enforcement, the obligations pertaining to the gift nevertheless should not and cannot be made into the conditions of the gift, as Mauss does. For even if it held that nowhere do we find the gift without an obligation to reciprocate, we cannot conclude that if there is no obligation to reciprocate, there is no gift. Obligations do not succeed in defining the *concept* of the gift. The gift is irreducible to them and to the reciprocity governed and characterised by them.

Don't get me wrong. I am not putting forth a reductionist argument about what the gift truly and genuinely is, nor am I saying, arrogantly, that Mauss does not know what he is talking about. My disagreement with Mauss and the Maussian

---

16 Revealingly, in the final chapter of his book Mauss himself writes that 'just as these gifts are not freely given, they are also not really disinterested. They *already represent for the most part total counter-services*' (Mauss 2008: 94; italics added).

tradition concerns not so much what the gift is – irrespective of the concepts with which we consider it – as the concept of the gift. I regard the concept of the gift with which Mauss operates as deficient, for it does not take seriously the opposition of free giving and exchange. Because of this, the distinction between the gift and debt/loan, just as that between the gift and the counter-gift, becomes close to non-existent in Mauss's theory.

And yet, the disagreement is not merely a matter of just providing the term 'gift' with an accurate definition. To paraphrase Nietzsche: instead of accepting the concept as a gift and at most merely polish and purify it, the notion of the gift must be invented and created anew.[17] Overall, to me, the ancient controversy between realism and nominalism appears as something of a badly stated problem. The 'gift' is neither an entity with some clearly identifiable properties, but a highly ambiguous 'object', which seems to evade clear-cut definitions and attempts at purification. Nor is the 'gift' merely a name for the discrete acts of giving, receiving and returning. There is a reality to which the word 'gift' refers, but it is not that of a completely independent entity. On the contrary, I hold that concepts strongly connect to what comes into existence with their use and to the practices of naming.[18] Or, as Gilles Deleuze and Félix Guattari (1994: 21) put it, concepts, though being 'incorporeal', are 'incarnated or effectuated in bodies'. And I sincerely believe that the potentialities and the space of possible ideas opened up by the concept of the gift suggested over the course of this book is richer than that proposed by Mauss.

Gift and Sacrifice

As he subsumes the gift to the order of exchange and under the figure of the circle, Mauss not only unintentionally disregards but even denounces unilateral giving without return and recompense. While in a sense it is perfectly justified to treat the gift in exchangist terms, insofar as most gifts are placed within existing relationships and thus almost always involve an expectation of reciprocity, the subjection of the gift to the order of exchange – in the very same gesture – nevertheless also nullifies the gift. For isn't the gift always in some respect annulled in and by circulation? Whenever the gift returns, it negates itself as a gift. In *Given Time* (1994: 7), Derrida notes of this the following:

> If there is gift, the *given* of the gift [...] must not come back to the giving [...]. It must not circulate, it must not be exchanged, it must not in any case be exhausted, as a gift, by the process of exchange, by the movement of circulation of the circle in the form of return to the point of departure. If the figure of the circle is essential to economics, the gift must remain *aneconomic*.

---

17   Cf. Nietzsche (1968: 409).

18   Following Ian Hacking (2002), this standpoint could be termed 'dynamic nominalism'.

Why is this so? Because wherever and whenever the gift returns (and/or brings back a profit), it is 'turned into its opposite' (Cixous 1986: 87). The 'gift is annulled in the economic odyssey of the circle' (Derrida, 1994: 25): when the gift is 'paid back', the gift-relationship comes to an end and becomes a pure circle of economic exchange, which involves the 'settling of scores' and 'accounting' (Godbout and Caille 1998: 198). As soon as there is a guarantee that a gift once given will be compensated, we are no longer dealing with the gift-relation, but with exchange.

The gift, in order to be possible as a gift, thus necessitates *loss*. If there is a guaranteed compensation for loss, in the strict sense there is no gift, for in such a case nothing would really have been given away. I hold that there always has to be a *sacrifice* of some sort involved; the gift has to remain without return.[19] In the absence of a sacrifice, the gift negates itself. When the gift turns out to be beneficial for the donor, the act of giving stops being generous and gratuitous. Instead, the given thing becomes merely a means of exchange, perhaps even an instrument for gaining profit. The act of giving must therefore not come back to itself; there has to be something in the giving and in the given thing, which is lost, something that does not return to the giving subject. For there to be a gift, the donor should not profit from the gift. Getting rich by donating is a contradiction in terms. If it is to remain pure the gift must interrupt the circle of exchange rather than be subsumed under it.

Let me be clear. What I mean by sacrifice is not the ceremonial offering, internally linked to violence involving a sacrificial victim, whether animal or human.[20] In anthropological scholarship and religious studies, sacrifice is typically understood as a religious rite the purpose of which is to establish or nourish a relationship with a divinity through an offering.[21] For the sake of the conceptual

---

19   In *The Gift*, Mauss sees sacrifice as a crucial motive in the practice of destroying at the potlatch, but he does not elaborate the notion nor does he grant it a central role in the structure of the gift. In contrast to this, in an early work *Sacrifice: its Nature and Function* (1964 [1899]) Mauss co-authored with Henri Hubert, he does provide a very detailed account of sacrifice. Interestingly, much in the same way that later Mauss was to interpret the gift, Hubert and Mauss consider sacrifice on the basis of debt. They picture sacrifice ultimately as a discharge of a debt to a divinity: a sacrifice is offered because of owing to the deity.

20   In *Violence and the Sacred* (1979), René Girard explores this linkage between sacrifice and violence in greatest detail and breadth. According to Girard, sacrifice is essentially a mechanism of replacement. By way of sacrifice, the community tries to protect its members from spontaneous, uncontrollable violence by channelling violence to a relatively harmless sacrificial victim. In Girard's reading, sacrifice is violence-turned-sacred. The English word 'sacrifice' is connected to the sacred also by its etymology. The term, first records of which date back to the mid-13th century, comes from Old French *sacrifise*. As for the French term, it is derived from the Latin *sacrificium* and *sacrificus*, 'performing priestly functions or sacrifices', which consists of *sacra*, the plural of *sacer*, 'sacred', and of the root of *facere*, 'to do, perform'. Hubert and Mauss (1964), too, note that to sacrifice is to render something sacred.

21   See for example Tylor (1871); Frazer (1976 [1890]); Hubert and Mauss (1964).

clarification of the gift that I am pursuing here, however, I will use the notion in a much more common and general sense, which does not confine it within religious rituals and unties it from relations between the profane and the sacred. Plain and simple, I consider sacrifice in terms of *expenditure*: as the giving up of something. To sacrifice is thus to dispose, abandon or surrender something. In line with established theories of sacrifice, I too stress that sacrificing involves destroying or killing,[22] though only in the sense that what is sacrificed always perishes for the person who gives it up. Sacrifice necessarily involves a loss.

So, to come back to the relation of the gift and sacrifice, let me repeat that in order for there to be a gift, the gift must involve a sacrifice. A gift always necessitates dispossession, the giving up of something, that is, giving with abandon. The giver must abandon the given, separate him/herself from it, otherwise no gift is given, as nothing is really given up. However, it is crucial to note that while the gift must always involve a sacrifice, sacrifice alone does not yet suffice to make up a gift. Sacrifice alone is not enough for a gift to take place. It actualises the gift only 'halfway'.[23] This is because the gift always assumes the *other* as its horizon of possibility, as I have stated above.[24] *The gift is a sacrifice offered to the other and for the other*, for the sake of the other. Otherwise the sacrifice only amounts to giving up, not to an actual giving (of a gift). If I just give up smoking, for example, there is no gift involved. However, if I do it for my family, the giving up becomes a gift.[25]

For a sacrifice to count as sacrifice, one must give up something valuable, desired or dear to oneself. Perhaps we could even say that sacrifice is inextricably intertwined with love. It is no sacrifice to destroy, abandon, put to death or get rid of something I hate. As Derrida (1995: 64) remarks: 'I must sacrifice what I love', otherwise it is no sacrifice. The link between the gift and sacrifice is established in an

---

22   In *The Gift*, Mauss, for example, uses the expression the 'killing' of property (see Mauss 2008: 142 note 141).

23   Jean-Luc Marion (2011: 73) notes the same thing though he speaks about the role of dispossession in sacrifice, not in the gift. My way of using the notion of sacrifice in the present text differs from Marion's more technical usage.

24   Here I depart from Hubert and Mauss (1964), who treat sacrifice itself as something always necessitating a (divine) recipient. It is not surprising, then, that they note that sacrifice is always also a sacrificial gift (*oblation*). They emphasise, however, that the reverse does not hold true, for unlike the sacrificial victim, not every sacrificial gift is destroyed (Hubert and Mauss 1964; see also Arppe 1992: 31).

25   Arguably economic exchange too is founded on sacrifice, though there sacrifice is not offered for the sake of the other, but for the sake of acquiring something one does not currently possess. In *The Philosophy of Money* (2004: 83) Simmel interprets economic life as being based on 'an exchange of sacrifices'. In exchange, one is able to attain a value only by sacrificing some other value. For Simmel, sacrifice is thus 'not only the condition of specific values, but the condition of value as such' (ibid.: 85). What importantly distinguishes the sacrifice encountered in the gift from the economic exchange of sacrifices is that in the latter, as Simmel notes, both parties win: each party receives more than s/he possessed before (ibid.: 82).

illuminating manner in Andrei Tarkovsky's *The Sacrifice* (1986). At the outbreak of an all-out nuclear war, the main protagonist Alexander (Erland Josephson) begs God to save the world from apocalypse. In return, he is offering to sacrifice everything:

> I will give thee all I have. I'll give thee my family, whom I love. I'll destroy my home, and give up Little Man. I'll mute, and never speak another word to anyone. I will relinquish everything that binds me to life if only Thou dost restore everything as it was before, as it was this morning and yesterday. Just let me rid of this deadly, sickening, animal fear! Yes, everything! Lord! Help me. I will do everything I have promised Thee.

Reminiscent of the story of Abraham in the Bible, who offers Isaac, his only son to God as a sacrifice (though to be replaced by a ram at the last minute) on God's command, Alexander is willing to sacrifice his family, his son, whom he loves; he is willing to dispose of everything. Both Abraham and Alexander would sacrifice out of love. And how could they not? They cannot but do so. Sacrifice must be painful to count as one; as said, to sacrifice what one does not love is not much of a sacrifice. However, the notable difference between the two men is that Abraham is ready to commit the monstrous, cruel, and hateful act of murdering his son in order to assume absolute responsibility, to fulfil God's will. God demands of Abraham that he sacrifice Isaac. His faith is put to test by an order to give the impossible, to give what he possibly cannot give, his son; and he is ready to give precisely that. The most unbearable thing. Alexander, by contrast, takes himself the initiative. It is *he* who makes an offer. It is he who *offers* the sacrifice. In fact, he does more than that: Alexander bargains with God. He proposes a trade-off: he makes the vow to give all he has in hope of a return, of a counter-service. I promise to believe in Thou if Thou promise to do what I ask of Thou – this is the exchange suggested by the praying person to God. Thus, it *pays off* to believe in God, if he fulfils the request.

The sacrifice that Alexander promises would be just as cruel as Abraham's, but wouldn't it also be a cowardly, most despicable act? After all, in the place of a more or less obligatory service not to speak of self-sacrifice, Alexander willingly offers to sacrifice his loved ones. Instead of proposing to put himself to death, to die for his loved ones, he would give his family, with the result that while the ones he loves would end up dead, he would only become mute himself. However, it is important to observe that Alexander is proposing no Faustian bargain here. He is not offering to sacrifice his loved ones for his own salvation. Alexander does express the wish to release himself from 'deadly, sickening, animal fear', but it can be argued that this is not the true recompense he asks for his sacrifice. He is indeed willing to sacrifice anything, but he is not offering it for his own sake. The release from fear would only be an effect. What he is, fundamentally, asking for from God is that God turn back time, prevent the apocalypse, 'restore everything as it was before, as it was this morning and yesterday'. What Alexander fears for is ultimately not himself, but for his loved ones and the world. So, the paradox of his offering, its madness and inconceivability, is that in order to save his loved ones,

Alexander offers his loved ones. He offers them to save them, for their salvation. He is willing to sacrifice the world to save the world.

Many critics have seen it as a sign of the film's narrative and logical incoherence that the vow to God does not coincide perfectly with the plot that follows.[26] After Alexander has proposed the bargain to God, he is paid a visit by Otto (Allan Edwall) later that night in his study. Otto, a postman and a collector of incidents, tells Alexander there is still some hope, one last chance to avoid the apocalypse and to reverse things to their previous state. What Alexander must do is to immediately go and sleep with Maria, one of the servant girls of his family. Otto asserts that she is a witch, 'of the best kind'. Alexander does as he is advised. He goes to Maria's house on the other side of the island and, by holding a gun on his head, succeeds in persuading her to have sex with him. When Alexander wakes up the next morning, he finds himself to be back in his house in his study. And he discovers that whatever either he or Maria did, it had worked: 'the electrical power has been restored and it appears in fact to be the previous day' (Moliterno 2001). However, despite things already having been restored as they were, Alexander nevertheless goes on to keep his side of the bargain with God: he sets his house in fire and becomes mute. At the end of the film, he is apparently taken to a mental asylum in a van that has come to pick him up.

So, there is an incoherence of some sort, at the very least, between the two sacrifices: copulating with the witch and burning the house. The one is completely redundant in the light of the other. Having already trusted his fate in the hands of God, the sexual intercourse with Maria the witch seems absolutely superfluous. And, the other way around, when everything had already been restored as it was, it does not seem compulsory for Alexander to make the other sacrifice anymore. Hence, as for example Johnson and Petrie (1994: 172) lament,

> … an unexplained double sacrifice is created when Alexander *both* sleeps with the witch, as encouraged by the new soothsayer, the postman Otto, *and* burns down his house and becomes mute, thus fulfilling his vow with God. This results in a frustrating absence of thematic and philosophical coherence that ultimately damages the film.

Tarkovsky did indeed make some changes to the original story line. In fact, in 1983, three years before the premier, the project was still titled *The Witch*. At some stage, he changed the name to *The Sacrifice*, and the apocalyptic scenario was added to it. However, is the double sacrifice present in the final film only due to confusion between the original narrative and the additional one? Is it a mistake, a slip? Was the sick artist, already diagnosed with terminal cancer at that point, getting sloppy in the editing stage?

While all this may be true, I also think that a more empathic interpretation is possible. What if we took seriously the double sacrifice in all its inconceivability?

26　　See for example Strick (1987); Johnson and Petrie (1994); Moliterno (2001).

It should be remembered to whom Alexander has proposed the pact: God. A transcendent giver is not like anyone else. In the Judeo-Christian belief, God is conceived of as an absolute Other. Alexander cannot possibly know God's will. He does not know whether God has heard him. To be sure, Alexander cannot even know whether God will or has fulfilled his side of the bargain. Even after everything has been restored as it was, it remains uncertain whether this is of the makings of God or Maria the witch. God may want to prevent the apocalypse or not, he may agree to what Alexander asks from him or not, but in no way is he obliged to decide in Alexander's favour. He does not have to explain his reasons, whatever it is that he decides. His workings and will remain always in secrecy and inconceivable to people. What an unjust pact. What is more, in the beginning of the film, Alexander appears uncertain, to say the very least, in his faith. In his encounter with Otto the postman he tells the latter that his relations with God are non-existent. In a sense, then, Alexander is torn between two conflicting sides, and it is because of that, one could argue, that he seeks help from two directions: Alexander the new convert calls upon God, and Alexander the non-believer turns to a witch.

All in all, to go back to the conditions of possibility of the (unconditional) gift, isn't the mad doubling of sacrifice precisely what unties Alexander's gesture, in either one of the instances, from simple exchange? When it comes to his pact with God, the sacrificing of the love for and intimacy with his wife by making love to the witch is completely redundant. And, as things had already been restored to their previous state, there was not necessarily any need for Alexander to burn his house and become mute anymore, but he did it anyway. Isn't it precisely this redundancy, this excess, which ultimately makes each sacrifice a sacrifice and also a gift? For wherever the sacrifice remains subordinate to the order of exchange, it does not amount to a pure gift, a genuine sacrifice. Only a sacrifice that exceeds reciprocity, obligation and return is a sacrifice in the true sense of the term. This is a highly important point, crucial for my whole argument in the book. I will let Otto the postman deliver my take-home message here. When Otto pays Alexander a visit at his remote house, in the movie, he gives his host a gift, an enormous, framed map of Europe from the 16th century, to congratulate Alexander at the eve of his 50th birthday. First, Alexander proclaims all the things one is supposed to utter when presented with a gift: 'But it's far too dear a gift. I don't know if I can … […] it's far too much! Too much, Otto!' Indeed, the gift is by definition 'too much', an excess, an extra, more than we deserve and more than we need, perhaps even more than we can handle, and therefore it might often seem preferable to refuse a gift than to accept one. However, then Alexander continues by making public what should remain in secret: 'I know it's no sacrifice, but …' (only the giver may say so, and s/he announces it without really meaning it). Otto immediately objects and, for a moment, becomes my key informant and, even more than that, a fellow philosopher and sociologist: 'And why shouldn't it be? Of course it's a sacrifice! Every gift involves a sacrifice. If not, what kind of gift would it be?' A gift that would involve no sacrifice would annul itself. Sacrifice is a precondition of the gift, and a sacrifice for the sake of the other amounts to a gift.

Of course, insofar as the gift can never remain without relation, it always also has a relation to the circle of exchange. There is no gift that would not weave a relation of some kind, no matter how abstract or anonymous, between the donor and the donee. Nevertheless, unless the gift gets annulled, it must eschew exchange. It can never be reducible to the order of exchange and debt. As Derrida (1994: 9) writes, 'wherever *time as circle* […] is predominant, the gift is impossible'. While having a relation to exchange, the gift, if there is any – that is, if there is indeed something like the gift and not only counter-gifts and instruments for discharging debts and getting even, which we more or less mistakenly and imprecisely call gifts – should itself remain outside the circularity of exchange. In *relation to* the circle the pure gift designates *exteriority*. The gift, as Derrida expresses it, is 'this exteriority that sets the circle going, it is this exteriority that puts the economy in motion. It is this exteriority that *engages* in the circle and makes it turn' (ibid.: 30). While perhaps initiating the circularity of exchange, the gift itself is not a point on the circle, nor it is immersed in the circular motion, but resists and even opposes it.

To be sure, such a relation of exteriority to the circle of exchange may indeed be impossible. It is quite possible that there is no outside to exchange, that it is not possible to keep a relation of foreignness to the circle, to remain a stranger to it. For does not exteriority designate nothing but a quality of the inside itself?[27] In this sense, the gift, as a pure gift, may indeed be impossible. This is the conclusion that Derrida reaches, and it is also his point of departure. According to him, the gift is '[n]ot impossible but *the* impossible. The very figure of the impossible. It announces itself, gives itself to be thought as the impossible' (ibid.: 7). The gift is the impossible, for it can never present itself as a gift. According to Derrida, it is crucial for the gift not to appear as one:

> *At the limit, the gift as gift* ought *not appear as gift: either to the donee or to the donor*. It cannot be gift as gift except by not being present as gift. Neither to the 'one' nor to the 'other'. If the other perceives or receives it, if he or she keeps it as gift, the gift is annulled. But the one who gives it must not see it or know it either: otherwise he begins, at the threshold, as soon as he intends to

---

27   It is interesting to note here that in *The Gift* Mauss is in contradiction with himself with regard to the ir/reversibility of the gift. On the one hand, Mauss is sure of himself that the acts of 'pure destruction' carried out in the potlatch defy all reciprocity. As he writes: 'The obligation to reciprocate constitutes the essence of the potlatch, in so far as it does not consist of pure destruction' (Mauss 2008: 53). For Mauss, in burning property or killing people, for example, the rivalry is no more 'a question of giving and returning gifts, but of destroying, so as not to give the slightest hint of desiring your gift to be reciprocated' (ibid.: 47). However, on the other hand Mauss notes that that 'acts of destruction are very often […] beneficial to the spirits', and they may also enhance the social standing of individuals and the family (ibid.: 53). Somewhat earlier, he notes the matter in even more explicit terms: 'The purpose of destruction by sacrifice is precisely that it is an act of giving that is necessarily reciprocated' (ibid.: 20). This would seem to suggest towards the impossibility of the pure gift.

> give, to pay himself with a symbolic recognition, to praise himself, to approve of himself, to gratify himself, to congratulate himself, to give back to himself symbolically the value of what he thinks he has given or what he is preparing to give. (ibid.: 14)

However, it is significant to observe here that to say that the gift – in the sense of gratuitous and free giving – is impossible is not the same thing as to say that there are no gifts (see Derrida in Derrida and Marion 1999: 59). Derrida is not referring here to the gift as an empirical phenomenon, but he only speaks of the concept of the gift. He is not saying that he is speaking about the gift though there is none. On the contrary, he is only saying that the gift is not to be reduced to presence. On the contrary, it must avoid being present (as a gift). And here we encounter a paradox, for sacrifice, so it seems, needs to be *felt* to count as one: can one sacrifice without knowing so?

For Derrida, the gift is a gift only provided that it is not recognised as one. It cannot be con-ceived nor per-ceived – intended any more than re-ceived – as a gift; and for this reason, so Derrida argues, the gift cannot be grasped fully in phenomenological terms.[28] The gift remains 'unpresentable': 'a gift that could be recognised as such in the light of day, a gift destined for recognition, would immediately annul itself' (Derrida 1995: 29).[29] It doesn't take a payment in kind for the gift to be annulled; it already suffices that the other gives back – or even that the giver gives him/herself – a *'symbolic equivalent'* 'in the place of the thing itself' (ibid.: 13; italics added). Consequently, the truth of the gift is simultaneously its untruth. The essence of the gift is that it must not conform to its essence.

To sum up, the problem with Mauss's account of the gift is, basically, that it is ultimately incapable of distinguishing the gift from loan and debt. Of course, Mauss seems to operate with an altogether different concept of the gift than I do: while the aim of the present book is to explore the possibility of irreversible, unilateral and free giving, Mauss gives primacy to the reversibility of exchange. In other words, whereas for Mauss reciprocity is what is essential in the gift, the book at hand insists that for there to be a gift, the gift must abhor or suspend reciprocity and return. However, in a sense Mauss is perfectly justified to treat the gift as a token of exchange, insofar as the notion of gratuitous giving did not yet exist for the archaic people, on whose practices he bases his own concept of the gift. The archaic people, as argued by Jean Baudrillard (1993 [1976]: 48 note 25)

---

28   In his attempt to reconfigure phenomenology and its possibilities, Marion (2002) disentangles the event of the gift from the experience of the subject. For him, the conditions of impossibility of the gift described by Derrida – no giver, no given, no givee – precisely make up its conditions of possibility in his analysis of the gift as 'givenness'. On the dispute and differences between Derrida's and Marion's conceptions, see also Moore (2011).

29   In the subsequent section I will return to this by briefly discussing the gift's relation to secrecy.

knew 'nothing of the gratuity of the gift'.[30] On the contrary, in the archaic systems studied by Mauss, every gift was compensated, and giving was unavoidably reversible.[31]

Nevertheless, Mauss gets into trouble precisely the moment when, based on the empirical material he utilises, he makes the effort to develop a general theory of the gift by reducing the concept of the gift to the archaic practices of exchange. It remains questionable to what extent the model of the archaic gift still holds today for the practices of *giving* in present societies. What is more, as long as we are interested in clarifying and delineating the notion of the gift, the Maussian edifice remains insufficient. *The Gift* remains blind to any possible gap, incompatibility or rupture between the gift and exchange, and therefore the difference between the gift and loan/debt becomes close to non-existent in it. Of course, Mauss is not alone in modelling gift-giving in accordance with exchange. It is rather quite common in sociological studies that the concepts of gift-giving and exchange are used interchangeably, without making any explicit distinction between them.[32] Nevertheless, the confusion significantly undermines the concept of the gift (see Marion 2011: 75 for more on this), because it nullifies, as I have argued above, the sacrifice, the giving up and dispossession involved in giving.

---

30   However, I disagree with Baudrillard on his claim that the idea of the free, irreversible gift is nothing but fiction, a *myth* invented by the modern political economy. According to him, 'The gift is our myth, the idealist myth correlative to our materialist myth' (Baudrillard 1993 [1976]: 48–9 note 25) First of all, it can be argued that the notion of gratuitous giving is irreducible to capitalism, but its roots go much further in history. Second, as becomes evident throughout the book, I hold that gratuitous giving is not merely a myth, but it does occur, even though it would be the occurrence of the impossible.

31   Accordingly, as a related point, while Derrida laments that in *The Gift* Mauss 'speaks of everything but the gift', a more affirmative take would be to say that in it Mauss speaks of *much more* than just gift-giving. The notion of the gift by no means exhausts the complex systems of exchange-relations imbued with obligations that Mauss treats in *The Gift*. All in all, it might be reasonable, as Marcel Hénaff (2010: 114–5) suggests, to distinguish gift-giving and ceremonial gift-exchange from one another (in his fantastic book, Hénaff focuses on the latter). As Hénaff puts it, 'What matters [in ceremonial gift exchange] is not giving per se but the launching or continuing of a procedure of reciprocal recognition'. It may indeed be that is not at all appropriate to consider this ceremonial reciprocity in terms of giving alone.

32   For just one example, see Sinardet and Mortelmans (2004). The authors repeatedly use giving and exchange synonymously. For instance, the very first sentence of the abstract to their article reads: 'At first sight, gift-giving looks like an altruistic exchange of objects'. Altruistic exchange is an unhappy contradiction in terms.

The (un)Truth of the Gift

Is there any chance for giving to be reconciled or coincide with the circle of exchange? In other words, can irreversibility and reversibility ever co-exist? In his account of the gift, Pierre Bourdieu (1990) insists that they can. Bourdieu suggests that the idea(l) of the gift as free and gratuitous is in fact a necessary condition for the functioning of gift-exchange. For Bourdieu, the failure of the objectivist analyses of the gift, such as Lévi-Strauss's structuralist approach, is precisely that they fail to acknowledge the experience of the disinterestedness of the gift as a crucial component of gift-exchange, as part of its nature. They do not take seriously the views of the agents, and therefore they 'ignore the fact that the agents practice as irreversible a sequence of actions that the observer constitutes as reversible' (ibid.: 104). The experience of the practice of gift-exchange does not respond to mechanical and reversible 'cycles of reciprocity' (ibid.: 98), but the gift is experienced and desired as disinterested, irreversible giving, as a 'refusal of self-interest and egoistic calculation, and an exaltation of generosity'. The gift is intended as gratuitous and unrequited as much in individual experience as in public judgment.

And yet, at the same time, 'objectively' seen, the seemingly disconnected series of acts of giving, receiving and returning do make up a cycle of exchange. Accordingly, Bourdieu argues for a truly objective analysis of the gift. Such an analysis must take seriously the ambiguity of the gift, its *dual truth* (Bourdieu 1997: 231). It has to account for how it is possible that objective exchange is experienced as a discontinuous series of gratuitous acts of gift-giving. The participants who like to think of the gift as free and generous nevertheless act in accordance with the logic of objective exchange.

Grounding his account on a theory of practice, Bourdieu suggests that there are two 'truths' of the gift 'quite opposite' (Bourdieu 1990: 107) to one another. The subjective truth of the gift is that it is free and irreversible. The gift is pictured in terms of disinterested, voluntary and generous giving, distinguished from interested, egoistic and strictly balanced exchange. And yet, the objective truth of the gift is reciprocity, that is, the 'objective "mechanism" of exchange' (ibid.: 105), interlocking the seemingly discrete acts of giving, receiving and returning. According to Bourdieu, for gift-exchange to be possible, a deliberate, conscious denial and oversight of the mechanism of exchange is presupposed. As he writes: 'Gift exchange is one of the social games that cannot be played unless the players refuse to acknowledge the objective truth of the game' (ibid.: 105). For Bourdieu, gift-exchange is even 'the paradigm of all the operations through which symbolic alchemy produces the reality-denying reality that the collective consciousness aims at as a collectively produced, sustained and maintained misrecognition of the "objective" truth' (ibid.: 110).

To say that the rules of the practice of giving cannot be made public is not the same as to say that people would be completely unaware of them. On the contrary, according to Bourdieu the disinterestedness of the gift amounts to a quite deliberate individual and collective self-deception. It is the conscious misrecognition of the rules of the gift that makes gift-exchange 'viable and acceptable' (Bourdieu 1997: 232). Bourdieu suggests that irreversible giving and reversible exchange can be reconciled above all thanks to *time*. This relates his account to that of Derrida's. Just as Derrida, Bourdieu stresses the significance of time to giving, but interestingly with a completely different emphasis and with the exact opposite results. Both stress that giving takes time and takes place in time. However, whereas Derrida thinks that wherever cyclic time prevails there can be no gift, Bourdieu suggests that it is the lapse of time between giving and returning that makes possible the deliberate misrecognition of the objective truth of the gift. For him, the co-existence of the subjective and objective truth of the gift owes its possibility to a lapse of time: 'the *interval* between gift and counter-gift is what allows a pattern of exchange that is always liable to strike [...] as *reversible* [...] to be experienced as *irreversible*' (Bourdieu 1977: 6).[33] The deferment of the return is an 'instrument of denial' (Bourdieu 1990: 107) that makes it possible to conceive of the self-interested and forced exchange as a series of disinterested and voluntary acts. Were the gift returned immediately, the practice would not amount to gift-exchange.

It is interesting to note that, just as for Derrida, for Bourdieu the gift is essentially bound to secrecy. For both, the objective truth of the gift must never be recognised. It must always remain a secret. In *The Gift of Death* (1995: 29–30) Derrida writes: 'The gift is the secret itself, if the secret *itself* can be told. Secrecy is the last word of the gift, which is the last word of the secret'. However, it is noteworthy that Derrida's and Bourdieu's conceptions could not diverge more on the question of what is the truth of the gift. Whereas for Derrida the objective truth of the gift is (impossible) generosity and goodness, for Bourdieu it is calculation and exchange. Thus, while for Derrida the truth of the gift must be equal to its untruth, to a non-gift (since the very identification and recognition of the gift as generous and good immediately suffices to annihilate the gift by forcing it under the order of exchange), for Bourdieu gift-exchange amounts to the successful co-existence of the subjective and objective truth of the gift, provided that the latter is never recognised in the light of day.

The problem with Bourdieu's theory is that while he stresses the problems resulting from stopping short at the objectivist model of the gift and insists on paying attention also to the subjective experience of actors, he ultimately gives the actors' views much less weight than the assumedly 'objective' gaze of the observing sociologist. He takes subjects' experience seriously only to the extent that he thinks it performs the function of obscuring the true nature of the gift, which he regards as a necessary precondition for the successful existence of the subjective and objective truth (Elder-Vass 2013). The actors' view of the gift as gratuitous giving is for Bourdieu a misconception of the objective truth of the

---

33   In the English translation of *Le sens Pratique*, titled *The Logic of Practice* (1990), an unfortunate mistake is caused by the fact that the terms 'irreversible' and 'reversible' have swapped places in the sentence (see Bourdieu 1990: 105).

gift as a form of exchange. He never takes seriously the possibility that the actors might in fact be *right* about the nature of the gift (ibid.).

On the face of it, Mauss seems to perceive the gift in a manner that stands in agreement with Bourdieu's subsequent view. After all, Mauss remarks in *The Gift* (2008: 4) that generosity and disinterestedness is just a form of 'polite fiction, formalism, and social deceit'. However, his account is not quite as economistic as that of Bourdieu's. *The Gift* does begin from the rebuttal of voluntary and irreversible gifts by arguing for the precedence of exchange and reciprocity, but towards the end Mauss increasingly stresses the voluntary nature of gifts. Thus *The Gift*, as Godbout and Caillé (1998: 197) put it, 'makes a sort of strange loop, like its object of study':

> At first [Mauss] sets himself in opposition to the idea of the arrow to counter the widespread view that the gift involves no return and so is disinterested. He insists that there is an obligatory return. Thus he plunges into the circle of the gift. Then he progressively distances from the gift as a type of economic exchange. To do this, he emphasizes the voluntary nature of the return – which leads him back to the arrow. (ibid.: 196)

The striking difference between Bourdieu and Mauss is revealed by their very different views on the ambiguity of the gift. While Bourdieu dissolves the opposition between free and obligatory in temporal terms and in practice, on a principal level he very much retains it in all its force – and thus downplays the significance of the actors' views and beliefs. Mauss, on the contrary, eschews the very opposition: 'These concepts of law and economics that it pleases us to contrast: liberty and obligation; liberality, generosity, and luxury, as against savings, interest, and utility – it would be good to put them into the melting pot once more'. Mauss argues that the notion of the gift prevalent among the Trobriand people, for example, is neither that of free, disinterestedness giving, nor that of utility seeking and interestedness, but 'a sort of *hybrid*' (Mauss, 2008: 93; italics added). For Mauss, then, the gift is a 'sort of' middle term, a third between categories. So, what is radical in his theory is that he suggests that we need to treat conjointly what we usually perceive in mutually contradictory terms: we need to think of the gift at once as voluntary *and* obligatory, free *and* laden with expectations of return, disinterested *and* interested.

For Mauss, then, the gift is irreducible to social deceit, hypocrisy and masked self-interest. In a sense, *The Gift* (2008) even reads as a *critique of calculative reason*. From the archaic practices of exchange, Mauss wishes to discover an alternative 'morality' of giving and solidarity as against utilitarianism and the calculative reason prevalent in modernity (I will discuss this at greater length in Ch. 5).[34] According to Mauss, the morality of the gift 'still function[s] in our own

---

34   In French sociology, the legacy of Mauss in this respect is most explicitly taken up and kept alive by the research group MAUSS (Mouvement Anti-Utilitariste dans les Sciences Sociales), which attacks utilitarianism within the social sciences and of economics in

societies, in unchanging fashion and, so to speak, hidden, below the surface'. He believes to have found in the gift 'one of the human foundations on which our societies are built' (ibid.: 5).

Nevertheless, to conclude, the problem with Mauss is that he does not take seriously the incompatibility of the gift and exchange. Expenditure cannot be reconciled with appropriation.[35] And gifts are primarily given, not exchanged. Counter-gifts do not follow gifts automatically, but the counter-gift remains, just as the gift itself, a surprise, an event. Thus, the arrow between the giver and the recipient is a more elementary relation than the circle of exchange. '[B]eneath exchange, there lies a gift', as Godbout (1992: 259) has argued.[36] Bourdieu does acknowledge the incompatibility of the gift and exchange, but he ultimately regards giving merely as a subjective supplement to the objective phenomenon of exchange, and therefore he never even comes to consider the possibility that the actors might be right in assuming the gift to be gratuitous. However, 'the phenomenon of the gift', as Jean-Luc Marion (2011: 76) has stressed, is 'much more than exchange'. If one considers the gift as solely an element of exchange, it is deprived of its excess and expenditure. Individual and collective self-deception of the objective truth of the gift is not enough but, as I have suggested above, there must always be a sacrifice, a loss involved in giving for there to be a gift. The gift must be beyond measure and the calculus of *do ut des*. It must perish for the donor. If the giver does not detach him/herself from what s/he has given, or if what is given comes back to the giver, nothing has really been given up at all.

In countering in this chapter the prevalent anthropological and sociological approach for which the gift is always already placed within the framework of reciprocity, I found it useful to draw on some of the insights by Derrida. Mauss's and Derrida's accounts are diametrically opposed to one another. Whereas Mauss's conception of the gift implies thorough circularity, Derrida insists that, for there to be a gift, the gift must separate itself from circularity. While exchange may indeed be the empirical truth of the gift, at the same time the concept of the gift is not reducible to exchange, for exchange tends to nullify the gift. Here we arrive at what is perhaps the most basic one of the several paradoxes characterising the gift: *the gift is neither reducible nor irreducible to exchange, and it is neither reducible nor irreducible to free giving*. While the gift, almost without exception, occurs within exchange, when it is explained entirely based on exchange, the gift is annulled, for

---

particularly. Alain Caillé, the co-author of Jacques T. Godbout in *The World of the Gift*, is the founder of the group. The problem with utilitarianism is, simply, as Godbout and Caillé (1998: 16) note, that it focuses 'systematically on the acts of the isolated individual, of the "ego"'. Thus it ignores the ways in which any act of receiving is always preceded and preconditioned by a giving. In Chapter 4 I consider this in terms of the relation of parasitism to the gift.

35   The relation of the gift to appropriation will be discussed in the context of economy in Chapter 6.

36   Picking up from this, Pierpaolo Donati (2003) emphasises that '*it is necessary to understand that exchange is based on free giving and not vice versa*' (italics in the original).

in exchange nothing is really given, irrevocably and without return. And, the other way around, when one looks at the gift solely in terms of free giving, dissociated from relations of reciprocity, one fails to see the circles of exchanges in which the gift takes place and to which it gives rise. Thus, the gift cannot be what it 'in reality' is (reciprocity/exchange), and it is what it cannot be (free giving).

Although claiming to be writing on the gift, ultimately Mauss never speaks in *The Gift* about the gift as such, but only about counter-gifts: every giver examined in the essay is already a recipient, every act of giving is already an act of reciprocating and every gift is a repayment. Mauss arrives at the game when it already has begun. Starting in the middle of things, *in medias res*, is a preferable strategy everywhere else apart from the thinking of the gift, for the gift, if there is one, is precisely (in) the beginning of things; it is the kick-off, the first mover. Perhaps, when studying actual things given in actual relations, where each action is an assemblage, a confederation of a multiple agents from various times and places and of various materials, it is even impossible to get to the beginning of the game, to the initiative that sets the game going and gives it its movement. Perhaps one indeed is inevitably always already in the game. However, without a gift placed, not within the game but in its beginning, there is no game at all.

Chapter 3

The Generosity of the Given

Without a given, no giving nor giver.

In the previous chapter, the discussion of the gift remained one-sided, at best, for the chapter treated the gift only in terms of giving, without taking into consideration what is given in the giving, that is, the 'given' of the giving. In this chapter, therefore, I will turn attention to this given and examine the gift as a *given thing*. Giving is inextricably linked to the given (the reverse, however, may not always hold true, as not every 'given' necessitates an act of giving).[1] Each act of giving implies a given thing, that some-thing is given, and every gift-exchange requires a token of exchange. Of course, as already suggested in Chapter 1, this 'thing' is not always necessarily a concrete, physical object. Besides tangible objects, there are also other kinds of gifts, such as care, hospitality, emotional support, friendly gestures, promises, rituals, dedications, invitations, feasts, dances, speeches and expressions of love. Nevertheless, it is important to note against the widely accepted view that gifts can in fact never be 'non-material'.[2] This is so for the simple reason that, in our being, we human beings as much as any other entities are inextricably immersed in various kinds of materials. Our actions and representations are not so much bestowed upon materials as being co-emergent with them. There is therefore also no relation between 'the social' and 'the material', for human relations are always already entangled with an array of heterogeneous materials. As Tim Ingold (2011: 24) elegantly puts it, 'human beings do not exist on the "other side" of materiality, but swim in an ocean of materials'.

In this chapter, my suggestion is that Mauss's *The Gift* is helpful in thinking our immersion in the variety of materials. It is well known how Mauss acknowledges the material world in his famous piece on the techniques of the body (Mauss 1973). Besides paying attention to the materiality of bodies, in the paper Mauss also discusses the 'instruments' or 'supplementary means' of bodily techniques. He remarks that various techniques presuppose an object: techniques of digging, for example, depend on the spade used, techniques of sleeping and experience of insomnia on the bed, techniques of sitting on the chair and the table and techniques of marching on the bugle. Further, in *Sacrifice: its Nature and Function* (1964) Hubert and Mauss interestingly stress that any relation to the deity necessitates things. What is more, Hubert and Mauss also suggest that things are not isolated

---

1   For the relation of givenness and the gift, see also Marion, *The Reason of the Gift* (2011).

2   For an example of such a view in sociological literature on the gift, see Komter (2005, 2007).

substances detached from humans and their relations: 'The sacred things in relation to which sacrifice functions, are social things. And this is enough to explain sacrifice' (Hubert and Mauss 1964: 101).

The world of materials is very much present in *The Gift* (2008) as well. Instead of assuming a rigid polarity between mind and matter, the essay shows with great lucidity – though most of the time only implicitly, as if without Mauss knowing it – how the representations that the people it studies have emerged and arisen from the ways in which they engage themselves with various materials. Mauss acknowledges the role of objects in group-making and facilitating associations by paying attention to how the economic and moral relations of the people, just as their relations with ancestors and gods, are mediated by objects. What is more, he also shows how these people come to know politeness, honour, power and obligations precisely through the copper objects, shields, blankets, arm-shells, necklaces, boats, boxes, eagle feathers, sticks, combs and bracelets that circulate among them. Generosity is always mediated by and manifested in some materials.

The intimate connection between giving and a given becomes evident in Derrida's formulation of the necessary conditions for the gift that I cited in Chapter 1, according to which there is no event of the gift, unless someone gives something to someone other. Furthermore, I would claim that the *what* of the giving is indispensable for both the *that* of the giving (*that* one gives; *that* there is a gift, an event of the gift) and the *who* of the giving (that there can be *someone who gives*). This is the generosity, if you will, of the given. Without the given, there is no giver and no event of the gift either, for there is no sense to giving (by some one to some one other), nay, no giving, without a given thing, without some thing being given, without there being some-thing to give. The given not only gives the giving its sense, but it also 'gives' or constitutes the donor and the donee: there is no giver or receiver before the occurrence of a giving of this given. The giver and the recipient must therefore be thought as being contemporaneous with the giving of some thing. This is of course something very different from Derrida's Heideggerian perspective and his critique of the philosophy of presence. Derrida's point of departure in his exploration of the gift is no real object that is present and appropriable, but 'being' (*Sein*) that gives and belongs to no one. In his exploration of the gift, Derrida commences from Heidegger's formula: *Es gibt Sein, es gibt Zeit.*

As already noted, Mauss clearly acknowledged the importance of paying attention to the given. Let us recall here the two closely intertwined questions that he asks in the beginning of *The Gift* (2008: 4): '*What rule of legality and self-interest, in societies of a backward type, compels the gift that has been received to be obligatorily reciprocated? What power lies in the object given that causes its recipient to pay it back?*' Mauss was confident that it is above all the indigenous Maori notion of *hau* that answers the latter of the questions. He explains that the *hau* translates as 'spirit'. It is tantamount to 'the spirit of things, and especially that of the forest and the wild fowl it contains' (ibid.: 14). Mauss suggests that it is precisely the *hau* that forces gifts to be repaid.

Next we will take a closer look at Mauss's rendering of the *hau*. The purpose of my exploration of it is not to explicate its particular thesis, but to use it as a point of departure to think the nature of the gift-object, the given thing, in more general terms, and sketch a stance that takes into account the role of the gift-object in the birth of the social relation and the collective. Mauss's view of the things passed on in the archaic societies as 'animate' will be discussed in connection with the more recent debates on the so-called *new materialism*, and in particular with the notion of *quasi-object* employed by Serres. Instead of invoking indigenous views on spirituality, I will consider the active, generative power of things in terms of their materials *and* their intermingling with relations. The gift is a not an inert 'object', but itself a social bond, a relationship instead of a substance residing completely in itself.

The *Hau*

Mauss's account of the *hau* depends almost entirely on a Maori text collected by the ethnographer and eminent Maori scholar Elsdon Best (1856–1931). The text is by Tamati Ranaipiri, a sage, who according to Mauss is 'one of the best Maori informants' of Best. Mauss suggests that Ranaipiri offers us 'completely by chance, and entirely without prejudice, the key to the problem [of the *hau*]'. (Mauss 2008: 14) Because of the central place of the text in Mauss's interpretation, it deserves to be quoted in full length here. I use the English translation by W.D. Halls to the 1990 edition of *The Gift*:

> I will speak to you about the *hau* … The *hau* is not the wind that blows – not at all. Let us suppose that you possess a certain article (*taonga*) and that you give me this article. You give it [to; O.P.] me without setting a price on it. We strike no bargain about it. Now, I give this article to a third person who, after a certain lapse of time, decides to give me something as payment in return (*utu*). He makes a present to me of something (*taonga*). Now, this *taonga* that he gives me is the spirit (*hau*) of the *taonga* that I received from you and that I had given to *him*. The *taonga* that I received from these *taonga* (which came from you) must be returned to you. It would not be fair (*tika*) on my part to keep these *taonga* for myself, whether they were desirable (*rawe*) or undesirable (*kino*). I must give them to you because they are a *hau* of the *taonga* that you gave me. If I kept this other *taonga* for myself, serious harm might befall me, even death. This is the nature of the *hau*, the *hau* of personal property, the *hau* of the *taonga*, the *hau* of the forest. *Kati ena* (But enough on this subject). (Cited by Mauss 2008: 14)

What makes the text intriguing is, first of all, the fact that it lays out, though only in a different register, the very same precondition of the gift that was discussed in the previous chapter: the thing given must be given 'without setting a price on it'. The parties 'strike no bargain about it'. Second, and what interests us the most here is that the text clearly indicates that, in the practices of Maori gift-exchange, it is the given thing itself, embodying the spirit of the donor, which obliges restitution. According to Mauss, 'What imposes obligation in the present received and exchanged, is the fact that the thing received is not inactive. Even when it has been abandoned by the giver, it still possesses something of him' (ibid.: 15). The *hau* is a 'special intrinsic power' in the things given, which 'causes them to be given[3] and above all to be reciprocated' (ibid.: 49). So, for Maori people, what obliges the receiver to repay the gift one has received is, above all else, the spirit inherent in it. It could even be said, as the elderly Maori remarks, that counter-gifts *are* the *hau* of the article that initiated the exchange. Counter-gifts, in this sense, are literally *return*-gifts: the return-gift, figuratively speaking, is the spirit of the first gift *returning to its point of origin*. Mauss notes that 'the *hau* […] wishes to return to its birthplace' (ibid.: 15).

What is especially interesting in the account of the *hau* given by Ranaipiri is the introduction of the third person. Mauss states that this is the only 'obscure feature' in the text (ibid.: 14), though he adds that in order to understand this intervention, 'one need only to say', as he cites Ranaipiri:

> The *taonga* and all goods termed strictly personal possess a *hau*, a spiritual power. You give me one of them, and I pass it on to a third party; he gives another to me in turn, because he is impelled to do so by the *hau* my present possesses. I, for my part, am obliged to give you that thing because I must return to you what is in reality the effect of the *hau* of your *taonga*. (ibid.: 15)

The quotation addresses an important point. The spirit of the given thing obliges not only the recipient in a dyadic relation, but it has a hold over anyone to whom the article (or its equivalent) is passed on. When a person passes a gift one has received from someone on to a third person, the return-gift given by the third person to him/her embodies the spirit of the gift that was given first. Adding the number of persons involved does not change anything. All the gifts that may follow are equally compelled by the spirit of the first gift and are counter-gifts, return-gifts, because of that. They all embody the *hau* of the first giver.

For Mauss, gift-exchange is thus essentially about things intermingled with souls: 'Souls are mixed with things; things with souls […] This is precisely what contract and exchange are' (ibid.: 25–6). For example, the system of gifts among the Maori people presents a 'mixture of spiritual ties between things that to some degree appertain to the soul, and individuals, and groups that to some extent treat one another as things' (ibid.: 17–18). The crucial thing here is that the bond arises through the passing on of the gift. And this is so, Mauss argues, precisely because

---

3   To be exact, the *hau* only explains why gifts are reciprocated; it provides no reason to giving or to receiving (see also Sahlins [1974] 2004: 150). Accordingly, with reference to the discussion in Chapter 2, the above quotation is yet another example indicating that for Mauss, every gift is always already a counter-gift.

of the spirit inhabiting the given thing. As he notes of legal ties in the Maori juridical system: 'In Maori law, the legal tie, a tie occurring through things, is one between souls, because the thing itself possesses a soul, is of the soul' (ibid.: 16). Unlike money, as it is commonly perceived, the gift is not neutral, colourless and detached from the personality of the one who gives it,[4] but it remains bound to the giver. The gift is shadowed by the giver, who is shadowed by the gift.

If the gift is never completely detached from the person of the giver, but rather mixed with it, it follows that to give something to someone is always at the same time to give *oneself*, or *of oneself*. It is to make oneself into a gift; by giving some-thing as a gift one gives oneself, as a gift, makes a gift out of oneself. As Mauss puts it: '[T] o make a gift of something to someone is to make a present of some part of oneself' (ibid.: 16). In other words, 'by giving one is giving *oneself*', as Mauss notes later in the essay (ibid.: 59). This means, at the same time, that by accepting a gift one is willing to accept to become subjected to the giver in some respect, that the giver will exert a hold over you: 'to accept something from someone is to accept some part of his spiritual essence, of his soul' (ibid.: 16). However, the paradoxical nature of the gift prevails also here. While the gift to a certain extent always remains attached to the giver, it must equally detach itself from him/her. Otherwise there is no sacrifice, no giving up. The presence of the giver must withdraw from the given in order for I who receive it to be able to make it my own (Marion 2011: 77). Otherwise the object I receive will remain dirty, because of still belonging to the person who gave it to me and thus impossible for me to appropriate it (for more on the gesture of appropriation see Chapter 6). Therefore, giving embodies, paradoxically, a simultaneous loss of self and expansion of self: while there is real loss in the abandonment of the object (otherwise the gift would negate itself; the possession needs to be given up in order to appear as a gift), the given thing nevertheless remains symbolically inalienable from the person of the giver (and gives, therefore, the donor a hold over the donee). The gift is at once alienable and inalienable.[5]

Victim of Naïve Beliefs?

Much criticism has been levelled at Mauss's rendering of the *hau* over the years. That launched by Lévi-Strauss in not only among the very first readings of *The Gift*, but it is also definitely the most influential. For this reason it deserves to be examined more closely in what follows. Lévi-Strauss's critique also expresses an ignorance of the crucial role of objects in and for social relations that is typical of modern thought.

---

4   See, however, Viviana Zelizer (1994), who shows that not even money is a general, impersonal, neutral and homogenous means, but there are multiple moneys, as people give different meanings to it and use it in various ways depending on the relations they are involved in.

5   For more on gifts simultaneously given and kept, see Weiner (1992) and Godelier (1999).

According to Lévi-Strauss, the great contribution of Mauss's essay lies in its effort to go beyond the empirical observations to reach a deeper reality. Analysing the gift as a 'total social fact', which designates a totality of phenomena at once economic, juridical, religious, political, aesthetic and morphological, for instance, *The Gift* attempts an explanation of behaviour in terms of a collective unconscious, society's unconscious rules of exchange. Nevertheless, Lévi-Strauss (1987 [1950]: 45) suggests that, 'like Moses conducting his people all the way to a promised land whose splendour he would never behold', Mauss points towards structuralism without fully realising to do so. He stops halfway with his theory. He does not do as he tells others to do. For Lévi-Strauss, while showing the way beyond positivism, Mauss remained something of a positivist himself.

Therefore, for Lévi-Strauss, Mauss's essay ultimately amounts to a failure, despite its enormous potentiality. With all the right elements at hand, 'Mauss might have been expected to produce the twentieth-century social sciences' *Novum Organum*' (ibid.: 45). That is to say, *The Gift* had all the potential for creating an entirely new approach for the social sciences, akin to the masterpiece by Francis Bacon in 1620 in which he develops a new scientific method. But no, for the great disappointment of Lévi-Strauss. Mauss only manages to come up with a ramshackle construction consisting of some fragmented bits and pieces without accomplishing any comprehensive theory of society or the social.

For Lévi-Strauss, Mauss's failure stems from his unsatisfactory conceptualisation of exchange. While in his treatment Mauss seems to be guided by the notion of exchange as the 'common denominator of a large number of apparently heterogeneous social activities' (ibid.: 45–6), he nevertheless fails to acknowledge it as a 'primary, fundamental phenomenon' (ibid.: 47). Instead, he adopts the indigenous notion of *hau*:

> [I]n the *Essai sur le don*, Mauss strives to reconstruct a whole out of parts; and as that is manifestly not possible, he has to add to the mixture an additional quantity which gives him the illusion of squaring his account. This quantity is *hau*. Are we not dealing with a mystification, an effect quite often produced in the minds of ethnographers by indigenous people? (ibid.: 47)

As we can see, here the otherwise laudatory tone of Lévi-Strauss's piece changes. The accusations presented by him are harsh. They cannot be lightly dismissed, far from it. Lévi-Strauss reproaches Mauss not only for being too empirical but – what is even worse – also for being uncritical. That is, it is as if it was not enough that Mauss fails to grasp the underlying structure of exchange, as he sticks only to what he can observe (that is, the assumedly discrete obligations to give, receive and return). On top of that, he also falls victim to indigenous beliefs – the ones he was supposed to study! Thus, the ultimate sin and capital crime of Mauss in the eyes of Lévi-Strauss is his naïveté. He relies on indigenous reasoning, and rather uncritically at that. In Mauss, the mystical notion used by indigenous people to explain the obligations to give, receive and reciprocate is raised to the position of a scientific explanation. How could such naïveté not degrade science?

According to Lévi-Strauss, the *hau* is unable to provide a reason for exchange. He argues that it does not exist objectively. Instead of really explaining exchange, the *hau* is only what indigenous people think explains exchange: '*Hau* is not the ultimate explanation for exchange; it is the conscious form whereby men of a given society [...] apprehended an unconscious necessity whose explanation lies elsewhere' (ibid.: 48). Lévi-Strauss suggests that, by relying on the phantasmatic theories of indigenous people, which explain the gift in terms of some mysterious, animistic spirit occupying the subject, Mauss fails to see that the obligations to give, to receive and to return comprise nothing but parts of the total structure of exchange, which forms an underlying whole. According to Lévi-Strauss, an 'objective critique' alone will enable us to 'reach the underlying reality' that is the unconscious necessity of exchange (ibid.: 49).

In a sense, what this critique aimed at was some sort of 'disenchantment' of thought. It sought to shatter ill-founded beliefs and base our explanations on reason. In a dramatic tone, Lévi-Strauss describes the threat posed to sociology we must protect ourselves from:

> [W]e would risk committing sociology to a dangerous path: even a path of destruction, if we [...] reduced social reality to the conception that man – savage man, even – has of it. [...] Then ethnography would dissolve into a verbose phenomenology, a false naïve mixture in which the apparent obscurities of indigenous thinking would only be brought to the forefront to cover the confusions of the ethnographer, which would otherwise be obvious. (ibid.: 57–8)

Danger! Beware! We shan't let our guard down and let our reason be contaminated by indigenous mystery and magic, Lévi-Strauss fervently warns us, for if we do, we may be witnessing the end of sociology as we know it! Instead of explaining the three obligations involved in gifts through 'obscurities', as indigenous people did, Lévi-Strauss invokes pure reason and science himself.[6] He reduces the *hau* to a sheer *fetish*, that is, a false projection of beliefs. A fetish, as Latour defines it, is 'nothing in itself, but simply the blank screen onto which we have projected, erroneously, our fancies, our labour, our hopes and passions' (Latour 1999a: 270). For Lévi-Strauss, things possess no intrinsic powers. The *hau* is merely a projection of indigenous beliefs onto objects that are inert pieces of matter. A bracelet is merely a bracelet, and a necklace merely a necklace. This reminds, of course, of Marx (1975 [1867]: 83) who, a century earlier, had defined commodity

---

6   The criticism levelled by Lévi-Strauss has been hailed for instance by Maurice Godelier (1999: 20), who notes that '[Lévi-Strauss's] criticism of Mauss [...] we can only share'. Godelier goes on by affirming Lévi-Strauss's warnings concerning the 'path of destruction' as '[s]age remarks, accompanied by a definition of scientific knowledge to which we can only adhere' (ibid.).

fetishism as a 'social relation between men, that assumes, in their eyes, a fantastic form of a relation between things'.

However, to me Lévi-Strauss's critique has at least two serious problems of its own. The first concerns his conviction that the social scientist alone is critical and reflexive, while the people studied are uncritical and unreflexive, even naïve.[7] Nay, Lévi-Strauss accuses *not only* indigenous people *but also* Mauss of naïveté: the first naïvely believe that objects possess a spirit, and the latter is naïve enough to accept this naïve belief as an explanation of the gift. Such a belief in the naïveté of others is characteristic of what Latour has called 'critical thinking' or 'critical sociology'. Critical sociology seeks to dispel delusion and liberate people from their illusions. As Latour writes in *We have never been modern* (1993: 51) in a sarcastic tone:

> Social scientists have for long allowed themselves to denounce the belief system of ordinary people. They call this belief system 'naturalization' (Bourdieu and Wacquant 1992). Ordinary people imagine that the power of gods, the objectivity of money, the attraction of fashion, the beauty of art come from some objective properties intrinsic to the nature of things. Fortunately, social scientists know better and they show that the arrow goes in fact in the other direction, from society to the objects. Gods, money, fashion and art offer only a surface for the projection of our social needs and interests. At least since Emile Durkheim, such has been the price of entry into the sociology profession (Durkheim [1915] 1965). To become a social scientist is to realize that the inner properties of objects do not count, that they are mere receptables for human categories.

Nevertheless, to be precise, the critical thinker shows off to naïve ordinary people not only once, but twice (Latour 2010a: 12). Latour ridicules the critical thinker for having a forked tongue:

> The human actor thinks he is determined by the power of objects, a power that tells him how to behave. Fortunately, the critical thinker is watching out for him, and denounces the actor's double-dealing, which, 'in reality', projects the power of his own action onto an inert object. One might believe that the work of denunciation is over. Sobered up, freed, de-alienated, the subject takes back the energy that used to belong to him and refuses to grant his imaginary constructions an autonomy that they can never again recapture. The work of denunciation does not stop here, however; it starts again, but now in the other direction. The free and autonomous human subject boasts, a little too soon, that he is the primal cause of all of his own projections and manipulations. Fortunately, the critical thinker, who never sleeps, once again reveals how determination works, beneath the illusion of freedom. The subject believes that he is free, while 'in reality' he

---

7   In anthropology, this preconception has traditionally taken the form of biased, ethnocentric attitudes of non-Western people as 'primitive' or 'naïve'. More recently, such conceptions have been critically addressed and challenged. See for example Strathern (1988).

is wholly controlled. In order to explain the determinations involved, we must take recourse to objective facts, revealed to us by the natural, human or social sciences. The laws of biology, genetics, economics, society and language are going to put the speaking object, who believed himself to be master of his own deeds and acts, in his place. (Latour 2010a: 13)

What an arrogant figure this critical thinker is! In his effort to denounce false beliefs and break illusions, it is implied that it is he who knows best, while the people studied know nothing. And if the actors object to his social explanations, for the critical social scientist this is 'the *best* proof that those explanations are right' (Latour 2005: 9). So, for him the actors do not ultimately have to be taken into account. Their 'presence or opinion has made no difference in the analyst's account' (Latour 2005: 57 note 58). However, it would be mean and erroneous to regard the critical thinker as malevolent. Quite the contrary, for the great amazement of everyone, he pictures himself as a great liberator. In his eyes, all the work of denunciation is only for the great benefit of the people. It is his gift to them, for he carries it out all for them and for their sake.

One does not really need to stretch one's imagination much to be able to see Lévi-Strauss as an embodiment of this figure of the fierce critical social scientist. He is convinced about the naïveté of others. He believes that others naïvely believe. And he triumphs twice over this naïveté. First, he accuses indigenous people (as much as Mauss) of being mistaken about the origin of the power of objects. Lévi-Strauss shows, with the powers vested in him by the facts, that the *hau* is merely a fetish. It is nothing in itself; it is only a phantasmatic projection of rules and obligations of very human making, nothing but a human construction. Second, he reminds the subjects that they are not the masters of this projection. The subjects are not free to develop and construct their rules, relations and societies as they wish. It is not their minds that freely and autonomously have produced the *hau*, but the *hau* is rather a creation of society's rules.

Latour suggests that for the iconoclasm and complacent paternalism of critical sociology, social scientists should substitute a very different strategy. What social scientists would need to do according to him is to take seriously what actors say and do. This is announced by one of his favourite slogans 'follow the actors' (see for example Latour 2005: 68). As he explains in *Pandora's Hope* (1999a: 287): 'The simplest explanation for all the attitudes of humanity since the dawn of its existence is probably that people mean what they say, and that, when they designate an object, that object is the cause of their behavior – *not* a delusion to be explained by a mental state'. What this means is that instead of believing, rather pompously, to be the one who has all the knowledge and all the explanations, the social scientist should try to learn from the actors whom s/he is studying by giving close attention to how they explain the world and their actions to themselves and to others (Latour 1999b: 19–20). Otherwise it is hard to justify why one should bother to do any actual research in the first place. Latour even goes as far as claiming that we have to let those who we study do our sociology for us: 'You see my friend, how precise and sophisticated our informants are [...] They know everything. They're doing our sociology for us, and doing it better than we can; it's not worth the trouble to do more. You see? Our job is a cinch' (Latour 1996: 10). So, in Latour's view, the social scientist is not in the business for explaining. The actors make everything; they have their own theories, frames and interpretations. The researcher should not play the judge and say which of the actors' explanations are right and which are false, but only to provide an account of what the actors do and say. A bit of naïve undertaking, for sure, but it may be wise to take the word of Serres on this, who declares as some kind of credo of his in *The Five Senses* (2008: 41): 'A little bit of naivety is better than suspicion'.

Don't we find a germ of such an attitude on display also in *The Gift*? Mauss explicitly bases his theoretical ideas on indigenous views. He is no iconoclast accusing anyone of believing in non-existent things. He is not assuming – or naïvely believing – that others naïvely believe, nor does he want to disillusion the actors. On the contrary, Mauss took seriously the reasons provided by the actors themselves for their actions. Instead of denouncing their beliefs, Mauss took it at face value that if people say so, things really make them do things. Everything that the subjects experience mattered to him. Of course, for the sake of fairness let it be noted that in *The Gift* Mauss too performs his share of the critical work of denunciation, as he debunks the common wisdom of the gift as free and gratuitous. While people wish to think that they give gifts out of sheer generosity and disinterestedness, Mauss contends that 'in reality' any gift entails an expectation of repayment. However, Mauss does this without disregarding the representations and experiences of people. He is not saying that the idea of the voluntary, disinterest gift is merely an illusion, whilst the reality of the gift is to be found in the rules of exchange. Like Bourdieu, too, argued, the idea of the gifts as free, disinterested and voluntary is not due to naiveté, but the Trobriand people, for example, were perfectly well aware that a gift is always accepted with a burden attached. What Mauss ultimately suggests is that we need to think the gift in an altogether different way, in terms that we usually perceive as mutually contradictory: freedom and obligation, interest and disinterest and subjects intermingled with objects.

The Vibrancy of Things

Next I would like to draw attention to another point on which I disagree with Lévi-Strauss's criticism of Mauss. Lévi-Strauss's approach is problematic not only in that he believes – and rather naïvely at that, I am tempted to add[8] – that

---

8   Of course, one could criticise my own criticism of Lévi-Strauss on the same grounds as I criticise him. In other words, don't I myself at least equally naïvely believe that Lévi-Strauss naïvely believes that others naïvely believe? To this I will only say: I know that you are not that naïve to believe that I would naïvely believe in naïve belief!

others naïvely believe, but its major problems also concern the *content* of those beliefs. Lévi-Strauss's account reproduces a total, sharp-cut separation of humans and objects. For him, the foundation of human relations cannot possibly reside in objects. For Lévi-Strauss, social life, as Godelier (1999: 18) puts it, is 'built on "exchange" and is composed of symbolic systems [...] articulated by unconscious mental structures'. Hence, by denouncing the *hau* as merely a projection of the rules of the deeper-lying structure of exchange, Lévi-Strauss's critique has the downside of throwing the baby out with the bathwater. It renders the question of the gift-object into a false problem. As Derrida (1994: 74) has noted, '[Lévi-Strauss's] criticism tends to eliminate with a wave of the hand the difficulties regarding the question of the gift. For a logic of the thing [...] Lévi-Strauss substitutes a logic of relation and exchange which causes all difficulties to vanish and even the very value of gift'. Lévi-Strauss is an archetypical critical sociologist insofar as for him objects are ultimately '*made of* social ties' (cf. Latour 2005: 249).

Of course, it is not fair to blame it all on Lévi-Strauss. It seems to be somewhat typical of traditional anthropology as a whole to assume that while in traditional societies persons and things are profoundly mixed, that is not the case in modern societies. To pick just one example, in his testimony of Mauss, Godelier (1999: 10–11) acknowledges that the power Mauss described had 'hold of both persons and things', but he nevertheless hastens to quickly add that '[Mauss] was speaking of course of societies where there seemed to be no absolute boundary between the two, and therefore no radical separation. Things were an extension of persons, and people identified the things they possessed and exchanged'. What the statement implies, then, is that our own societies are to be sharply contrasted with the kind of societies that Mauss was speaking of. In other words, it makes the assumption that in our own contemporary collective existence there is an absolute separation and boundary between subjects and objects.[9]

In more general terms, such a view reproduces what Alfred North Whitehead (1964 [1920]: 31) has called the 'bifurcation of nature'. According to him, the bifurcation of nature is something that modern thought unquestionably accepts. It cuts the world in two: on the one side, it puts the causal and objective realm of natural objects and inert matter, and, on the other side, the perceptions, views, beliefs and representations of subjects. Bifurcation posits the object–subject divide as the fundamental rift or gap that structures reality (Whitehead 1933). This is also, roughly put, the main claim of Latour's ideas regarding the 'modern constitution'. He argues that the divide between Nature and Society is an artifice,

---

9 Nevertheless, there are significant exceptions, too, and therefore Latour's claim about the incapability of anthropology to acknowledge the intertwinement of humans and non-humans is slightly too totalising and simplifying. Anthropologist Marilyn Strathern (1996), for example, has argued that anthropology is perfectly capable of following the intermeshing of phenomena, her own work perhaps being the best proof of that. She suggests that any object or event is constituted by the 'tracery of heterogeneous elements' (ibid.: 521).

a product of modernism. For Latour, to be modern means above all to uphold two asymmetries: on the one hand, to separate the present radically from the past; and, on the other, to assume an absolute gap between Nature and Society. These two 'Copernican revolutions' (see Serres with Latour 1995: 137–9, 143–6; Latour 1999a: 305) are not separate, but crucially intertwined. The first stems from the latter: we tend to assume that, unlike in traditional societies, the various dimensions of our own existence are strictly separate. Nature and society, as well as science and politics, it is insisted, are incapable of crossing paths. The facts of nature and social relations appear as distinct ontological zones. This has found its way also to the interdisciplinary division of work: only natural scientists have the right to speak in the name of nature, purified of all that is social; and only social scientists and politicians have the right to speak in the name society, purified from all that is material (Pyyhtinen and Tamminen 2007).

The problem with bifurcation is that, if we reduce objects to social relations, our understanding of them is left hopelessly opaque and inadequate, for those very relations are populated by objects that significantly contribute to establishing and weaving them. Reality is not divided into the sphere of inert matter on the one hand, and the social sphere on the other. On the contrary, objects or non-humans such as technology and natural phenomena could be said to constitute an integral part of the existence of humans. This is so to the extent, Latour (1993: 136) maintains, that 'the human [...] cannot be grasped and saved unless that other part of itself, the share of things, is restored to it'. It is altogether futile to oppose humans to non-humans, for we are largely dependent on the capabilities of various non-humans in our most mundane activities.[10] For example, in order to be able to type these words, I must join forces with a whole swarm of all kinds of materials, ranging from word processors and books to the tiny components of my laptop, a stable electricity grid, ancestors within the Indo-European language group, a grant enabling a sabbatical leave and even food. What is the human, then? Literally, a 'fold', a 'crossbreed' (see Serres 1994: 47; 2008: 22).

Therefore I think that in order to really be able to pursue the gift, one has to pay attention to how our collective existence is thoroughly mixed in with objects. And, by taking seriously the notion of the *hau*, this is precisely what Mauss was doing. He avoided the reduction of things to relations. His theory of the gift takes seriously the logic of the thing. The gift necessitates that there is a thing given. As Mauss (2008: 65) himself puts it, 'there must be a thing or service for there to be a gift, and the thing or service must place one under an obligation'. All in all, the reversal of direction that Mauss suggested with regard to objects by emphasising the *hau* is instructive. Instead of looking at how human subjects give shape and meaning to objects and how they master them, in *The Gift* Mauss draws attention to the working and creative powers of things.

So, Mauss does not associate things with passivity. In *The Gift*, objects do not appear as inert, but invested with generative powers. Instead of picturing them as

---

10   See also Pyyhtinen and Tamminen (2011).

passive and inert matter, Mauss contends that 'things themselves [...] are animate' (Mauss 2008: 62). He repeats the idea on several occasions in the essay. For instance, when discussing Roman law, he notes that in it, 'things themselves had a personality and an inherent power. Things are not the inert objects that the law of Justinian and our own legal systems conceive them to be' (ibid.: 63). The *res*, thing, dealt with in juridical texts should not be conceived merely in its physical, tangible thingness:

> [O]riginally the *res* need not have been the crude, merely tangible thing, passive object of transaction that it has become. It would seem that the best etymology is one that compares the word to the Sanskrit *rah*, *ratih*, gift, present, something pleasurable. The *res* must above all have been something that gives pleasure to another person. Moreover, the thing is always stampered by a seal, as a mark of family property. (Mauss 2008: 64)

To pick another example, in the North American potlatch, Mauss suggests, 'the things exchanged [...] possess a special intrinsic power, which causes them to be given and above all to be reciprocated' (ibid.: 49). In the 'things exchanged during the potlatch, a power is present that forces gifts to be passed around, to be given, and returned' (ibid.: 55). The copper objects which are the basic goods for the potlatch 'are alive and move autonomously, and inspire other objects to do so'. They are 'animate things' (ibid.: 57).

However, whilst Mauss emphasises the active, generative and productive powers of things, his account of them is not fully satisfactory. If we wish to get a grip at materials as active constituents of social relations between humans, Mauss takes us only halfway. This is because in his understanding of the vitality proper to objects he ultimately comes to regard their animating principle as *additional* to the objects themselves (cf. Ingold 2011: 28–9). In the last instance, for Mauss, the powers of objects are more or less 'fairylike qualities' (Mauss 2008: 57).[11]

In order to gain a fuller understanding of the active workings of materials, it is necessary to turn away from Mauss towards sources of more recent origin. I find the most intriguing the so-called *new materialisms*, greatly inspired by such thinkers as Spinoza, Bergson, Whitehead, Deleuze and Guattari, who put emphasis on the materiality of phenomena, activity and relations.[12] New materialist scholars reject the idea of matter as passive and mechanistic, distinct from active, free and self-moving human subjects. As Diana Coole and Samantha Frost describe in

---

11   Cf. Godelier (1999: 16): 'To be sure, Mauss reminds us that this [that copper objects are alive and move autonomously; O.P.] is true only in the framework of a mythological vision of the cosmos and society'.

12   The plural 'materialisms' instead of the singular 'materialism' is intended. New materialisms comprise no unified doctrine or a school, not to speak of a paradigm, but they rather amount to a set of diffuse views, theories and approaches that not only share an interest in materiality, but also approach it along somewhat similar lines.

their introduction to the edited volume *New Materialisms* (2010: 8), 'an overriding characteristic' of the thinkers who could be labelled as new materialists is 'their insistence on describing active processes of materialisation of which embodied humans are an integral part, rather than the monotonous repetitions of dead matter from which human subjects are apart'. Objects and their materials do not only restrain, resist, block, inhibit and prevent the will and actions of humans, but also enable and authorise them to do things. They possess an effectivity that transcends the mastery and control of humans (see for example Latour 1986; 1999a and b; Barad 2007; Bennett 2010).

So, to recap, new materialisms break with the Western tradition of treating objects as passive, lifeless and mechanical as opposed to the active, living and free human subjects. In the ordinary sense of the word, the term 'object', derived from Latin *ob-* 'against, before' and *iacere* 'to throw', designates something presented, put or thrown before or against the mind or sight. The object is conceived as an isolated, self-contained and self-identical piece of matter that stands or is placed against or before the subject. 'Each substantial thing', as Whitehead writes in *Adventures of Ideas* (1933: 169), 'is thus conceived as complete in itself, without reference to any other substantial thing'. Such an understanding of objects derives significantly from Aristotle and his dictum, according to which a substance is 'neither asserted of a subject nor present in a subject' (Whitehead 1978 [1929]: 50). In the 17th century, Descartes conceived of substance in much along the same lines. According to his definition, a substance is 'an existent thing which requires nothing but itself in order to exist' (Descartes 1983 [1644]: Part 1 § 51). It is arguably from Descartes that the idea of objects being inert stems. Descartes considered objects in terms of corporeal substance having a certain length, breadth and thickness. Unlike human subjects, objects are not considered as being capable of self-movement. In Newtonian physics, for example, 'objects move only upon encounter with an external force' and according to the calculable laws of motion determined by causality (Coole and Frost 2010: 7).

Of course, as we have seen, Mauss, too, perceives a vitality proper to objects, but the crucial difference between his stance and that of new materialisms is that while for Mauss the enlivening and active force is *in* the materials of objects, for new materialist thinkers it is *of* them. Accordingly, instead of calling it, to quote Mauss, the 'spirit of things', it would be more exact to say that for him the *hau* is rather the 'spirit in things'. For Mauss, it is not because of their materials and in their own right that objects are active, but because of a spirit that has come to inhabit them. New materialist thinkers, amongst whom I would also count myself, by contrast, do not conceive of the vitality of objects as a non-material force bestowed upon the objects, but we examine objects as active by their very materials. New materialist approaches 'do not [...] look beyond the material constitution of objects in order to discover what makes them tick' (Ingold 2011: 28).

To get a better idea of how new materialist thinkers perceive the active powers of materials, it is informative to look at the work of Gilles Deleuze and Félix

Guattari. With their provocative notion of 'material vitalism', Deleuze and Guattari (1987) famously challenge the opposition between – and bifurcation into – active life on the one hand, and dead matter on the other. Material vitalism suggests a material reconfiguration of life, a way of thinking life in terms of 'matter-energy', 'matter flow' and 'matter in variation that enters assemblages and leaves them' (ibid.: 407; see also Bennett 2010). Material vitalism assumes a vitality that 'exists everywhere', 'a life proper to matter' (Deleuze and Guattari 1987: 411). By evoking a 'prodigious idea of *Nonorganic Life*', Deleuze and Guattari are after a vitality that is not solely and primarily organic. For them, 'everything is alive' (ibid.: 499), but this is so not because everything would be organic. Quite the contrary, impersonal life or 'a life' is not only inorganic in character but also immensely more vital than any organism. According to Deleuze und Guattari, any organism is a 'diversion of life' that imprisons life within an actual form or organisation (ibid.). With the notion of anorganic life, Deleuze and Guattari thus eschew the very distinction between organic und anorganic, active and passive or living and non-living at an ontological level.

Whether one buys the idea of anorganic life or not, the notion nevertheless addresses an important point: that the powers of objects are very material and very real. Yet, while stressing the materiality of objects and their productive, inventive powers, new materialist thinkers (at least not all of them) do not reduce the agentic effects of objects to their raw physical stubbornness. The famous example by Latour – who, unlike Deleuze and Guattari, does not consider the capacity of non-humans in terms of vitality but on the basis of effects – of the speed bump found on the campus is instructive here:

> In artifacts and technologies we do not find the efficiency and stubbornness of matter, imprinting chains of cause and effect onto malleable humans. The speed bump is ultimately not made of matter; it is full of engineers and chancellors and lawmakers, commingling their wills and their story lines with those of gravel, concrete, paint, and standard calculation. (Latour 1999a: 190)

It is not only due to its physical, solid resistance that the speed bump is able to save lives on the campus. That is to say, the speed bump is capable of changing the drivers' actions not only due to the fact that it is impossible for them drive through the concrete, but also because in it, various intentions and goals – to reduce road deaths, ensure obedience to traffic regulations and thereby guard public morality, for example – are folded into concrete. This is not the same thing as to say that the agency of the speed bump would be reducible to human intentionality. The speed bump is no neutral extension of human will. On the contrary, by translating the respect for law and for the life of students into concern over the suspension of one's car, it fundamentally modifies and shapes the initial enunciations. First, as Latour notes, it brings about an 'actorial' shift: the speed bump is not a policeman, nor does it resemble one (even though in French it is called a 'sleeping policeman'). Second, it forges a 'spatial' shift: 'on the campus road there now resides a new actant that slows down cars (or damages them)'. Finally, it accomplishes a 'temporal' shift: the bump is constantly present and acts, day and night, independent of the engineers, the policemen and the lawmakers who have disappeared from the scene (Latour 1999a: 188).[13]

Overall, it is important to note that in dissolving the human-centred notions of action and agency, the point to be made is not that non-humans, be they living beings or material objects, too, have intentionality or that humans invest them with intentional properties. Rather, what is suggested by the idea of the active powers of objects and their materials – be they considered in terms of vitality or in some other way, such as by looking at the agentic effects of non-human actants – is a way of reconsidering action and agency not in terms of intentionality but in terms of relations, assemblages, confederations and flows. This is not to deprive human agents of intentionality or cognition, nor is it to deny the existence of several crucial differences between humans and non-humans. Humans do have certain specific features such as introspection, the capability to make one's own experiences the object of one's cognition, but cognition or intentionality should not be privileged when conceptualising action. Intentional action is only one specific case of action. In other words, we need to challenge the very privilege accorded to intentionality, free will, mind and the like when thinking of action and agentic effects. And I will suggest that it is profitable to look at the gift, too, in this way. The gift is a given thing whose passing on establishes and makes visible a bond between human subjects, and a thing that, quite literally, makes people do things. Instead of focusing exclusively on the intentions of the one-who-gives or the one-who-receives, we need to follow the movements of the gift-object if we are to see the relations woven by the gift.

Quasi-object

Latour's example of the speed bump importantly suggests that it is not fruitful to consider materiality only in terms of brute matter. As Coole and Frost (2010: 9) nicely put it, 'materiality is always something more than "mere" matter: an excess, force, vitality, relationality, or difference that renders matter active, self-creative, productive, unpredictable'. Such an understanding of materiality also impels us to radically alter our way of thinking about objects. To me, the most powerful and illustrative reconceptualisation of objects along relational lines without, at the same time, compromising their materiality has been offered by Serres. I feel that it is interesting, and necessary, even, to complement Mauss's ideas with those of Serres (an undertaking, to be sure, made somewhat controversial due to Serres's disparagement of Mauss's *The Gift*).

According to Serres, objects significantly constitute what it is to be human: 'We only become human by means of objects. We remain animals by our

---

13   I have discussed the matter also elsewhere (see Pyyhtinen and Tamminen 2011).

representations. Men are animals who have found the object' (Serres 1991: 209). To elaborate this further:

> Man, it is said, is a political animal, meaning simply that the man who is exclusively political is bestial – I mean attached, linked, bound with no recourse and no other horizon to the relations within the group. He is the pure idealist, for whom the object is nothing but a social representation. I believe – but I could be wrong – that this is why animals, even the higher animals, even those living in a strong collectivity, never have an object. When the object appears, another man appears. (Serres 1991: 209)

The claim that humans are the only ones who have objects would seem to be somewhat exaggerated, as various other animals, too, have their objects: primates their tools, dogs their bones, cats their spool and cattle their pasturage, for example. What is nevertheless insightful in Serres's idea of the entanglement of humans with objects is the way how for Serres this challenges human exceptionalism and the human-centred notions of action. As he writes in *Angels*: 'No, we are not so very exceptional. What old books used to call our faculties are to be found here, outside of us, scattered about the universe, both the inert and the man-made' (Serres 1995a: 48). It is not only humans that know, for instance, but objects, too:

> The spindle of the sundial, using the sun, but acting on its own, marks the hour of the equinox and the position of the given location; memory is found, dormant, in libraries, in museums, behind the screen of my computer, and in language, both written and spoken; this memory is awakened and brought to life when the power is switched on; imagination lights up, goes out or fades on our television screens … (ibid.)

Thereby, Serres insists on the redistribution of agentic capabilities. Objects are no sheer passive 'objects' of our actions, but they have active and generative effects. They do things: 'a panpipe warbles, a clarinet sings, a violin weeps, a bassoon sobs, the sensitivity of brass, strings and wood' (ibid.). Instead of humans standing as the sole creators of things, objects significantly shape our human capabilities and what we are. Serres terms this view 'pragmatogony', derived from the Greek terms *pragma* (thing, matter) and *agnos* (that which is begotten, the created) (Serres 1987; see also Beer 2010: 6). Given the effects that objects obviously have, they necessarily possess some creative powers: 'Do you really think that machines and technologies would be able to construct groups and change history if they were merely passive objects?' (Serres 1995a: 48).

Serres insists that the term subject as much as that of object need to be furnished with the prefix *quasi-*; subjects are essentially quasi-subjects and objects quasi-objects. With regard to the thinking of objects and materiality, especially the notion of the quasi-object suggests two very important points. First, the prefix quasi- underlines that while objects are real and material, they nevertheless cannot be reduced to brute matter or to some reality 'out there'. Objects consist not only of 'matter', but they are also significantly constituted in and by relations, both in terms of their internal make up (as each object is a temporary arrangement between various components) and their dependence on other entities in their existence. Objects are not detached from the collective and its relations, but they are always part of its life, weaving its relations and providing those relations with stability; objects are invested with hopes, fears and labour, they mobilise humans and enable them to do things they would not be able to do without them. Therefore, objects cannot be properly understood when stripped away of their relations and detached out of their environment; for it is in and through relations that they ultimately receive their meaning and effectivity. We never encounter anything out of its specific circumstances; we only ever experience and encounter mixtures, compounds and foldings (Serres 2008: 27–9).[14] Nothing exists solely in and by itself independent of all other things, but everything exists only in relation to other things.

Second, by sticking to the notion of 'object' instead of simply employing the seemingly much more convenient 'thing' as Heidegger did,[15] Serres is able to stress that while constituting itself in relations, the quasi-object never stops *also* being a 'mere' object. It is irreducible to human relations or to language and signification. In this sense, the object always remains to some extent a *given* for the relation. It has effectivity, force and trajectories that are irreducible to humans and their actions and intentions, or to relations in general. For example, even though the intention behind any given gift remains human (though one can also give without knowing it; for Derrida, as we have seen, it even amounts to a condition of possibility of the gift that it remains secret, not recognised as a gift),[16] there is also an element of *surprise* in the gift. We can never fully anticipate the effects produced by the gift. This is also the reason behind the difficulty of the art of gift-giving; we can never know for sure how the gift will be received. The gift always manages to surprise, both the donor and the donee. No object and no gift is perfectly loyal, merely a passive instrument of human action, but also resists our intentions and interpretations.

Objects (and subjects) are always mixtures and crossbreeds, placed both in the world of nature or matter and in society (which of course nowhere stops being also

---

14   Serres pictures each and every entity as a *fold* (*pli*). He borrows the concept from Deleuze (see Serres 1994: 49). Like Deleuze, Serres stresses that the fold is the germ, origin or core of all forms, though it is itself merely an assembly of other folds (ibid.: 48). An organism, for example, presents a system which receives, restores, exchanges, and gives away energy and information in their various forms from sunlight to the flows of food, oxygen, heat, and messages that go through the organism (Serres 1982: 74). Humans too are folds: 'I live in folds, and I am myself nothing but a collection of folds' (Serres 1994: 47).

15   See Heidegger (1971).

16   As Derrida notes in 'On the Gift' (Derrida and Marion, 1999: 60): 'A gift is something you do without knowing what you do'.

'material'), and existing at once in relations and out of relations. Hence, the object is not only a matter of collectivity, but also matter that is bound to remain to some extent strange and impenetrable to humans. As Serres poetically puts it, the object is always also 'a thing of this world; it is a flesh of incarnation, a light captured, seized, and barred within walls', within its own 'interior' (Serres 1991: 59).

Serres's insights of the quasi-object have great relevance for the social scientific thinking of the community. The notion of the quasi-object suggests that there is no community 'as such', as no community can emerge without attaching itself to objects: 'No human collectivity exists without things; human relations go through things, our relations to things go through men' (Serres 1995c: 45). For Serres, the initial condition of the community lies therefore in the object, not in the subject, contract, shared essence, common identity or some collective will (Serres 1991: 106). As he writes in *Genesis*, 'the object [...] stabilizes our relationships, it slows down the time of our revolutions'. The objects 'makes our history slow': instead of 'social changes [...] flaring up every minute', our togetherness has stable forms (Serres 1995b: 87). One can argue that this is mainly so because objects have a temporality of their own that is distinct from the experience, memory and interactions of humans (see also Stiegler 1998). 'To the stability of objects corresponds the lability of relationships' (Serres 2008: 44). The object crystallises the fluctuating, labile energies of the multiple: 'The mob fluctuates and the institution is made of stone' (Serres 1995b: 106). Because of objects, humans are not forced to constantly reproduce and maintain their mutual relations with the help of sounds and touches (Latour 2010b; Lehtonen 2012). And, the other way around, when relations are not marked with an object, they waver in immediacy, evaporate and vanish.

Although in the above quoted formulations Serres emphasises the stability of objects, for him the object is not always and necessarily a relatively fixed, stable and immutable element around which the multiple is gathered, but it can also be a mutable, moving element circulating from one subject to another. In both cases, it is the object that, literally, *collects* the community together, something which is underlined also by the concept Serres uses for the community: *collective* (French: *collectif*). Accordingly, Serres suggests that the best way to grasp the birth of the collective and how relations get spun is to follow the motions of quasi-objects. The community, invisible and nothing in itself, becomes visible only in the quasi-objects, and what becomes visible in it is precisely the community in its entirety.

Serres proposes that the object and the collective are co-constituted. There is no object without a collective, and no collective without an object. You do not get the one without the other. Objects receive their meaning, abilities and stability as they travel in the relations of the collective, and the objects circulating from subject to subject knit the collective together. In his books, Serres's favourite example of the entanglement of the collective and the object is the ball in football. Without the ball, there is no game, and one cannot 'play ball' all by oneself. On the one hand, the ball is the centre around which the game shifts and is alive: 'Around the ball, the team fluctuates quick as a flame, around it, through it, it keeps a nucleus of organization. The ball is the sun of the system and the force passing among its elements, it is a center that is off-centered, off-side, outstripped' (Serres 1995b: 87–8). In the movements of the ball, the collective at once expands and contracts, spreads out and comes together, as the ball assembles it by travelling from player to player. And yet, on the other hand, the ball is what it is only in the middle of the game, in touches, kicks and hits, in being passed on from player to player. The ball that is in the attacking zone becomes hot and dangerous, in contrast to the controlled, relatively harmless and safe ball shuttling back and forth in the middle of the pitch. It is important to note that the ball is no passive 'object', but it is active. In a sense, the ball itself is playing, playing with the players. The best, most skilled players do not manipulate and force the ball to go with them. On the contrary, they 'serve' the ball and its movements; when the 'preceding one is shunted aside, laid out, trampled', the next one carries on (Serres 1995b: 88). To play is to make 'oneself the attribute of the ball as a substance' (Serres 2007: 226). It is only the bad players who treat the ball as if it was only an object and are therefore clumsy with the ball, or they are too selfish and hold it all to themselves.

In its circulation and movements, the ball creates relations, expressed by different prepositions. As the players serve the ball, it connects them *with* each other and welds their team together: instead of everyone looking out for themselves, the players play *for* their team. In its movements, the ball also connects the teams in their rival aims: it makes the teams play *against* each other. Nevertheless, the ball not only weaves the collective, but it also stands as a sign of the subject: 'it marks or designates a subject who, without it, would not be a subject' (Serres 2007: 225). When completely detached from the ball, the player is in the dark. The 'I' is a token passed between players: the one who has the ball is marked. S/he is 'marked as the victim', as the one to be chased and tackled (Serres 2007: 226). Hence, it is thanks to the ball that we know in the game 'how and when we are subjects and when and how we are no longer subjects' (ibid.: 227).

Any Object and No Object

To come back to Mauss and the gift, Mauss clearly acknowledges the role of the gift-object in group-formation. He repeatedly shows in *The Gift* how the bond emerges through the passing on of a thing: the gift-relation is 'a tie expressed by things' (Mauss 2008: 63). In Maori law, for instance, Mauss notes, 'the legal tie, a tie occurring through things, is one between souls, because the thing itself possesses a soul, is of the soul' (ibid.: 16). The obligations pertaining to giving, receiving and returning are brought into play through objects. 'The contracting parties are bound by them' (ibid.: 62). Thereby Mauss's account of the gift already points towards a theoretical understanding of the share of objects in our relations and collective existence in general, though without him being fully aware of that. Indeed, like Moses, Mauss was leading his people to a promised land, the splendours of which he would never contemplate and realise himself, but the promised land in question was not (only) that of structuralism, but of *materiology*[17] or *object-oriented sociology*. For Mauss, gift-exchange is all about circulating objects that give rise to a network of relations. Unfortunately, Mauss's object lessons have been obfuscated over the years by the criticism that his reliance on the mystical, indigenous notion of the *hau* has faced. His gesture of taking seriously the gift-object thus needs to be revitalised.

Nevertheless, it is no wonder that the objectness or thingness of the gift has been not been paid much attention by the previous studies on the gift. After all, as soon as something is being offered as a gift, what matters is not so much the object and what it is as the relation established between the giver and the receiver who accepts the gift. It seems that the gift is more a relation than a tangible, brute thing; it is more of a bond than of substantial matter. Indeed, it is as if the gift appeared *in re*, in the matter of a thing, without being itself a thing. This is emphasised by the practice, very common in many contemporary Western cultures, of identifying gifts as gifts with wrapping. As David Cheal (1988) has observed, the purpose of the wrapping is to draw attention away from the object itself to the gesture of giving. 'It is the thought that counts', as the common saying goes, meaning that the act of giving and the expression of generosity is more important than the object and its material value. The wrapping underscores this by hiding the object and placing it in secrecy.

All in all, the gift is at the same time *any object*[18] and *no object*: while any object may be given as a gift, no object is merely and nothing but a gift, but every gift is always also some-thing else. Therefore, the gift is not an object of the same stripe that books, balls, computers and tables, for example, are. Unlike these other objects, the gift lacks any inherent qualities. What makes an object a gift is not what John Locke (1979 [1689]) called an object's 'primary', intrinsic qualities, but that it is offered and passed on without demanding any explicit payment for it. The assumed primary qualities, as it were, are secondary, while it is the so-called 'secondary' qualities that are of primary importance. The inversion of primary and secondary qualities is of course sheer wordplay, as we must undermine the very divide if we are to understand the gift, or any object, for that matter: what things/gifts in themselves are can be grasped only in the specific relations and circumstances they are entangled with. Nevertheless, the wordplay alludes to an important point. While books, balls, computers, and tables may be offered as gifts, it cannot be said that balls, computers, and tables are books. 'Giftness' is not a property of any specific object. The gift is not attached to any object in particular. On the contrary, in principle any object may appear as a gift. Therefore, as Gasché (1997: 101) puts it,

> All the denominations and all the conceptualization brought to bear do not succeed in defining the 'object' which, instead turns out to be unnameable. [The gift] always shows up as an other, as a non-object […]. At most, all that

---

17   The term is from Latour (2013: 221).

18   Aafke Komter (2007: 94), too, notes that, 'Virtually anything can be given as a gift'.

can be reported is the ambiguity, which in and of itself eludes any attempt at enunciation and conceptualization.

So, in a sense, the gift is a blank figure or, in the parlance of Serres (1991: 93), a 'joker', a 'blank domino'. Just as the joker in a pack of cards can be an ace, a king, a queen, a jack or any number, the gift can take on any value and determination, depending on the relations in and by which it is constituted. It is undetermined; it lacks any specific, intrinsic qualities in itself – it is any object and no object (this effect is further reinforced by the wrapping). The gift-object is determined by the ensemble in which it moves. With the exclusion of money, there is perhaps no other object that would embody relations to the extent that the gift does. The gift is relational, it receives its meaning and abilities from relations. The gift is so inextricably entangled with social relations that it cannot be grasped as something completely in itself without paying attention to the ties that accompany it. The reason for giving is not internal to the given object itself, but the gift-object serves the creation, nourishment and stabilisation of relations. By imposing obligations, the gift establishes a relation between the donor and the donee. When we receive a gift, we immediately feel obliged: we are supposed to return the gift; the gift must somehow come back to the donor, if not in the form of an actual, concrete counter-gift then at least in that of a symbolic equivalent of the gift received. There is no gift outside relations. In addition, the meaning of a gift is significantly dependent on the nature of the relationship between the one who gives it and the one who receives. A gift has a very different feeling to it depending on whether the giver is of inferior or superior rank to the receiver (Godelier 1999: 13), and whether they are strangers or lovers, for instance, even if the gift-object in both cases was apparently the same. Furthermore, the significance of relations testifies also to the fact that a gift may be refused not only for not being what the receiver needs or desires (for being of poor quality, for instance), but also the awareness of the unwanted relationship it might produce may make it appear repulsive or unpleasant. In other words, it may not always be due to the object itself that the gift appears as undesirable to the recipient, but even the otherwise most desirable thing may appear as undesirable, if it is offered by a person one does not wish to feel obliged or bound to.

And yet, all this notwithstanding, the gift is irreducible to a relation – there is no gift-relation without some-*thing* that is given, received and often also reciprocated, and there is no gift collective, no community of gifts, without an object circulating through the collective. There must be some thing that is given and passed on. Therefore, while being a relation, the gift is also the *origin* of that relation. It is precisely the movement of the gift which establishes the bond between the donor and the donee; the gift-relation is produced by the gift-object being passed on from the giver to the receiver. What is more, as it establishes a relation, the gift also tries to free itself from all relations; while there is no gift that would not bind the donor and the donee, the gift also must be out of bounds. This is because the bond, in the form of an obligation, a debt, as we have seen, always threatens to annul the gift.

Substituting Alliance for Violence

The problem any culture and civilisation must solve is that of the possibility of co-existence. How is it possible for us to live together peacefully? How can we exist side by side in the world without killing one another? In order to survive, collectivities must find ways to suppress and limit violence; otherwise they are doomed to extinction. For violence produces ultimately nothing but more violence, 'vengeance begets vengeance and never stops' (Serres 1995c: 13). Here we have the eternal return as the infinite cycle of violence.

Co-existence is thus essentially conditioned by the cessation of violence. One of the contributions of Mauss's *The Gift* is that it ties the gift to this. In the essay, Mauss shows repeatedly how the refusal to accept a gift or to return one equals a declaration of war. In the archaic gift, the acts of giving, receiving and repaying constitute themselves in relation to the ever-present threat of conflict. Nevertheless, for Mauss archaic gift-exchange is not only constantly accompanied by the threat of violence. Rather, it is ultimately the gift that presents for Mauss the assurance of peace and protects us from violence. He thinks that peaceful co-existence comes down to 'substituting alliance, gifts and trade for war' (Mauss 2008: 105). The gift teaches us 'how to oppose' without slaughtering one another (ibid.: 106). Exchange presupposes and necessitates the laying down of one's weapons: 'To trade, the first condition was to [...] lay aside the spear' (ibid.: 105). Gift-exchange offers a way out of the endless reproduction of violence: 'one lays down one's arms and gives up magic, or one gives everything, from fleeting acts of hospitality to one's daughter and one's goods' (ibid.: 104).[19] So, the archaic gift is tied to violence with a double bind: while the inability or the refusal to reciprocate runs the risk of sparking violence, functioning exchange succeeds in resolving and preventing conflicts. A formulation by Lévi-Strauss (1969 [1949]: 67) captures this well: 'Exchanges are peacefully resolved wars and wars are the result of unsuccessful transactions'.

In *Stone Age Economics* (2004 [1974]), Marshall Sahlins draws an interesting parallel between Mauss and the political philosophy of Thomas Hobbes. According to Sahlins, like Hobbes, 'Mauss debates from an original condition of disorder' (ibid.: 169). Sahlins finds in Mauss's gift a primitive analogue of Hobbes's social contract. Whereas for Hobbes, peace was secured by the social contract, for Mauss it is the gift that assures peace in the archaic societies: 'For the war of every man against every man, Mauss substitutes the exchange of everything between everybody' (ibid.: 168). As we saw in the previous chapter, Mauss suggests that in the archaic societies, the phenomenon of the gift is extended to everywhere, everyone and everything. It covers all aspects of the lives of the people there. So, unlike Hobbes, Mauss does not think that social order requires consent to

---

19 Girard's (1979) analysis of sacrifice has several affinities with the presented way of looking at the gift. For Girard, sacrifice appears as a means to intercept the cycle of violence.

an authority, to a sovereign third party, but peaceful co-existence is achieved through reciprocity: the gift itself appears in Mauss's essay as a symbolic third party replacing contract. No Leviathan has to step in between subjects to prevent violence from bursting, but they manage to suspend violence solely by themselves as they engage in exchange of gifts.

It is easy to agree with Mauss and Sahlins in their views on the gift as a means to peaceful co-existence. While violence causes the social bond to be destroyed, the purpose of the gift is to establish, settle, maintain and solidify relations. 'The gift is alliance, solidarity, communion – in brief, peace', Sahlins writes (ibid.: 169). However, his reliance on Hobbes imports a problematic feature to Sahlins's thinking of which he is apparently not aware. That he accepts Hobbes's terms not only makes Sahlins's conceptualisation of the original condition of disorder somewhat unsatisfactory, but it also makes him miss a crucial aspect of Mauss's account.

By drawing from the insights of Serres (as well as Girard), one can argue against Hobbes and Sahlins that the original condition of disorder is not the war of all against all, but a state of primitive, uncontrolled and freely fluctuating *violence*. (So, perhaps, in the beginning was violence, not the apple? Or, is it rather the alternation of peace and violence that we find in the beginning, as Serres would have it?) 'When everyone fights against everyone, there is no state of war, but rather violence, a pure, unbridled crisis without any possible cessation' (Serres 1995c: 13–14).[20] War always already represents order. 'By definition, war is a legal state' (ibid.: 8), Serres notes. He elaborates this claim in *Genesis*:

> War is decided, it is declared, ordered, prepared, institutionalized, made sacred, it is won, lost, concluded by treaty. War is a state of order, a classic state of lines and columns, maps and strategies, leaders and spectacle, it knows friends, enemies, neutrals, allies, it defines belligerence. (Serres 1995b: 83)

We do not find in war the primal state that precedes order and social contract, for war already presupposes a contract. War represents a pact and involves alliance. War is ordered, organised and regulated in so many ways and objectified into institutions. To be able to wage war, there is at least a tacit agreement presupposed by the belligerents. They 'decide, by a common agreement [...] to devote themselves to battles'. According to Serres, Hobbes (and we could say the same of Sahlins as well) was thus 'off by a whole era' by mistaking the war for the original state of disorder. We do not proceed from war to social contract, but from primitive violence to contract and war. As Serres encapsulates the sequence: 'Violence before; war afterwards; legal contract in the between' (Serres 1995c: 13).

---

20 Serres's conception of violence in certain respects clearly owes to Girard (1979). Girard's idea of the precedence of violence has been heavily criticised by Godbout and Caillé (1998), who, while seeing the gift as an alternative to violence, nevertheless regard violence as secondary to the gift – for Godbout and Caillé, in the beginning is the gift, not violence.

So, in contrast to what Hobbes and Sahlins maintain, peaceful co-existence is not born of the cessation of war, but of the cessation of violence. According to Serres, war itself is in fact a solution to the problem of primitive violence: 'A society makes war to avoid at all costs the return to th[e] state [of uncontrolled fury]' (Serres 1995b: 83). In this, war is parallel to religion and exchange. For Serres, battle, the sacred and exchange are 'social universals' (each of the terms being also included in the other two), which establish order by suspending violence: 'The sacred shields us from human and global violence, it is produced by it; the military protects us from violence external or internal to the group; the exchange makes our needs flow through channels that, without them, would bring us harm' (ibid.: 87).

Significantly for our object lessons, Serres stresses that each of the social universals is attached to a corresponding object: religion is tied to a sacred object, war to weapons and exchange to values or tokens of exchange. It is in the objects that these pacts become visible: 'Nowhere do I see the sacred without a sacred object, a war or an army without weapons (there are no weapons [...] formed expressly for the originating violence), and exchange without values' (ibid.: 88). Each of these objects is a quasi-object in the sense discussed above, and each of them freezes the frantic flame of the energies and relations of the multiple.

Of course, one can always argue that the entire interpretation of Hobbes's view of the original condition of disorder is based here on one single term, 'war', that is not even very important in his theory; he might as well have used the term 'violence'. Nevertheless, the difference between violence and war stressed above is of great relevance especially with regard to Mauss's conception of the gift as a vehicle of peaceful co-existence. By positing the gift against war, Sahlins, as I already suggested above, not only mistakes war for the primal state before any pact, but also misses a crucial feature in Mauss's account of the gift. While in some places in *The Gift* Mauss does oppose the gift to war, when discussing the potlatch, as we remember from Chapter 2, he draws an explicit connection between the two. In an important short passage placed in the endnotes, Mauss goes as far as to equate the gift with war. According to him, 'the potlatch is a war'. It is a 'war between properties': by 'killing' property (and sometimes even people), the participants are trying to humiliate their rivals (Mauss 2008: 142 note 141).

The parallelism Mauss draws between the gift and war has two essential implications. First, it suggests that war is not conceived here as some kind of primitive, pre-contractual state of disorder. On the contrary, the war between properties is strictly regulated. Second, and even more significantly, it forces us to reconsider the gift itself. The gift is not peace as opposed to war, solidarity as opposed to strife and alliance as opposed to animosity, but these mutually exclusive terms merge in the gift: the gift is at once *both* peace *and* war, *both* solidarity *and* strife, *both* alliance *and* animosity. This does not mean that these conceptual antagonisms reach a final, reconciled synthesis in the gift. Rather, the gift retains the contrasts in force. It expresses the constant tension between the opposing poles. Thus, gift-exchange provides a solution to the problem of primitive, uncontrolled violence not only by way of creating solidarity, but also by offering us ways to 'oppose without massacring one another'. Besides designating friendship and alliance, gift-exchange is also, as the example of the potlatch shows us like no other, a ritualised, sublimated form of warfare. Gift-exchange is a continuation of war by other means.

To be sure, at first sight, in the so-called 'civilised' societies the gift's ability to function as a remedy to violence would appear to have become obsolete. For, in contrast to the archaic societies, it seems that in the modern societies the threat of violence is not omnipresent. It does not accompany the dealings and lives of humans to the extent that it perhaps used to in the past. We do not live in a world where the smallest errors may have the most horrifying consequences, and where social relationships are therefore marked by extreme caution. It may be speculated that the ever-present threat of violence was perhaps even the reason for the dominance of the gift in the archaic societies. In them, everything was organised around the exchange of gifts. The threat of the outburst of conflicts and tensions inspired to give and urged to reciprocity: the greater the (threat of) hostility, the more extravagant the generosity. Conversely, it can be speculated that the respective decrease in the threat of violence might explain the diminished visibility of the gift in our contemporary Western societies.

However, while it is not self-evident that archaic societies were any bit more violent than the present ones, I think it is downright mistaken to assume that today the constitution of the community or the collective would no longer depend on the exclusion of violence. The cessation of violence pertains not only to archaic societies and to the avoidance of uncontrolled fury. On the contrary, pacification and the suspension of tensions is something that needs to be repeated over and over again – it is only that the gift may no longer be the most compelling means in achieving that. Solidarity and community must be constantly maintained. The gift offers itself as one means to accomplish this, as it not only solidifies flaring relations, but it also offers an assurance of peaceful co-existence. Peaceable co-existence is conditioned by exchange, by the acceptance of the communal obligation, *munus*, to give. A kinsman interviewed by Lorna Marshall (1961: 245) for her study expresses this nicely: 'We give what we have. That is the way we live together'.

To sum up, the gift is placed at the heart of the question of the collective. Perhaps one could even say that, better than any other phenomenon, it shows how the birth of the collective is intertwined with the object. It is the things in circulation and in motion – or the things standing still, around which the fluctuating multiple circulates and gathers itself – that make visible and enable us to trace the network of relations constituting the collective. All in all, our relations to our fellow humans are mediated by objects. This also means that the way we are with, and treat objects also affects our relationships with our fellow humans:[21] the acts of showing our disappointment at a gift we have received, putting it out

---

21   See Lehtonen (2008).

of sight, giving it to someone else, selling it, destroying it or refusing it outright – all ways of responding to bad gifts – are usually deemed offensive to the donor.[22] In addition, just as there is no collective without an object, our relationship to objects is always mediated by our fellow humans. Objects are not only of the physical world but essentially also of *us*. They are always a matter of relations and the collective. While being produced by relations, things also weave relations. They are at once constituted by and constitutive of relations. Therefore, it is profitable to look at things in their relations to us and to other things instead of just looking at them in themselves and for their own sake. However, instead of invoking indigenous views on spirituality, as Mauss did, I have suggested above that the active, generative power of things should be considered in terms of their intermingling with human relations and the collective. The gift is a quasi-object.

---

22 See Sinardet and Mortelmans (2005: 256–5). Bad gifts will be discussed in more detail in Chapter 5.

Chapter 4

Parasites' Paradise
(aka Lice Hopping on the Beach)

By taking without giving, the parasite gives the giving of the given.

As we have seen, the starting point typically taken for granted – as a 'given' – by the theories of the gift is that one has to start from giving or from the one-who-gives, not from receiving or from the one-who-receives, if one is to understand the gift. In this chapter, however, I will purposely depart from that tradition. If one pays attention solely to the act of giving and to the motives of the giver, one inevitably misses the phases, equally crucial to the event of the gift, that follow the giving in the process: the transfer of a possession (the appropriation[1] of the given by the other) as well as the effects of the gift (for example the feeling of delight, gratitude, embarrassment or discomfort caused by the gift, and the bond created or threatened by it). The realisation of the gift is thus not up to the giver alone; it depends not solely on giving but as much on taking.[2] What is abandoned by me needs to be accepted by the other in order for a gift to appear. If the possession that I abandon is not accepted by the other, there is no true giving and hence no gift, but only giving up.

In what follows, I will align the notion of the gift with that of the *parasite* by Serres. The concept of the parasite reverses the irreversible order of beginning with giving when thinking of the gift. Instead of starting from the individual giver and his/her generosity and the will to give, it gives precedence to *taking* and *receiving*. As Serres (2007: 24) remarks, the parasite is '[a]lways taking, never giving'. I will discuss the connectedness of the notion of the gift with that of the parasite in the context of or, better, in conjunction with the film *The Beach* (2000), directed by Danny Boyle. The film, based on a best-selling novel of the same name by Alex Garland, was Boyle's fourth movie. Before it, he had done such cult hits as *Shallow Grave* (1994) and *Trainspotting* (1996), and his subsequent works include for instance the post-apocalyptic horror film *28 Days Later* as well as the victorious *Slumdog Millionaire*, for which he won the Academy Award for Best Director. In the chapter, I'm concerned less with 'analysing' the movie by applying Serres's concepts than with reading Serres through and with the film in order to think the interrelatedness of the gift with the parasite. The word 'parasite'

---

1   The notion of appropriation will be discussed in more detail and at more length in Chapter 6.

2   This becomes obvious for instance in the case of gift failure. As Dave Sinardet and Dimitri Mortelmans (2005: 252) note in their article on failed gift exchanges, 'a gift only becomes a failure when it reaches the hands of the receiver'.

comes up only three times in *The Beach*, and yet one can argue that the whole film is marked with parasitic relations. In a sense, the film maps a system of these relations – of giving and taking, gifts and abuse – and I will describe them to the smallest detail, deliberately to the limit at which the richness of the description begins to turn into noise. It is as if everything in the movie, down to its very production process, as we will see, was a question of the parasite.[3]

Let us pause here. Parasite? The choice of words might strike odd or unusual, to say the very least, given that the science bearing the name parasitology reserves the term only to invertebrates like tapeworms, fleas, vermin, flukes and lice. However, in *The Parasite* (2007: 6; orig. *Le Parasite*, 1980), Serres suggests that parasitism is not restricted only to these small animals, but that all relations – human, animal, relations of communication, you name it – are parasitic in essence. Take humans, for example. We are universal parasites, as everything and everyone around us is hospitable space: not only do we make plants and animals our hosts for instance when we eat and milk them and clothe ourselves in their skin or wool, but we even want to parasite our own kind, our fellow humans, just as much as they enjoy our own hospitality (Serres 2007: 24). What is more, according to Serres parasitology 'bears several traces of anthropomorphism' (ibid.: 6), as it 'uses the vocabulary of the host: hostility or hospitality' (ibid.: 193). Its understanding of parasitic relations is thus to a great extent shaped by our sense of ancient customs and habits related to hospitality, table manners, hostelry, and relations with strangers. Animal parasitism is all about guests and hosts: 'The animal-host offers a meal from the larder or from his own flesh; as a hotel or a hostel, he provides a place to sleep, quite graciously, of course' (ibid.: 6). To parasite is to eat next to the host, intervene between him/her and his/her nutrition. Serres grounds this idea on the etymology of the word 'parasite', in which the 'prefix *para-* means "near", "next to", measures a distance. The *sitos* is the food' (ibid.: 144).

The neighbouring function of eating is, of course, making noise: the open mouth that eats also emits sound. From the mishmash of abusive animals, social parasites, and noise we get three meanings to the word parasite in French explored by Serres in *The Parasite*: (1) in its biological sense, a parasite is an organism feeding on another one; (2) in the anthropological sense, an abusive guest (unlike the biological parasite, the social parasite does not necessarily live *in* its host, but just *by* it, for instance by being housed, fed, or sheltered by one's host); (3) and in information theory, it designates noise, static, a break in the message.

However, to get to the entwining of the three meanings of the notion of the parasite, we have to rewind. *The Parasite* begins with Serres's recapitulation of a fable by La Fontaine of the city rat who has invited the country rat for a visit. The rats chew and gnaw their meal with delight on a Persian rug. The meal consists of nothing but scraps, bits and leftovers, but for the country rat, at least, it makes a

---

3   Parasitism is mainly an addition – and thus a gift, an extra – made to the film. Many of the parasitic relations appearing in the film are absent in the novel. In addition, in the latter the word parasite is not mentioned once.

royal feast, since in the country they only eat soup. However, the feast is cut short, as the rats hear noise from the door. The noise made by their cutting and nibbling has woken up the head of the house, the tax farmer, who has now got out of bed to determine the origin of the disturbing sounds. Now, let us have a look at the story with the above three meanings of the word parasite in mind. The country rat, though being an animal, is a parasite in the anthropological sense: a guest at a banquet, exploiting his host, the city rat. The city rat, living in the tax farmer's house and feeding on his leftovers, is a parasite in the biological sense: the city rat taxes the tax collector. But the tax farmer, too, is a parasite. He has produced nothing in his own right, neither cheese nor ham nor oil but, by the powers of his position and the law, he only profits from the work of the peasant, himself a parasite of the earth and its fruits. And, finally, the noise that the rats make is parasitic in the third sense of the term, namely that employed in cybernetics, as it wakes up the tax farmer from his sleep, and he in turn becomes a parasite interrupting the feast. One parasite chases another out one after the other. The parasite 'is the noise of the system that can only be supplanted by a noise' (ibid.: 79). There is no immediate connection between the three meanings, but rather a similarity of form, an isomorphism: in each case as well as at each point of La Fontaine's story, the relation is of a similar kind: *an arrow with only one way.*

Excluding the Parasite

The Beach is a travel story of the pursuit of a lost world, of finding one's way out from the modern world filled with noise to a serene paradise. The film is also a narrative about how every para-dise inevitably ends up being para-sited, for no secret is ever safe for good. The link between paradise and secrecy is by no means accidental, but the two are internally bound to one another: paradise is possible only on the condition that it is kept secret, and a secret is a small paradise for those who share it. And, just as every secret, keeping paradise intact has a price. Something remains a secret only on the condition of exclusion.[4] As a relation, the secret is always a matter of first and second persons, whether in the singular or in the plural. According to its structure, it is something between 'us', all others barred, which amounts to saying that secrecy always implies separation: while tying together those who share it, the secret also unties them from the world, from everyone else, from the outside. To every secret there is thus an excluded third. A secret between 'us', whether consisting of two or multiple members, presupposes an excluded third and is made possible only by its exclusion. A secret can be kept and remain a secret only insofar as all thirds are constantly excluded. And yet, as *The Beach* shows, no secret lasts forever, and no paradise remains un-parasited for long. Walls have ears and the air is full of eyeballs. The parasite is always there, in-between, in the position of the third, interfering and intercepting

---

4   For more on secrecy, see Simmel (1992: 383–455).

(ibid.: 63). It is always on the channel, plugged into the relation. The world of *The Beach* is a world populated by parasites. However fictional, it is not a monstrous or nightmarish world, but a quite realistic one, very similar to our everyday world. In a sense, the film transports our imagination from our parasitic now-here to an un-parasited paradise, which for the viewers is a utopian no-where.[5]

The movie begins with a scene from the streets of noisy Bangkok by night with the main protagonist Richard, a young American backpacker played by Leonardo DiCaprio, strolling aimlessly from entertainment to entertainment, from water balloon wars to a drinking contest where the contestants are challenged to drink snake blood. Richard has left his ordinary life and old world in order to get to another one. And so he has landed on Thailand. But, as soon as he has got there, he realises that just crossing the ocean does not suffice. This is because the comforts of his home have followed him on his way, along with the alike-minded fellow American homebodies: 'you cross the ocean and cut yourself loose […]. The only downer is, everyone's got the same idea. We all travel thousands of miles just to watch TV and check into somewhere with all the comforts of home. I just feel like everyone tries to do something different, but … you always wind up doing the same damn thing'. People wish to go out to the world without being deprived of the comforts of modern life. And, therefore, no one ever actually leaves indoors. Today, we're packed into cities. Our life takes place in homes, offices, banks, bureaus, supermarkets, cars, airports, airplanes, buses, trains, metros, stations, lavatories, nightclubs and hotels. People, as Serres sarcastically puts it in *The Natural Contract* (1995c: 28), are '[i]ndifferent to the climate, except during their vacations when they rediscover the world in a clumsy, arcadian way'.

But Richard wants to escape the fall into repetition. He wishes to leave indoors, cut former relations and get in contact with the Real, the real world. In the voiceover narration to the opening scene, Richard says he is 'looking for something more beautiful, something more exciting, and yes, I admit, something more dangerous'. Our ordinary world is forgiving and safe. Even when we rediscover the world in a 'clumsy, arcadian way', it must be cleared up for us in advance. Chaos and disorder must be excluded and order must be created. In the film, Boyle underscores this nicely in a scene where Richard, having just checked into a guesthouse, enters the guest facilities. The other residents are watching *Apocalypse Now* from a screen. Lieutenant Colonel Bill Kilgore (Robert Duvall), shirtless and wearing a Stetson, comfortingly shouts his comrade(s) in the midst of the flames of the battlefield: 'We'll have this place cleaned up in a jiffy, son. Don't you worry'. Serres notes that our ordinary world is like a 'bedchamber', where 'everything is forgiving, the bed and the pillow, the armchair and the rug, supple and soft. A thousand causes with nonexistent effects' (Serres 1995c: 111). Such a world puts one to sleep, to a stupefying slumber that makes one numb and dumb. The tranquillity of that world seems to chase off death. And, with the flows of tourists, *The Beach* suggests that world has been spread everywhere, like they

---

5   For more on the dynamics of no-where and now-here, see Olsson (2007).

had been carrying an infectious disease. Each place is populated by tourists. For the traveller, they are a global nuisance. Whether moving in crowds or pairs, they are literally to be found everywhere, with their cameras scanning the scenery for potential snapshots. For travellers and backpackers like Richard, tourists are the most despicable of human kind, if not even the ultimate enemy. They represent the miseries of human civilisation. Tourists are the consumers of the passage, the unavoidable bane, the scum of the earth, the fools with thick wallets. The tourist is someone from whom the traveller must set him or herself apart. A traveller has to deny the tourist in oneself, for the traveller is a sucker for the authentic.[6] The tourists, on the contrary, just 'want it all to be safe. Just like America', Richard complains. Any paradise is just waiting to be invaded by tourists and turned into a holiday reserve or an attraction, a safe and soft indoor space, as it were. By transforming everything real and authentic into 'touristy', tourists annihilate and demolish all that which the traveller lives off and for. Consuming space, the tourist of *The Beach* is a parasite that threatens to eat away any paradise. The tourist is, paradoxically, a parasite who is welcomed – welcomed because s/he *gives*, brings in the money. Indeed, it is ultimately money that allows the tourist to play the position of the parasite: 'Pay them in dollars, fuck their daughters, and turn it into Wonderland', as Daffy, a character played by Robert Carlyle announces his anti-touristic motto in the film.

The paradise that *The Beach* exhibits is not a state of future bliss, but an actual place of perfection, contentment and happiness. The paradise pursued by Richard is a secret, secluded island with a perfect, white beach, crystal clear blue water and more dope one can ever smoke. There is something very familiar in this island, isn't there? Without having to force it, the film's paradise island located in the Gulf of Thailand evokes Utopia, an imaginary island in the Atlantic Ocean described by Thomas More in his 1516 book of the same title. Of places, More notes, Utopia is 'the happiest in the world'. The homophone of utopia, *eutopia*, designates a good place, a place of felicity; in Greek, εὖ means 'good' or 'well' and τόπος 'place'. However, while being related to it, the paradise island in *The Beach* is to be sharply distinguished from both Utopia the island and utopia the notion. In the term utopia, the prefix u- of utopia is derived from the Greek οὐ ('not'). Thus, utopia designates, literally, a no-place, a no-where. Utopias are unreal spaces, spaces without any real place in the world. They 'are emplacements having no real place', as Michel Foucault (2000: 178) puts it in the piece 'Different Spaces'. In a political sense, a utopia presents an ideal, perfect community, usually one that is projected to the future. The paradise of *The Beach*, by contrast, could perhaps be described as a *realised utopia*. Like utopia, it reverses the miseries of contemporary society but, unlike utopias, it is a localisable, real place. In the

---

6   Interestingly, to some extent *The Beach* echoes anti-touristic attitudes that were prevalent in tourism studies especially in the 1980s, with authors such as Feifer (1985) and MacCannell (1989) bemoaning the loss of authenticity. For a critique of anti-touristic attitudes, see Veijola and Jokinen (1994).

Foucauldian parlance, the paradise imaged in the movie could be characterised as an 'other space' or 'heterotopia': it is a place different from and 'outside all places', but it nevertheless can be localised (ibid.). The paradise turns the nowhere of utopia into a now and here.

However, until he ultimately really gets on the island in the film, the very existence of the beach remains uncertain for Richard. Even at the point when he is already holding a drawn map of the island in his possession, Richard is still unable to authenticate the story; in other words, to know for sure whether the beach really is a paradise and not only a utopia. In the film, the story of the beach circulates among backpackers as an urban myth (indeed, as a quasi-object of some kind). One evening, when Richard arrives at his hut at a beach resort in Chaweng in heavy rain he notices that he has lost his key. Zeph and Sammy, two American surfer guys from the next hut along from Richard's (in their parlance somewhat emulating the iconic popular culture fictional figures Bill and Ted or Beavis and Butthead) show him hospitality and invite him over to their porch for a beer and a joint. Zeph asks Richard:

> – I presume you know the story of the Kentucky fried mouse.

> – Yeah. Woman bites into a chicken leg and it turns out to be uh … a mouse. Right? It's an urban myth.

> – Exactly. It always happened to a friend of a friend of someone else.

> – So?

> – So, I guess there's this urban myth goin' around here at the moment. It's about a beach. Yeah?

> – Uh-huh.

> – And this beach is … perfect, man. It's on an island, right? Hidden from the sea. Now, imagine. You got pure white sand. Crystal-clear water. Palm trees.

> [Sammy:] – Yeah, with coconuts and shit. Yo, tell him the best part, dawg.

> – Plus, enough dope, Richard, to smoke, all day, every day for the rest of your goddamn life.

> [Sammy:] – Yeah! Mad weed!

> – There's only a few people who know exactly where it is, and they keep it absolutely secret. Of course no one's actually ever met any of these people, only met someone who has, you know what I mean?

[Sammy]: – Exactly. It's a Kentucky fried mouse!

[Richard:] – Hm.

– [Zeph:] Although, I must say if I had a key to a place like that I'd keep it to myself cos … you don't want every fucking asshole in Thailand turnin' up! Boo-boo!

A prerequisite of any paradise is that it must be enclosed. The word 'paradise' arrived to English from the French *paradis*, which is derived from the Latin *paradisus*, Greek *parádeisos* (παράδεισος), and ultimately from the Old Persian word *pairidaêza*. The literal meaning of the word *pairidaêza*, compound of *pairi-* ('around') and *daêza-* ('to make, form (a wall)'), is 'enclosure, park'. The idea of walled enclosure was not preserved in later usage, yet the word park, which is of the same family as paradise, is from Old French *parc*, probably ultimately from West Germanic *parruk*, meaning 'enclosed tract of land', and refers to a deliberately enclosed area. In fact, to be precise, the word *parruk* originally referred to the fencing, not to the place that is enclosed with fences. What is more, the Greek word *parádeisos*, which was originally used to refer to an orchard or hunting park in Persia, was used in Septuagint, the Greek Old Testament, to mean 'Garden of Eden'. And the word 'garden' comes from Old English *geard*, 'enclosure'. Paradise thus designates a demarcated and finite space. It is a space protected from the openness of chaos by enclosure.

In *The Beach*, the idea of enclosure is rendered evident. Sealed in from the sea by cliffs, the beach is hidden from view. The cliffs appear as a borderline demarcating the inside from the outside. As a border, they have a dual role: while they protect the inhabitants of the abode with their softness, with their hardness they also keep possible invaders out (cf. Serres 2011: 43). It is only by being cut off from this world by a border that the beach is able to remain a paradise. It must be kept secret and intact. The first time Richard hears about the beach is from a former resident of the colony inhabiting it. The man, speaking with a Scottish accent and travelling with the fake name Daffy Duck on his passport, assures Richard that the beach is secret and must also remain that way: 'See it's like a … a lagoon. Ya know, a tidal … lagoon. See it's sealed in by cliffs. Totally fuckin' secret, totally fuckin' … forbidden. And nobody can ever, ever, ever, ever go there. Ever'. Otherwise the beach would be immediately invaded by tourist-parasites. Tourists would instantly take possession of the island by soiling it with pollution, both hard (garbage, filth, excrement, exhaust from mopeds and cars and so on) and soft (signs, images, logos, billboards, advertisements and loudspeakers, for example) (cf. Serres 2011). It is only later that Richard, at that point already living on the island himself, realises what Daffy really meant. When paying a short visit to the outside world in order to stock up on food and equipment, Richard is nauseated by the noise of the world he used to belong to. Garish neon lights, bazaars, bars, criss-crossing cars and mopeds howling, partying and vomiting tourists all over the place, prostitution, techno raves on the beach … 'I'd really been looking forward to air conditioning and some cold beer, but when we got to Ko Pha-Ngan, I just wanted to leave again. In one moment, I understood more clearly than ever why we were so special, why we kept our secret. Because if we didn't, sooner or later, they'd turn it into this. Cancers. Parasites. Eating up the whole fuckin' world'.

While paradise shields us from violence, it is also produced by it: the peacefulness of any paradise constitutes itself by and in relation to the violent act of excluding the parasites. This is to say that community significantly depends not only on the inclusion achieved by the circulating gift and the related obligation to give – *munus* – but also and equally on exclusion: prevention, demarcation, exclusion, expulsion and distancing. No community can be absolutely inclusive. As sad as it is, and against much cherished Western political utopias, a completely open, inclusive community without any exclusion could not survive. It would crumble and collapse in a minute. If at least some of the parasites were not kept out, chaos would break loose. Order is possible on the condition that chaos is excluded.

At the same time, however, no inside is ever inviolable. No inside is ever fully sealed. All borders have holes, passages, portals and porosities. Through them, things may enter and leave. That Richard himself, a parasite in his own right, manages to enter the island is a token of that. Because of the existence of pores and holes, no paradise is ever fully secured from parasites. The total elimination of parasites cannot be attained. All attempts at their permanent and absolute exclusion are doomed to fail. It is only a question of time when the parasites come back in. Therefore, to maintain order and to keep chaos out, the gesture of exclusion has to be repeated incessantly, again and again.

Yet, it is questionable whether the total extermination of the parasite would even be desirable, since the total extermination of the parasite can be achieved only by exterminating the system (Serres 2007). For instance, while regional accent, mumbling, stammering and cacophony tend to disturb oral communication, just as writing is liable to the noise of spelling errors, ill-drawn graphs and bad penmanship, speech and writing could be rid of perturbations of this kind for good only at the expense of eliminating voice and graphs that are essential to speech and writing (Serres 1982: 66–70).[7] As long as there is a relation, the parasite is there as well. We see one instance of this in the film when Richard calls home from a phone booth in Ko Pha-Ngan. The line is bad; there is noise on the channel. But to eliminate all noise, one would have to eliminate the channel of communication, the telephone line, itself. All in all, 'There is no system without parasites. This constant is a law' (Serres 2007: 12). This is to say that the parasite is not external to a system, merely a transitory, marginal nuisance, but part of the system itself. It is at once necessary for the system and an obstacle for its proper functioning (ibid.: 79).

---

7   The parasite also individuates: what makes one's voice unique, just as one's identifiable handwriting, is these features designated as 'noise'.

Because the total exclusion of parasites can never be achieved, it would be inexact to describe paradise in terms of a perfectly inviolable place completely devoid of parasites. In *The Beach*, paradise is not a homogeneous stasis of perfect and balanced exchange. It is not a place from which all the parasites have been successfully chased out. Rather, it is a place where one and one's brethren get to be the only parasites. The beach is an enclosed world from which *all the other* parasites apart from oneself and one's community are sought to be made absent. The paradise of *The Beach*, to quote a catching phrase by Deleuze and Guattari (1987: 30) that they utter in a wholly different context, amounts to a colony of '[l]ice hopping on the beach'. It is a 'beach resort for people who don't like beach resorts', says Richard in a voice-over. For the traveller-parasite, Nature is not an enemy, but the most generous of hosts. It is a hospitable place surrounding the traveller: one gets to lie in the sun on a secluded beach, feel the gentle gust of wind on one's skin, swim in the refreshing turquoise water and get high on the endless reserve of cannabis. But to be able to live off these fruits of the para-disiac nature one has to, para-doxically, evict the para-sites. My paradise is conditioned by the fact that I am the sole parasite of it. To ensure that the host will keep on giving, I have to chase out the other parasites. Or, to rephrase, the paradise can be a state of balanced and equitable exchanges amongst the residents, but such a condition can only be achieved by excluding (other) parasites.

The Beach itself does not exempt itself from the parasitic relations that it displays. To a certain degree, allegedly the production process of the film was parasitic in its own right. The 20th Century Fox film company faced fierce opposition from environmentalists, pro-democracy groups and local residents in Thailand for making prohibited changes to the protected natural landscape of Maya Beach in Krabi's Phi Phi Island national park for the purposes of shooting the film. The paradise exhibited in the film was, paradoxically, a creation of breaching the peace of a natural paradise. 20th Century Fox 'bulldozed the beach, removed native plants and planted some 100 coconut trees because the film script called for a perfect tropical beach, large enough to play football on it'. According to environmental activists, the effects of the actions were severe: 'During storms that hit the area by the end of the rainy season, the environmental consequences already became evident: The sand dunes dug up and stripped from their natural vegetation collapsed and were washed into the sea. The transportation of equipment and fully-grown coconut trees to the island also damaged coral in Maya Bay'.[8] Furthermore, subsequently the beach became crowded by tourists who wanted to visit the paradise beach they had seen in the film. It made no difference that the beach itself depicted in the film was fictional (for example, the cliffs surrounding the bay were digitally added). So, the consequences of the movie to the filming location were reminiscent of the events taking place in the film: the paradise was spoiled.

---

8   http://www.twnside.org.sg/title/beach-cn.htm (consulted in Aug. 2012).

The Kula Ring Reversed

Where does the gift reside in and amongst all these parasitic chains? In the story of the city rat and the country rat recounted by Serres as well as in the film *The Beach* – and in whatever relation, for that matter – the gift is placed in the beginning of any relation, as their initiative. Every parasite is preceded by a gift. The host or the donor comes before every parasite. The parasite is conditioned by the gift, as abuse and exploitation is only possible on the condition that something has been *given*. In the parasitic chain, every parasite is followed by another as if in a stepladder formation (Serres 2007: 27). The system of parasites is not very different from the system of the gift. One could even say that the parasitic chain is the *kula* ring reversed, where the cyclical movement of the gift is viewed as a series of stills. Every parasite (givee) is also a host (giver) for the next one: the city rat for the country rat, the sleeping tax farmer for the rats eating his food, the taxed peasant for the tax farmer, the cow, the crops and the tree for the peasant and so forth, along the parasitic chain (ibid.: 14).

For the parasite, then, the gift is a *given*, a cause and precondition for its existence. In this sense, the gift is not only given *to* the parasite, but *the gift 'gives' the parasite*: the parasite is born from the gift. The parasite needs a hospitable space around it. Its very life and existence depend on it; when the giving ends, parasitism ends too. Accordingly, Serres importantly distinguishes the parasite from the predator. While the predator goes for the prey, the parasite is dependent on giving: 'The host is not a prey, for he offers and continues to give' (ibid.: 7). The parasite does not hunt, but lives on, with and by its host. Serres plays with the twofold meaning of the French word *hôte*, which means both guest and host. For him, parasitic relations are all about guests and hosts. 'The host, the guest: the same word; he gives and receives, offers and accepts, invites and is invited, master and passer-by' (ibid.: 15). He further stresses that there is no exchange between the guest and host, but they only 'exchange places' (ibid.: 16); each gives/receives in his turn. The relation between the guest and the host therefore goes always only one way, never the other. Thus the aforementioned simple, irreversible arrow is the perfect image for the parasitic relation. A further token of the link between the gift and the parasite is that a semantic ambivalence reminiscent of the one that marks the term *hôte* also characterises the expression 'to give'. Émile Benveniste (1997 [1948–49]: 34) notes that in the early phase of Indo-European languages, the verbs '[t]o give and 'to take [...] were originally linked by their polarity and [...] susceptible of the same expression', derived from the root *do-*. It 'properly means neither "take" nor "give" but either the one or the other, depending on the construction'.

Unlike the gift, the parasite does not incite reciprocity, but defies it. The parasite is a reverse of the gift and the obligation to give depicted by Mauss. While the gift is a token of generosity, parasitism is all about abuse and exploitation. And while the gift, in its purest, absolute meaning amounts to the gesture of giving or to some-thing given with no expectation of return, the parasite takes without giving. As Serres puts it, the parasite is the one who 'receives everything and gives nothing in exchange' (ibid.: 26). This is to say that the parasite self-exempts itself from the communal *munus*. The parasite is 'immune', as it were, to the obligation to give. The parasite contracts out of it, and thus self-establishes immunity. As Esposito notes, 'He is immune who is safe from obligations or dangers that concern everyone else, from the moment that giving something in and of itself implies a diminishment of one's own goods and in the ultimate analysis also of oneself' (Esposito, Campbell and Paparcone 2006: 50–51).

Who among us are parasites, then? Who is a donor and who is a parasite, who is a host and who is a guest? Parasitism does not necessarily involve any intention to abuse, as we will later see. In addition, it is important to note that parasiteness is no fixed quality of this or that creature, nor is it a fixed position. Overall, it is not always clear, whether one gives or takes; the line between giving and taking is drawn upon the water. For instance, who is to tell whether the charming prince resurrecting Snow White from her glass coffin actually stole a kiss instead of giving one? For he did seem to want something from her after all: the kiss was a farewell, a goodbye, which, however, miraculously brought her back to life. In any case, in the parasitic circle, anyone and anything is a parasite in its turn. The parasite is a circulating epithet, a token passed over and moving back and forth along with the gift. As Serres (2007: 16) remarks, 'Hosts and parasites are always in the process of passing by, being sent away, touring around, walking alone'. They constantly swap places. It is first and foremost the gift that appears as the marker of the parasite. Whenever and wherever a gift is given, the parasite is also there: the gift turns the recipient into a parasite.

The gift also attracts parasites. This makes gift-giving a dangerous business. By giving, the donor always exposes oneself to the risk of being abused; the gift travels 'in a channel that is already parasited' (ibid.: 80). The gift-relation is simultaneously an abusive relation, with either the recipient or the donor in the position of the parasite. No disinterested, unselfish giving can rule out the possibility of being taken advantage of. On the contrary, to some extent generosity even *invites* parasitism. Generosity is an invitation that makes the other a receiver/parasite; when it is turned down, the gift is annulled. Further, a relation without exchange, a gift with no expectation of return and therefore with no possibility of compensation, as we noted in Chapter 2, also tends to give the donor the upper hand. It gives the donor a hold over the recipient. In such a case, by giving, the donor receives more than one has given. Benefiting and parasitism are already present also in a situation where the gift is always weighed, measured and calculated, that is, where the giver expects a guaranteed return. So, in any event, the parasite is contemporaneous with the gift, or with the relation itself. As Serres writes: 'The original relation is that of abuse. It never stops. It is contemporaneous with the relation; it is the relation itself and the opening of the system' (ibid.: 85). Therefore, we have to try to do away with the one-sided negative connotations of the term parasite, and be as neutral as possible. The parasite is not only an obstacle for the relation but also its precondition. By accepting the gift, the parasite *gives* the giving of the given.

A Gift Anterior to the Logic of the Gift

Let us look at the parasitic circle exhibited by *The Beach*. Where is the first gift in the film? And where is the parasite? The gift that really sets Richard off in his search for the paradise beach takes the form of a map. One day, as Richard is returning to his room at the guesthouse he has booked himself into, the cleaning lady tells him in the hallway that he has a letter on his door, fastened with a thumbtack. And when he opens the letter with a picture of armed Daffy on its cover he finds out that it contains a map of the beach island. But the gift-map is preceded by another gift, the offering of a joint. And even before we get to the first gift, we are plunged into noise. The night before, Richard is kept awake by a noisy French couple making love and groaning with pleasure in a room next to his. Then, the noise they were making is suppressed by an even louder noise coming from the corridor. Blustering Daffy, drunk, making ridiculous martial arts moves and kicking up a fuss, shouts with a Scottish accent: 'Everybody happy?! Everybody having a good time, eh? Fuck you! Fuck you!' A woman's voice tries to quiet down the clamour: 'Please shut up, OK?' But this only foments Daffy and gets him more heated up: 'Bastard parasites! Viruses! That's fucking great. Cancers! Bastard cancers!'

Having entered his room after the noisy episode in the corridor, Daffy tears a hole in the mosquito screen running at the top of the wall separating his room from Richard's and asks whether he has got anything to smoke. Richard indignantly answers that he doesn't, but this doesn't bother Daffy: 'That's nae problem, pal, because, er … I've got loads of the fuckin' stuff'. When Richard finds the letter on his door the next day, he notices that it includes a drawn map of the island Daffy had been talking about in the heat of the night when they had their smoke and chat. The map, drawn on a creased piece of paper, reveals the location of the beach, marked by an X on an island next to Ko Samui and Ko Pha-Ngan in the Gulf of Thailand.

The map Daffy passes down to Richard is surely a strange gift. It is a gift without a tie and without obligation and, provided that it belongs to the logic of the gift that a gift involves a debt, it is also a gift that is 'anterior *de facto* and *de jure* to the logic of the gift' (Gasché 1997: 111). It does not oblige the one who has received, and it never comes back to the giver. It defers circulation. It goes without doubt that from the Maussian perspective, such a gift would amount to nothing but a non-gift. However, insofar as the gift must essentially remain gratuitous, without a price, it must also untie itself from the bond and from exchange. Daffy is in the position of an initial donor, who remains outside the cycle of gift-exchange. While inaugurating the circle of exchange, he stands in a place that is not yet situated in the cycle. By leaving Richard the map Daffy did not particularly seek to establish a bond with Richard. The gift that Richard is left with – the gift that he inherits from Daffy – inevitably remains without restitution. It cannot be responded to. It does not invite or lead to further reciprocity, because when Richard, baffled for having found the letter, immediately goes over to Daffy's room, he finds Daffy lying dead on the floor with his wrists cut open and blood all over the walls, bed and floor. The present received by Richard is received at a present from a giver who is not present anymore, and therefore it would be completely wrong to say that in this case the gift was given for the purpose of creating or nourishing a social bond. The gift does not put Richard in debt, nor does it impose any obligation upon him. Richard does not owe Daffy anything. The moment Richard received the map Daffy's life had already gone up in smoke, like the joint they shared the night before. When they had their smoke, Daffy was already as good as dead. When telling Richard about the beach and its perfection, Daffy, deranged and already a half-spectre of a man, at once overheated and tranquil, inhaling the smoke like his last strokes of breath, asks Richard, like a preacher whose faith is being put to the test, whether he believes in that place. No, he does not. Richard is a non-believer. But he expects that persuasion and an attempt at conversion will ensue. How wrong could he be? He doesn't realise that he is attending the last rites of a preacher who does not care anymore. It makes no difference what a man as good as dead thinks anymore. At this point, it's completely up to Richard. It is up to him, whether he wants to believe in the beach or not, and, later, after receiving the map, it is also up to him whether he decides to search the beach and set his foot on it or not. Neither Daffy the dead nor the gift-map obliges him to it.

The map Richard finds the following day is a key to just what he has been craving for: something more beautiful, exciting and dangerous. But, what is important, he did not yet know that. Even the very sight of Daffy's room leaves him numb. After seeing so many dead bodies in the movies (as well as in the news and in television shows), when we actually see one, it feels unreal, something seen in the movies and not in real life: 'You hope, and you dream, but you never think something's gonna happen to you. Not like it does in the movies. And when it actually does, you want it to feel different. More visceral. More real. I was waiting for it to hit me. But it just wouldn't happen'. As for the gift-map, Richard has neither requested nor asked for it. It is imposed upon him. Like the offering of a smoke the night before, the gift-map anticipates Richard's wish. And it is precisely by anticipating the request that the gift – and the giver – truly becomes virtuous. The virtue of the offer preceding any wish is depicted in a perceptive manner in the eulogy on tobacco, the opening scene in Molière's *Don Juan* (and discussed by Serres [1982: 4–5] and Derrida [1994: 112–13] alike). In the opening of the play, Don Juan's servant Sganarelle praises the joys and noble effects of tobacco. According to him, 'It not only clears and delights the brain; but it also inclines the heart to virtue, and helps one to become a gentleman'. And then Sganarelle explains how it is that tobacco succeeds in this miracle: 'Haven't you noticed how, as soon as one begins to take it, one becomes uncommonly generous to everybody, ready to present one's box right and left wherever one goes? You don't even wait to be asked, but anticipate the desires of others […]' (Molière 2008: 33).

However, loony Daffy, babbling on unceasingly, is no honest gentleman. Far from it. By giving Richard the map, isn't he betraying his own, that is, his former brethren? Instead of keeping the secret of the beach strictly to himself, he reveals it to a stranger, an odd 'travellin wank' he had only formed a momentary alliance with, a union which was dissolved, gone up in smoke, when the joint, the object binding them to one another, was consumed. The non-reason of Daffy is that he contradicts himself. In one and the same gesture, he simultaneously renders the island both sacred and profane. He provides both prohibition and access. He both encloses the island and lets the parasites in. For after insisting that the island must be kept intact, that no one can ever enter it, he leaves Richard the map that leads to the island. Or perhaps for Daffy the beach was already a paradise lost. Perhaps the parasites were already there. Daffy did his best to heal the island's immunity system from an infection when he was on it. He pictured himself as a sort of medicine man or a physician of the community: 'See I-I was the one that was trying to find the cure. Procurer of the cure. And I said to them: "You've got to leave. You've got to leave this place." But they wouldnae listen'. The immunity system had already failed. The assumedly rightful inhabitants of the paradise, the men and women with ideals, were parasites just like any other, for they too came from the outside. As Daffy tells Richard: 'Ideals, eh? We were just fuckin' parasites! The big, chunky Charlie!'

The Ethical as a Temptation One Should Resist

Let us return to the map received by Richard. What a strange gift indeed. The law of the gift, as we saw in the two previous chapters, usually commands that gifts must keep on moving. The ethics of the gift says that it is immoral to withhold and keep a gift for oneself. One must never hang on to what one has received, but always give it away, sooner or later. Ultimately, the gift or its (symbolic) equivalent must always return home, to its origin. However, the gift Richard receives from Daffy insists just the opposite. It demands of the receiver to violate the law of the gift. It asks that it should never move, never be passed on to a third person. So, it is correct, and even essential, for Richard to withhold, to keep back. The map must never enter exchange relations. It must never circulate. Otherwise the gift would, as it were, negate and annihilate itself. All these prohibitions are for the sake of protecting the beach. For if the gift travelled from hand to hand, sooner or later the paradise would be destroyed, as every traveller and tourist in Thailand would join in.

To be able to use the map and consume the passage, one has to be on the map oneself. But the gift-map is not a magic carpet that would fly one to the destination. This takes us to the gift number two. Richard makes his peace with the parasites by going over to the French couple who had kept him awake the night before to invite them to accompany him to the beach. Françoise (Virginie Ledoyen) and her boyfriend Étienne (Guillaume Canet) gladly accept the invitation. Nevertheless, the generous invitation is partly motivated by the prospect of parasitism. When Étienne opens the door, Richard produces a Freudian slip out of nervousness: 'Hey! You want to take a hike? Uh, a-a trip, a journey? With y-your girlfriend and me? I mean the two of you and me. Together'. So, in the blink of an eye, the host himself is turned into a parasite. And indeed, later in the film Richard ends up coming in-between the French couple (in the novel he is attracted to Françoise, but never acts upon his crush). But also at this very early stage he is already parasiting Étienne. Richard couldn't have reached the destination just by himself. As he confesses in a voiceover to the occasion of inviting Françoise and Étienne to accompany him: 'I realised that I had absolutely no idea of how I was gonna get there'. Étienne organises the whole journey: 'tickets, timetables, the whole damn trip'. And yet, Étienne and Françoise are just as dependent on Richard as he is on them, since without him and the map he has in his possession they would not only never have found the beach, but also never even known anything of its existence. So, Richard, who is like a cripple, and Étienne and Françoise, who make one blind person, strike a bargain, as it were, by exchanging legs for eyes and knowledge (cf. Serres 2007: 37). Together, they form a functioning unity, as if one able body: the blind will carry the cripple, who will be the guide.

But, to be exact, the gift does not coincide with the bilateral and self-interested contract. Rather, the contract negates the principle of the gift and is its direct opposition (Esposito 2010: 29). The common *munus* is not motivated by self-interest and consideration of benefit, but derives, as Esposito argues, from *fear*. Reminiscent of Heidegger, Esposito considers fear essentially as the fear of death. What we have to fear is death, that 'of no longer being what we are: alive' (ibid.: 21). In *Being and Time* (1962), Heidegger suggests that what distinguishes human beings from other living beings is that we know in advance that we shall die. And thus the mode of being of humans is *Sorge*, care, anxiety, or concern. Esposito picks up this lead and maintains that it is fear, the fear of death that defines us as mortals: 'what does it mean that we are "mortals" if not that we are subjects above all *to* fear' (Esposito 2010: 21). According to him fear is '*terribly originary*': 'fear is ours in the most extreme sense that we are not other from it. We originate in fear'. Up to a certain point, the community, so we like to think, protects us from this fear. In the community that survives the death of the individual, the common 'we' secures the individual a certain kind of immortality: people find comfort in the idea that one does not die, at least not completely, insofar as the social whole (family, fatherland, humanity and so on) of which one is a part lives on (cf. Blanchot 1988; see also Pyyhtinen 2010: 105). The morning after getting stoned on their porch with Zeph and Sammy, his fellow Americans, Richard, as a way of paying back courtesy, draws a copy of the map and slips it under the surfer guys' door together with the T-shirt they were kind enough to loan him. 'I told myself that spreading news is a part of traveller's nature. But if I was being completely honest, I was just like everybody else: shit-scared of the great unknown. Desperate to take a little piece of home with me'.

Thus, against common wisdom, perhaps even against the standard philosophy of ethics, the ethical is here a *temptation* one must refuse: Richard should have resisted the call to responsibility (cf. Derrida 1995: 61). Or, to phrase the matter otherwise, the map is accompanied by an entirely different ethics altogether, one that is alien to obligation and exchange instead of being opened up by them. So, instead of acting responsibly and yielding to the obligation to pass on the gift, to pay it forward, Richard should have, out of responsibility, not responded. Duty demands here, paradoxically, that one refute the call to responsibility. Richard should have refused the communal *munus*. Hence, obeying the ethical order of the gift makes him irresponsible. Isn't this our most common, everyday experience of responsibility? That is to say, we cannot respond to the other without at the same time risking betraying others. I can be responsible to someone only by failing in my responsibility to another one (ibid.: 70). For while I may be responsible to the other, there are, as Derrida (1995: 68) remarks, 'also others, an infinite number of them, the innumerable generality of others to whom I should be bound by the same responsibility [...]. I cannot respond to the call, the request, or even the love of another without sacrificing the other, the other others'. Therefore, by responding to the obligation to repay the hospitality received from his fellow countrymen, Richard, in the same instant, betrays his future family on the island. Richard acknowledges this: 'Now, I know it wasn't a part of the plan, but I made a decision to leave a copy of the map. I'm not gonna say it was the best decision I ever made'. But one cannot blame him. Making a decision is always the hardest thing. The 'instant of decision is madness'.[9] There are no just decisions. A choice has to be made, but it is impossible to decide which choice is the best one: 'I can never justify the fact that I prefer or sacrifice any one (any other) to the other' (Derrida 1995: 70). Had Richard refuted the obligation to give, he would have fulfilled his obligations to his future family on the beach, but betrayed his fidelity to his fellow Americans he had befriended. Either way, by fulfilling his duty, he also betrays ethics. He is bound to both parties by the same responsibility and cut from them by the same betrayal. To decide is to bind by fulfilling one's duty, but it is also to cut.

'Hostpitality' and Paradise Lost

To get somewhere one needs more than instructions how to get there. The beach island that Richard, Étienne and Françoise are pursuing is in the national park and it is forbidden for tourists to go there. So they pay someone to take them on a boat to an island next to the one they are actually intending to go ashore, and decide to make the rest of the journey by swimming. And it is at this point that the adventure begins. Richard, Étienne and Françoise have to cross an arm of the sea, a distance of about one or two kilometres. They have to leave the shore behind, and it is only after they are so far that they cannot go back that they really have left their safe and forgiving home, let go of the feeling of security (cf. Serres 1997: 5). If they failed to finish the swim they would sink to the bottom of the sea and die.

After landing on the island, the island almost immediately reveals its wonders to the three travellers. At the same time, its system of parasitic relations begins to unfold. Richard, Étienne and Françoise discover an enormous cannabis field,

---

9   In several of his works, Derrida attributes the quote to Kierkegaard without, however, providing a reference to any specific text by the latter.

the size of a football pitch. However, the incredulous joy and amazement caused by the discovery is cut short. Richard, Étienne and Françoise realise that they were not invited, as Richard spots Thai gunmen on guard. Unwilling to listen to the staccato of assault rifles, the trio interrupts the bloodfeast before it gets started: they narrowly manage to save themselves and flee unnoticed. Parasites interrupting and driving away each other, one after the other. The greatest parasite is the one who expels all the others: 'Death to the parasite, some say, without seeing that a parasite is put to death only by a stronger parasite. Keep the noise down, says he, without perceiving that he has monopolized all the noise, without understanding that he thus becomes the head of all the fury' (Serres 1995b: 131).

When the trio finally finds their way to the beach, they realise that they are uninvited guest there as well: 'I don't know what we expected. People living in a cage, maybe even a few guys in tents. But nothing like this. It was like we arrived in a lost world. A full-scale community of travellers – not just passing through, but actually living here. I suddenly became aware that we weren't even invited'. Richard, Étienne and Françoise are surely trespassing. They are strangers violating someone else's home. Nevertheless, instead of being simply turned away, the intruders are welcomed as guests/enemies. Derrida (2000: 45) has employed the helpful term 'hostpitality' to express the ambiguity of guest and enemy. It manages to capture how hospitality and hostility are not foreign to one another, but closely linked. The guest, as long as he is a guest, is always also an intruder to some extent. Hospitality easily turns into hostility and, the other way around, absolute hospitality necessitates that one welcomes anyone, even one's enemy, as a guest. By letting the parasites arrive, the community interrupts interrupting. As long as the parasites are not too numerous, it is better to make one's peace with them, give them place (Serres 2007: 88). It is well known that an organism is safeguarded from a disease much more effectively through vaccination than through demarcation and keeping at distance. That is, immunity is achieved precisely by injecting the patient's organism with a tolerable amount of the same disease it is meant to be protected from (Esposito in Esposito, Campbell and Paparcone 2006: 51). The same goes to the communal body. Therefore, Richard, Étienne and Françoise are accepted, though not without reserve. They are taken to Sal, the leader of the tribe. She wants to make sure that there will be no more of their kind coming. That is the unspoken condition for a truce between them. When Richard shows the map and tells about the death of Daffy, Sal asks, as if casually: 'Do you think he gave the map to anybody else?' Richard answers 'I-I … No, I don't think so'. And when all three, Étienne, Françoise and Richard reply 'No' to her question whether they have shown the map to anybody, Sal is relieved: 'Good. We value our secrecy'. And she sets the map on fire.

As soon as the guests stop being in the state of coming, that is, as soon as they come and stay, they are no longer guests. Only a couple of days after their arrival, Richard, Étienne and Françoise settle in and make the beach their home: 'This became our world. And these people, our family. Back home was just one place we didn't think about. I settled in. I found my vocation: the pursuit of pleasure'.

For a while, it seemed like nothing could disturb their blissful happiness. As the voiceover narration provided by Richard tells us, 'There was a range of sporting and leisure activities to suit all tastes', anything from zip lines to video games, swimming, playing football and singalongs by the campfire, you name it.

Bliss nevertheless has its price. Unviolated, undisturbed happiness is itself a product of violence. It is only made possible by way of exclusion. 'In the perfect beach resort, nothing is allowed to interrupt the pursuit of pleasure'. The parasites must be kept away. Richard improves his position in the community by killing a shark that swam to their lagoon. Afterwards, he gets all the attention to himself by telling all others at the longhouse about his dangerous encounter with the shark. Hence, Richard becomes the greater parasite of the two: 'The parasited one parasites the parasite' and 'jumps to the last position' (Serres 2007: 13). However, immediately a new parasite jumps behind Richard's back. Sal's partner Bugs, their on-island carpenter, intervenes on Richard's glorious moment by belittling the feat of valor. It was only a baby shark, Bugs reminds, it had not really learnt to kill yet. It would be a whole different thing to face a full-grown mother, 'with a taste of blood on its tongue', Bugs further complains. But Richard has the last word. He ridicules Bugs for boring the others with his words of envy.

However, keeping parasites away is a full-day, non-stop business. It demands constant attention. One has to be constantly on guard, on shift around the clock 'without sleeping, without turning [one's] back, without leaving for a moment, without eating' (Serres 2007: 12). What makes the endeavour all the more difficult is that parasites not only keep flowing in from the outside; they also emerge from within. There are several serpents in the paradise, Richard himself being one of them. He comes in between Étienne and Françoise. Keaty (Paterson Joseph) intervenes between Richard and his libido by asking him to forget it, but Richard can't help it, the attraction he has developed for the beautiful Frenchwoman already has a hold of him: 'All in all, this really was paradise. Except for one thing. Desire is desire, wherever you go. The sun will not bleach it, nor the tide wash it away'. One night, Richard and Françoise sneak out from the camp to the beach, just the two of them, and end up kissing and caressing one another passionately. What happened on the beach that night was supposed to remain a secret, just between the two of them: 'That night, we promised ourselves, and we honestly believed, that no one would ever know'. However, the secret of their affair breaks, just as the two lovers did not remain underwater. Étienne knows. Everyone knows, without Richard and Françoise knowing it. While cutting branches with a machete, Étienne confronts Richard. For a moment, it seems that violence and bloodshed will follow. But Étienne notes that if Françoise's happiness is with Richard, so be it. He won't stand in their way.

So, the old order was transformed into a new one: Richard, formerly himself in third position, stepped in to the place of Étienne, and forced him to play the third. Étienne was cast off and a new pair was formed: Françoise and Richard. They became an item. 'For a while', as Richard's voiceover narration tells, 'we were untouchable in our happiness'. But no relation remains unparasited for long. The parasites keep turning up. One day Sal convenes the inhabitants to inform them about a situation. A fungus has contaminated some sacks of rice, and because of this parasite they have to make a journey to Ko Pha-Ngan to stock up on rice. There are no other volunteers but Bugs. However, Sal says that no, Richard will accompany her.

In Ko Pha-Ngan, the intimacy between Richard and Françoise is damaged and soiled. While Richard used to belong exclusively to Françoise, in Ko Pha-Ngan overnight he gives his body to Sal. However, it is not solely Sal who is a parasite here, but Richard, too, plays the parasite, for Sal is with Bugs. Although Bugs had seen this coming, Richard is a parasite more or less against his will. It is not out of passion but out of necessity that he sleeps with Sal. It is a pact. In Ko Pha-Ngan Richard encounters Zeph and Sammy when sitting at a bar. Zeph and Sammy can't believe their eyes. Zeph wants to introduce Richard to two German girls accompanying him and Sammy: 'Girls, I want you to meet the man! […] Hilda und Eva, das ist Richard! The man with the map.' 'Der Mensch mit der Wanderkarte?' one of the girls asks. 'Ja!' Zeph replies. Then Sammy continues by telling Richard that the girls are going to come with him and Zeph to the beach. And he apologises for the fact it has taken so long for them to get there, for they have been 'chilling out'. Richard realises that he has been busted. Now it comes clear to Sal that he lied about not showing the map to anyone. He tries to cover the tracks of his lie and claims that there is no beach after all: the beach was just a story, and the map was a fake. But Zeph won't buy it: 'You wouldn't be holding out on us, would ya? Let me guess. It's a fuckin' paradise!' And so Richard sleeps with Sal for her silence. (Richard does go to Ko Pha-Ngan in the book, too, but not with Sal. In the novel, Sal does not come in between Richard and Françoise, who never were an item in the first place, for that matter.) It was his return ticket to the island. Yet another duo bound by a secret. Sal tells Richard that 'I don't think we should tell anybody. OK? I think we should keep it between you and I'. The deal is that they both remain silent: both the map and the sex should remain a secret.

When they get back to the beach, Richard is giving out souvenirs at the longhouse like it's Christmas. Everybody is happy. Everything seems to be as before. 'So I started just where I left off. It was almost like my trip to Ko Pha-Ngan never happened. Almost'. Richard keeps the house of cards standing with two lies, both of which are about to rumble: to Sal he says Zeph and Sammy do not have a copy of the map, and to Françoise, who has been suspicious, he tells that nothing happened between him and Sal back in Ko Pha-Ngan. The paradise starts to collapse in consequence of a second shark intrusion. Two of the three Swedish guys in the tribe are bitten while fishing in the lagoon. And they are bitten badly: Sten is dead and Christo severely injured. The inhabitants bury Sten and hold a funeral, but things can't get back to normal any more. Sal won't agree to Christo's request that a doctor be called to the island to see him. On the contrary, she suggests that Christo somehow gets himself to the mainland and keeps their secret by not telling where the incident happened. But Christo is too scared to go anywhere near the water. And so they are stuck with Christo, for he isn't getting any better. This is the price of their secret. And Christo's moaning and suffering is starting to really get to the others. Being neither a host nor a guest, Christo – whose name is surely not devoid of religious connotations – is a parasite nevertheless. The others see him as a disturbing noise: 'You see, in a shark attack, or any other major tragedy, I guess, the important thing is to get eaten and die, in which case there's a funeral and somebody makes a speech and everybody says what a good guy you were. Or get better, in which case everyone can forget about it. Get better or die. It's the hanging around in between that really pisses people off'.

As a result, Christo is expelled from the community. He is stretchered into a tent in the middle of the jungle, where he lies in pain, with only Étienne keeping him company and tending to him. If people want peace, they need to banish the parasite. The parasite is our 'common enemy', a common nuisance we have to get rid of: 'we have to get together, assembling, resembling, against whoever troubles our relations'. The collective 'is the expulsion of the stranger, of the enemy, of the parasite' (Serres 2007: 56).[10] Of course, such an action is itself immoral. The tragedy of peaceful exchange, communication and dialogue is that it is possible only on the condition of the exclusion of the parasite, which is always an act of violence. But, as in so many other cases, the moral problems our actions may involve tend to be silenced by their effectivity: 'It would be a lot easier to condemn our behaviour if it hadn't been so effective. But out of sight really was out of mind. Once he was gone, we felt a whole lot better'.

The ultimate sign of the ruining of the paradise is the arrival of Zeph and Sammy together with the German girls on a neighbouring island. With binoculars, Sal notices that they have a copy of the map with them. Shutting out the parasites becomes Richard's mission. Sal orders him to keep watch in the bushes all day and night until they come and get the map back, no matter what. Unaware of his mission, the other inhabitants are getting suspicious and start talking about Richard. What is he doing all day? He does no work for the community. 'But he steals our food. I'm certain of it', a woman says. 'Idle, sponging, useless prick!' a man continues. Bugs, who had questioned Richard's usefulness for the community from the very beginning, joins in. All along Bugs the carpenter had regarded Richard as a useless parasite, who can make nothing and produce nothing.

At first Richard thought he would starve to death out there in the jungle. But in fact, '[l]ife up on the hill turned up to be a big improvement'. He is freed from the obligation to give and to contribute: there is no fishing duty, no gardening, no complex social relationships. He is playing his own game now. Compared to the life in the village, he finds much more exciting things to keep him occupied. The jungle becomes a massive 'gamespace'[11] for Richard. He sneaks around and spies the gunmen guarding the cannabis field. He likes to fool around: he imagines that

---

10   Serres's account could be regarded as a variation of Girard's notion of sacrifice. While for Girard the unity of the community is based on the exclusion of the sacrificial victim, for Serres it is based on the expulsion of the parasite.

11   The notion of gamespace is from Shaviro (2010).

he is playing a video-game, running in the woods, using sticks as guns, rolling on the ground, hiding behind rocks and dodging flying lizards. However, Richard has begun to lose it, just like Daffy had. The beach is too much for him. He cannot keep the abundance of input and sensation in control, but it keeps spilling out, just as it had happened with Daffy. He begins to see things. Daffy the spectre had already come to him in a dream back in the village, but now Richard is having actual conversations with him. Richard becomes obsessed with Daffy. 'This forest was my territory. Retrieving the map, my mission. And [the gunmen], my defenders. I was the only one with the overview of how it all fitted together. The island. Me. Them. The invaders. All connected. All playing the same game. And at the centre of it all, one man: Daffy'. Daffy, the initial donor, now the ultimate parasite, placed in the centre, stealing all the attention, taking up all space. The cycle is complete.

Richard the jungle warrior regards Daffy as his mentor. He thinks Daffy has led him the way, shown him the truth. So he owes Daffy after all. Richard reciprocates by living in faith. He won't betray the beach, most of all he won't let Daffy down. He's on the same side with Daffy. In the jungle, Richard hallucinates that he's walking in the corridor of the guesthouse back in Bangkok, and Daffy pulls him inside his room. The room is in the middle of a battleground. Light filters in through the gun-shot holes on the walls, and the wind is blowing. 'Viruses, Richard! Cancers! The big, chunky Charlie's eating up the whole world! Out there!' Daffy hands Richard a pair of binoculars and starts firing from the window with a machine-gun. 'Down on the beach! Down on the street! Pay them with dollars and fuck their daughters!' Together, Richard and Daffy will stop the parasites. Together, they will keep away the invaders: 'It starts with four, Richard! Four! But they multiply! They multiply! It's time to stop them! Year zero, kiddo!' Daffy shouts and keeps on firing. 'Year zero!' Richard repeats. Year zero is getting closer. Year zero: 'primal chaos, the state of things about to born […] a nascent state' (Serres 1995c: 51). Noise: the beginning and the end of it all.

Next, things evolved as if according to a law of nature. The paradise was about to be ruined, and there was nothing anyone could do about it. Having managed to build a raft and paddle to the island, Zeph, Sammy, Hilda and Eva are shot dead in the cannabis field by the guarding gunmen. It is only then that it really hits Richard. This time it is no game, nor does it feel like in the movies. This time it's visceral and real. The screaming, powerless fellow travellers are murdered in cold blood in front of his very eyes. Richard realises that it is about time to leave the island. He now sees that he has lost himself. He cannot remember the person he used to be. And he knows that, as long as he stays on the island, things will remain that way. He will never find that person again. (In a sense, for Richard, finding himself by way of escape becomes thus a gift, even the original gift, perhaps.) He heads back to the village to fetch Françoise and Étienne. And they arrange to meet by the boat. But before they can set off, Richard gives Christo the gift of death: he releases Christo from his suffering by suffocating him. However, paradise is not only protected from the outside, but it is also sealed from the inside. It is almost as difficult to escape as it is to get in. On their way to the beach, Françoise and Étienne are stopped by the gunmen, and Richard is knocked unconscious and taken to the longhouse.

At the longhouse, the gunmen walk in on the residents in the middle of a techno rave. The party is interrupted by the sound of gunshots fired into the air. The villagers had been celebrating the island and their communion. Sal had given a spirit-raising speech to strengthen their faith. It was time to look ahead. The problems they had had were now in the past. Or so it was, they thought. The farmer speaks up. He convinces them that he's not a bad guy, but a producer, a giver of gifts: 'Do you think I want to hurt you? I'm a farmer, that's all. Understand? I work. I send the money to my family. If too many people come to this island, it's trouble for me! I can't work, I can't send the money and my family don't eat!' He laments that the residents have not kept their side of the deal. That jeopardises his giving. 'I said no more people. But more people come. And you … You give them the map!' As a result, the times of generosity and abundance are over. The residents are to be banished from the paradise: 'Now, you all go home. Forget this island. Forget about Thailand!' However, Sal refuses. She is not willing to let go. She makes Richard the scapegoat, saying that it was all his fault, for it was he who copied the map: 'You let us down, Richard. You brought us trouble'. And what happens to scapegoats? Yes, they are sacrificed. The farmer hands Sal a revolver. The deal is that if she shoots Richard, they can stay. By killing him they would atone for their sins, make things right.

Sal pulls the trigger, but the gun clicks. The community instantly disperses and deserts her along with the longhouse. The situation reminds us of the paradox of paternal authority as depicted by Slavoj Žižek. In order to be experienced as actual, effective authority, authority must remain virtual, only a threat. As soon as it is actualised, it undermines itself and self-destroys. While the authority of a father, for instance, is based on and backed up by the threat of violence, as soon as he actually slaps his children or shouts at them, the father becomes ridiculous and loses all his authority.[12] In an analogous manner, the moment she pulls the trigger, Sal loses all her authority and potency. Like an empty cloth, she drops to her knees, weeping. After having occupied the spot of power, she suddenly no longer has any place. And, having no place, she no longer has anything. She has lost it all: her island, everything. Had the gun actually gone off, the consequence would have nevertheless remained the same: either way, Sal's action forced everyone to see, as Richard says, 'what it takes to keep our little "paradise" a secret'. While a paradise excludes violence, it is also based on violence, and Sal pulling the trigger made that explicit. Together, the former residents flee the island. They build a raft, swim back to the mainland and depart ways. The film ends with a scene from an Internet café, where Richard notices that he has received an email from Françoise. The message contains a photo of the beach community, with a handwritten inscription: 'Parallel Universe. Love, Françoise x'.

---

12   See http://www.youtube.com/watch?v=NXi46W51104.

A New Balance: The Logic of the Parasite

What is there for us to learn from the parasitic relations of *The Beach*, then? How does the film and the notion of the parasite help us better understand the gift and its relation to exchange? Most importantly, they show how both giving and taking are indispensable for the event of a gift. The actualisation of the gift depends not solely on the giver, but on the givee as well.

As the parasite is more than willing to accept the gift, the gift is anything but annulled by the parasite. As Richard utters in the voiceover narration to the scene in the beginning of the movie where he drinks snake blood with odd Thai men from the underworld: 'Never refuse an invitation'. It is the refusal of the offer that contradicts the gift. Turning down an offer offends the offerer and is equal to a declaration of war. Insofar as the gift needs to be accepted, empirically the parasite is even indispensable for the gift. The gift is possible because of the parasite, not in spite of it. It is the parasite which makes the given into a given; in the absence of the parasite, there is no given. The parasite *gives* the giving of the given. But wait a minute, doesn't the very act of accepting immediately negate the gift in the sense of giving without return, for it seems to imply reciprocity, the other *gives* his/her acceptance? So the parasite gives after all? Not quite. The parasite's giving turns out to be deceptive: the parasite gives only by taking.

The parasite merely gives the empirical possibility of the event of the gift. There would never occur any generosity, no gift would ever be given, if the giving was not followed by an acceptance and a minimal recognition (we are reintroduced here to the gap between the conceptual and the empirical, since conceptually the gift is disqualified by recognition, as we remember Derrida arguing). The acceptance needs to be signalled by the recipient uttering 'thank you'. As Serres explains this at length:

> No exchange could take place, no gift could be given in any of the languages I have spoken, if the final receiver did not say 'thank you' at the end of the line. The terminal offers thanks. The phrase is only a gust of wind; it is indispensable nonetheless. It throws this thank you on the scale of the freely given. Without it, there have been wars: the ingrates against the magnificent, the parasites against the euergetes. What purpose does giving serve, I ask you, if this minimal recognition did not recognize the superb and the generous? Moreover, the thanker moves away from the last position, one, by the way, that is rather difficult to maintain. To have the last word is to leave the last position to the other and to jump to the penultimate. Thus the host or the gift-giver quickly answers: 'Don't mention it; you're welcome; at your service', and thereby brings back the receiver to his place. (Serres 2007: 45)

'Thank you' – these are words of a parasite. While the utterance is obviously a token of gratitude, it is also a sign of the parasitic relation. The one who says 'thank you', the one who has the last word, plays the parasite. He violates 'the justice of the stomach': 'Solid for solid, substance for substance, and meal for coin of the realm; elsewhere, air for sound and vice versa' (ibid.: 35). The parasite invents a new logic: the word becomes worth the thing, 'the logical enters the secret of the material' (ibid.: 45). Turning non-equivalents into equivalents is the hocus-pocus of the parasite.[13] Here we are back in the order of exchange. But the exchange is far from being equal: 'The parasite is invited to the *table d'hôte*; in return, he must regale the other dinners with his stories and his mirth. To be exact, he exchanges good talk for good food; he buys his dinner, paying for it in words' (ibid.: 34). The parasite gives hot air and sound in return for solids and substances. 'The exchange of the logical for the material is a parasitic invention. The parasitic is there, at the very beginning of exchange and gift-giving, of gift-giving and damages; it switches the changes between what is not equivalent' (ibid.: 150).

This way, the parasite bends the logic of exchange for his/her own benefit (ibid.: 24). As we remember, the law of exchange was balanced reciprocity: for as much as I have received I must give back. The parasite, however, creates a new balance. According to Serres, its mathematical law goes like this: 'if I receive two without paying out the exchange value, I acquire four; if I take four and do not pay, I acquire eight'. Thus, by taking back what one is obligated to give, the parasite can acquire almost 'indefinitely' (Serres 1982: 9). The parasite interrupts just exchange and turns it into an 'unjust pact' (Serres 2007: 36).

So, it is obvious that the parasite violates the law of the gift, as presented by Mauss and Bourdieu alike. Within the (economic) order of relations, the gift is always supposed to be repaid (in kind). The one who only receives and either gives nothing in return or offers sheer hot air for things breaks the terms of the tacit agreement. The parasite never pays back in kind what s/he has received. However, while abusing the obligation to give to his/her own benefit, the parasite, as para-doxical as it first may seem, is in perfect compliance with the gift itself, when the gift is considered in terms of giving with abandon. Insofar as the gift gets annulled in the circulation, by preventing the gift to be transformed into transaction the parasite even retains the gift *as* a gift. In that sense, paratisism is empirically necessary for gratuitous giving: the free gift necessitates a givee who receives the gift without repaying it. Whenever and wherever we receive *a gift*, we are in the position of the parasite. If we did not remain parasitic (by receiving more than we give), the gift-relation would be turned into a relation of mercantile exchange, where there is an exact equivalency of values between what we give and what we receive.[14] This is also to say that one can also be a

---

13   It is therefore easy to see why money – making possible the exact equivalency of the most incommensurable of values – is the most magnificent of parasitic magicians.

14   The system of the gift is not one of balanced equality and equitable exchange, but one of 'alternating inequality' (Godbout and Caillé 1998: 33). Marion (2011: 76), too, notes that the gift 'free[s] itself from a logic of equality'. The gift is not egalitarian; it is in perpetual difference from equality. Now, you are the giver and I am the parasite. Next, I am the giver and you are the parasite. We swap places in a process that in principle goes

parasite against one's will. Being a parasite does not automatically presuppose malevolent intentions nor is it necessarily something desired. On the contrary, it may also be an unpleasant state, as parasitism involves dependency. Accordingly, in a sense the repayment of a gift can be seen as an effort to liberate oneself from the position of the parasite. By so doing one makes the previous host into a parasite, to whom one becomes a host oneself.

However, at the very moment of allowing for giving gratuitously, the parasite, by taking without giving in return, already reveals the impossibility of the absolute gift ever actually taking place. In a sense, then, the parasite at once violates and conforms to the logic of the gift, violates it by conforming to it. By accepting the gift without paying back, the parasite not only conforms to the notion of a unilateral gift, but also reveals the rules or the essence of the gift which must never become manifest, which must remain in secret (as discussed in Chapter 2), in order for there to be a gift, in the purest sense of the term. Therefore, to phrase the matter in the form of a paradox, the parasite reveals, empirically, in the realm of actual social relations, that *the essence of the gift is that it is not a gift*. The parasite reveals that there are no free gifts, at least not insofar as gifts always involve a debt, an obligation or demand for compensation of some sort. This is because the parasite becomes a problem only within the economy of exchange. The parasite contradicts only the gift that is indebted, the gift that is not free and disinterested, the gift that is not a gift in the pure and absolute sense. Were the gift constituted not only conceptually but also empirically by absolute generosity, excess and pure loss, the gift would be completely indifferent to the prospect of parasitism and the problem of abuse.

Two Gifts: Conditional and Unconditional

So, the gift is possible and impossible at the same time, and the parasite is at once a condition of its possibility and impossibility. With the help of the notion of the parasite, we are able to reveal an antinomy between two different notions of the gift: *unconditional* and *conditional*, the first being theoretical and the other empirical. The unconditional gift is absolute and unlimited. The unconditional gift means that one does not select to whom one gives: it means readiness and willingness to give without recognition, to *absolutely whoever*, to 'the absolute, unknown, anonymous other' (Derrida 2000: 25). The unconditional gift is liberated from the logic of exchange. It is to give without demand for any reward coming

---

on infinitely. Let me also refer here to Godbout and Caillé (1998: 211), who suggest that the gift always entails a 'surplus reception': 'we always receive more than we give, even if we do not want this to be so'. According to them, this is 'the most general law of the gift, observed wherever the gift is found and can function it is normal state'. So the law of the surplus reception suggests that, whether we like it or not, receiving always makes us parasites.

back to self. The conditional gift, by contrast, is based on selection. It is selective and limited in nature: one chooses to whom one gives, gives only to a specified, identified givee. Selection thus injects calculation to the incalculable: to whom do I give? How do I select to whom I give? Are you worthy of my gift? This is the gift of the gift-exchange and is conditioned by the exclusion of the parasite. In it, the giver and the recipient, a parasite in his/her own right, together form a system and chase out the (other) parasites. The unconditional gift, by contrast, does not distinguish between friend and parasite/enemy, the invited and the uninvited/abusive guest. It eschews the very distinction.

The contrast between the unconditional and the conditional gift thus appears absolute. They negate one another. For Derrida, as we remember, the gift can only be unconditional. Whenever and wherever giving is conditional, the gift negates itself as a gift. Nevertheless, in closer examination the relation between the two notions proves to be more complex. They at the same time presuppose and exclude each other. What Derrida has noted of unconditional and conditional hospitality, in my view also holds (and in this I thus to some extent read Derrida against himself) for the unconditional and conditional gift: 'They incorporate one another at the moment of excluding one another, they are dissociated at the moment of enveloping one another' (ibid.: 81).[15] This is also the reason why I have insisted above on the importance of studying also the actualisation of the gift in the dynamics of social relations instead of keeping solely to the analysis of its conceptual conditions of im/possibility; in the real logics of the social, the gift never appears as pure. The issue is not a matter of theoretical hair-splitting, but a very crucial one with concrete consequences if we think of for instance the justification (and erosion) of the welfare society, which has been under much debate and criticism during the last few decades. In addition, many of the current governmental actions against *personae non gratae*, such as turning away asylum seekers, exiling Romany refugees and forbidding public begging by law relate to the problems of the gift, hospitality and the parasite. What is at stake in these issues is the question, must we accept that the gift may be abused and taken advantage of (in order for there to be a gift)?

On the one hand, the gift is conditional, but it is conditioned in its dependence on unconditionality. The concept of the gift cannot be reduced to the logic of exchange. Even empirically, every gift would cease to be a gift were it not 'guided and given aspiration' by the ideal of the unconditional, absolute gift. If the giver held strictly to the symmetry and reciprocity of gift and counter-gift, if I gave only to those who give to me and to the extent that they give me, the gift would annul itself, for I would in fact *give* (up) nothing at all. The giving would be 'like a tax that is imposed or a debt that is repaid, like the acquittal of a debt' (ibid.: 106). And it would always bring back a repayment. To be sure,

---

15   The link between gift and hospitality is not arbitrary. On the contrary, as Benveniste ([1948–49] 1997: 36) has noted, 'An obvious connection joins the notion of the gift to that of hospitality'.

then, the gift would seem to be possible only on the condition that one avoids or suspends overt calculation and selection. Taken to its extreme, the conditional gift ends up negating the gift not only conceptually (as it necessarily does) but also empirically, just as the right to choose one's guests, when brought to a certain threshold, easily turns hospitality into hostility and xenophobia. Hence, for there to be a gift, it seems that one must at least on some level allow the possibility that the gift be abused and the exchange be interrupted. For it is only by stopping giving, by giving to no one, that one would be able to exclude with absolute certainty the possible abuse of one's generosity. Analogously, it is only by completely desolating the beach island that Sal or anyone else could have been able to prevent the paradise to be parasited in *The Beach*.

On the other hand, the gift always seems to require a certain amount of sovereignty, certain rights and duties, just as no hospitality is possible without the possibility of choosing one's guests, of welcoming whomever one wishes. Otherwise the gift, as Derrida remarks of hospitality, 'would risk being abstract, utopian, illusory, and so turning over into its opposite' (ibid.: 79). First of all, the gift is surely no *res nullius*, but a form of property. In order to be able to give something, one must first own and possess the thing. What I receive is therefore never originally mine. It always belongs first to someone else.[16] It may only become mine as it is given to me – though at the same time the given to some extent tends to remain in the possession of the giver even after s/he has given it, insofar as the given is shadowed by and even inalienable from the person of the giver. And ownership is based on exclusion, drawing boundaries, the cutting of relations (ownership, property and appropriation will be discussed in more detail and breadth in Chapter 6). Second, insofar as the gift to be given is not universally enjoyed, one can surely give some-thing to some-one, only provided that one not-gives (it) to someone else. The gift *selects*. One cannot give the other without sacrificing other others. In the act of giving, inclusion and exclusion thus seem to be inseparable. Giving *inasmuch as* holding back, inclusive *inasmuch as* exclusive, 'hospitable *inasmuch as* inhospitable' (ibid.: 81).

Therefore, as the notions of unconditional and conditional gift presuppose and oppose one another in one and the same gesture, I hold that what is called a gift are not two altogether different things, but unconditionality and conditionality, just as the conceptual and the empirical, need to be included as components of one and the same understanding of the gift. To repeat the theorem formulated in the form of a paradox in Chapter 2, the gift cannot be what it in reality is (conditional/ reciprocity/exchange), and it – conceptually – is what it – empirically – cannot be (unconditional/free giving).

16　Life is perhaps an exceptional gift in that it belongs to no one. Parents do not first possess it and then give it. The mother who 'gives' birth does not have in her possession the gift of life she is about to give, but she only 'delivers' it through her body at the instant of the birth of the newborn.

To sum up, the gift and the parasite are deeply intertwined. The one is the reverse of the other: while the absolute gift amounts to giving with no expectation of compensation, the absolute parasite receives without returning. What is more, the dynamics of gift-relations can be adequately described in terms of parasitism. Parasitism provides another vocabulary for dealing with the system and phenomenon of the gift. In both the gift and the parasitic relation, the arrow always goes the same way, never the other: from the giver to the recipient, from the host to the guest. The parasite both interrupts the system of the gift and is part of it, to a certain extent even helps to constitute it. Offering words for substance within the order of exchange, s/he interrupts balanced exchange, but those words also help to recognise generosity, a gift, a donor. However, at the same time, as we saw in Chapter 2, that very recognition in some respect annihilates, annuls and destroys the gift. A conceptual precondition of the gift is that for there to be a pure, free gift, it may even be necessary that the gift not be recognised as a gift, as the recognition already seizes the gift into the order of debt and exchange. The parasite is thus, in several ways, at once the beginning and the end of the gift. The parasite produces the end of giving in temporal terms. The parasite milks his/her host to his/her own benefit, and at least in principle the taking will go on, indefinitely, to the end of giving, until there is nothing more to give. And by doing so, the parasite also destroys the preconditions of his/her own existence.

With the help of the notion of the parasite, we are able to better take into consideration the uncertainty pertaining to gift and exchange. Return-gifts do not follow gifts automatically as if according to some mechanism or law of nature, but things may also proceed otherwise. The return-gift, just as the gift itself, is always to some extent an event, a surprise. Therefore, as Bourdieu has noted, 'To be truly objective, an analysis of exchange of gifts, words or challenges must allow for the fact that, far from unfolding mechanically, the series of acts which, apprehended from outside and after the event, appears as a cycle of reciprocity, presupposes a continuous creation and may be interrupted at any stage' (Bourdieu 1992: 105). Serresian parasitology offers a vocabulary for such an analysis. It enables us to conceptualise interruption, disturbance and unsuccessful transactions as something integral to the gift and exchange. The channel in which gifts travel is always already parasited.

Chapter 5

In/Exclusions: the Gift of Blood
and Alms for the Poor

The gift is inclusive only inasmuch as it is exclusive.

In 'The essay as Form' (2000: 93), Theodor Adorno notes of the essay genre that, '[l]uck and play are essential to it. It starts not with Adam and Eve but with what it wants to talk about'. I started with Adam and Eve and tried to retain luck and play nevertheless. And now I would still like to return to this arche scene of the gift and say something a bit more on the lovers. In Adam and Eve munching on the pome fruit we have the very first human relation. And not only that, but also the simplest relation, right? According to the myth, at that point there was no one else in the whole world but Adam and Eve. Only Adam and Eve: just the two of them. The book of Genesis tells us that it is from them that humankind evolved; yes, from only two, the entire world population, having now already reached 7 billion. What an amazing fable. The mother of all myths.

However, isn't it true that not even Adam and Eve's relationship was a matter of only the two of them? The apple, God and the serpent were surely there as well. First of all, in order for there to be Adam and Eve, there first had to be God who created them. But the serpent was there, too, to tempt them. So, Adam and Eve were preceded by two hosts, one benevolent, the other malevolent; one giving the lovers a place in his garden (though only to banish them in less than no time), the other, welcoming them to dine, as it were, at the other other's table as uninvited guests (and acting as a thermal exciter, who ultimately causes a split with the lovers and God).[1] But that was not enough. The apple was needed as well. It was ultimately the apple that bound the lovers together. The apple, by being passed on from the one to the other, confirmed the relationship between Eve and Adam.

So, in order for Adam and Eve to become an item, various third parties were required: God, the serpent, and the apple. And of course, simultaneously, the togetherness of the two also demanded that these third parties be excluded. In order for there to be two and only two, all possible intervening thirds had to be

---

1 Of course, it is not absolutely certain and clear that the serpent is malevolent. It is not uncommon in the exegetic literature to regard the serpent as God's creation. From another perspective, one could also ask, isn't it ultimately with the help of and thanks to the serpent that Adam and Eve are able to escape the oppressive restrictions of paradise? In fact, the serpent seems to give without restitution and return; he receives no counter-gift from Adam and Eve.

excluded: Adam and Eve fell out with God (or rather, were themselves excluded from the para-dise as disobedient and rebellious troublemakers and para-sites), discovered the serpent to be deceitful and thus cut relations with it, and, finally, even the apple was to disappear into immediacy and insignificance. In general, Serres (2007: 55–7) has noted that any relationship between two never amounts to anything but theatre. According to him, 'As soon as we are two, we are already three or four'. Every struggle, dialogue and exchange presupposes a 'mutual enemy' (for example noise, parasite), who the two parties try to exclude in agreement, and a 'mutual friend', whose existence is required as a mediating third term (Serres 1995c: 9).

The gift makes no exception here. The notion of the elementary gift-relation presented in previous chapters thus needs to be revised. It has already been noted that a gift-relation is never a matter of only two elements, the giver and the receiver. When we give and receive gifts in a reciprocal manner, we never stand in a relation just between the two of us, but a third is always there, included in the relation, insofar as the acts of giving, receiving and returning are grounded for example on certain obligations and rules that we have at least a tacit agreement on. Further, the gift-object itself operates as a third of such kind, as a middle term conciliating the two parties as it is passed on from the one to the other. But there is always also a fourth element to the assemblage. It is indiscernible like the included third mediating the exchanging parties and thus providing them with a common ground; not, however, because of being taken for granted, but because of being excluded. This element marks the outside or the exterior of the relation by not belonging to it. Every gift-relation is thus a constellation consisting of four elements, like a square or a cross (cf. Serres 1995c: 9). To every relation between a donor and a donee, there is an included third and an excluded third, a 'mutual friend' and a 'mutual enemy'. The first is an element presupposed by that relation (that is, the thing given, the obligations to give, receive and return), the latter an element excluded from the relation, a he or she or that or they that is left out. As they compete with one another in generosity, the two partners at the same time at least tacitly join their forces to exclude others from their communion.

Of course, in the case of Adam and Eve, one could also say that if one focuses on the relation between the two subjects one loses sight of the bigger picture: the evident, deterministic tension between good and evil to be solved. In the playing out of that tension, Adam and Eve are hardly anything but pawns. Nevertheless, with regard to the gift, it is the subjective axe, the relationship between subjects that is of greater significance here, for it draws attention to the fact of how the gift is inclusive only inasmuch as it is exclusive. This formula, *inclusive inasmuch as exclusive*, briefly mentioned already in the previous chapter, is what I will look into more closely in this chapter. It is not simply that the thirds are either included or excluded. They have to be included and excluded at the same time, being at once both a condition and an obstacle for the relation.

Gift between Strangers

It is a common thing in the research literature on the gift that authors oppose gifts and gift-exchange to commodities and market exchange.[2] While the gift is associated with personal, lasting relationships with friends and family members, relations within the market are regarded as impersonal, transitory connections between strangers. And while the gift is considered to establish a bond between people beyond the specific transaction, it is thought that in market transactions people are connected to one another only insofar as the transaction is concerned. What is more, while the gift entails obligations, with the help of money, so it is thought, we can buy ourselves free from personal obligations. As Simmel writes, contrasting the gift with money: 'The relationship is more completely dissolved and more radically terminated by payment of money than by gift of a specific object, which always, through its content, its choice and its use, retains an element of the person who has given it' (Simmel 2004: 378).

With only few exceptions, it is only fairly recently that the mutual exclusivity of the gift and the commodity as well as that of gift-exchange and market exchange has become questioned.[3] This is not to ignore their differences. In fact, comparing them to one another, as Healey (2006: 16) has suggested, 'is a good way to bring out the distinctive qualities of each'. It is only that the distinction between the gift and money should not be thought as a matter of opposition, but rather as 'a matter of degree' (Komter 2010: 18). The parallels as well as distinctive attributes of gift-relations and market relations will be discussed in more detail in the next chapter. In what follows, I will focus instead on a specifically modern feature of the gift, which does not fit the picture of the gift presented above. I am thinking here of the gift to *strangers*. According to Godbout and Caillé (1998), the most decisive difference between the modern systems of gift and the archaic ones is that while the archaic gift was associated with personal relationships, the gift to strangers is a quintessentially modern phenomenon.[4]

The tendency to associate the gift with personal relationships has been so prevailing in anthropological and sociological literature that Derrida (1994: 17 note 9), for example, has asked, whether the gift has in fact ever been thought

---

2 See for example Malinowski (1922); Sahlins (2004 [1974]); Titmuss (1970); Hyde (2007 [1983]; Cheal (1988); Gregory (1982); Godbout and Caillé (1998).

3 See for example Douglas (1978); Miller (1995a&b); Offer (1997); Komter (2005); Healy (2006).

4 While the roots of the gift to strangers may be found in religion, especially in Christianity, the modern gift to strangers is not tied to religion in any particular way, but is independent of it. In addition, in the Roman Empire there already existed a custom of the rich giving to the people. What distinguishes, however, the modern gift to strangers from this habit is that it is not a class phenomenon, but people from every social class participate in it (Godbout and Caillé 1988: 77–8).

outside the family.[5] It has been commonplace to assume that it is only in personal, close relationships that people give without keeping score; elsewhere, notably in the market, people tend to look out more closely for their own interests.

The idea of the family as the primary site for giving has also been contested (see for example Derrida 1994: 17–18 note 9). If giving only appears on the condition of a certain limited context, that is, if it is limited solely to the family relationship, then it seems that giving takes place within the order of reciprocity. Even though in the family repayment is not probably the explicit condition of giving, this is made possible precisely by the gift's embeddedness within an established and far-reaching system of reciprocity: the giving is either already a counter-gift to a certain preceding gift,[6] or in the relationships reciprocity is delayed, extending so far in time that it becomes less apparent.

If giving cannot be confined within the limited context of personal/family relationships, is it in the sphere of impersonal relations, then, that it takes place? In other words, does the gift to strangers present a form of gratuitous giving? In his now-classical book *The Gift Relationship* (1970), Richard Titmuss examines blood donation as a modern gift. He studies the people who give, supply or sell blood, and compares the blood transfusion and donor systems of various countries, especially Britain and the United States. The relation between the blood donor and the recipient are very different from the communal relationships of the archaic societies examined by the classic anthropological studies of the gift. In his book, Titmuss lists all in all 11 features which in his view make blood donation a voluntary, altruistic gift, but I will settle here on only recounting three of them, as for me these three are the ones by which blood donation is the most importantly distinguished from the archaic forms of the gift.[7]

First, as already insinuated, blood donation is *impersonal*. The gift of blood is given to an unspecified stranger, an unknown, anonymous other. As Titmuss expresses it: 'the recipient is in almost all cases not personally known to the donor'. And this is for good reasons, Titmuss claims. According to him, the danger in the donors and recipients knowing each other personally is that they might refuse to participate on religious, political, ethnic or other grounds. Second, blood donation is *unilateral*. It is characterised by the absence of reciprocity. Or, at most the reciprocity

---

5   Alvin Gouldner (1960), for instance, has suggested that it is only in the family that a transition from reciprocity to giving without expectation of return may take place.

6   Hyde (2007), for example, mentions a son who did not want any gratitude or any other kind of repayment from his mother, to whom he had donated an organ. The mother had already given him the ultimate gift of life, so how could he expect a counter-gift for what he had given her?

7   This is not to say that the gift to strangers would present an absolute, unconditional gift. In a Derridean sense, the absolute gift is a conceptual limit value, not a realisable fact. There is no pure gift 'in reality'. As we remember, Derrida suggested that the pure, absolute gift is conditioned by secrecy: it can never appear empirically. All empirical actualisations of giving are therefore compromises or hybrids of some sort.

is indirect and anonymous: one may donate blood by thinking that just as one's own contribution may save the life of someone, it may just happen that some day one is in need of a blood transfusion oneself, and then it would be preferable if others have donated as well. However, what is important is that in most systems of blood donation, there is no obligation imposed upon the recipient to reciprocate. What is more, in almost all cases the recipient is unable to make a corresponding gift in return even if they wanted to. (The donor may receive nominal compensation such as a rose or a badge, but this repayment, which is hardly equivalent to the donated blood anyway, is not made by the recipient but by the organisation collecting the blood.) Third, the gift of blood is *voluntary*. The absence of obligations to give and sanctions for not giving is characteristic of it. The giving of blood is not enforced by the government or by the organisations mediating the gift of blood.[8]

The case of blood donation is highly fascinating because it calls into question many of the ideas usually associated with the gift. First, it involves *no great sacrifice* from the donor. To the donor, the gift presents no significant loss, as the blood donated is quickly replaced by new blood produced by the donor's own body (to the recipient, by contrast, the gift may be a condition for their continuing survival) (Titmuss 1970: 74). Second, while the intrinsic entwinement of the gift and communal ties is usually taken as a given by most authors,[9] according to Titmuss the gift of blood does not establish any communal tie between the giver and the give. While Titmuss seems to ignore the indirect solidarity strengthened by blood donation as an *institution*, one may nevertheless argue that he is right in assuming that in the gift of blood there is no direct solidarity engendered between the donor and the recipient through a social bond, and no claims presented to the recipient, either. As Titmuss concludes on the differences between blood donation and the archaic gift: 'Unlike gift-exchange in archaic societies, there is in the free gift of blood to unnamed strangers no contract of custom, no legal bond, no functional determinism, no situations of discriminatory power, domination, constraint or compulsion, no sense of shame or guilt, no gratitude imperative and no need for the penitence of a Chrysostom' (ibid.: 239).

Third, the gift of blood seems to embody features that are usually assumed to belong only to gifts given to those close to us: it is unilateral and voluntary. Blood donation is a case that shows that we do not always only look out for our self-interest when dealing with strangers, but there is room for generosity as well. We do not always expect suitable compensation for our services from the recipient.[10]

---

8   Hence, those with a very rare blood type, as Titmuss (1970: 70) remarks, have to depend for their very lives on the willingness to donate of a very few strangers with identical blood.

9   See for example Mauss (2008); Sahlins (2004 [1974]); Hyde (2007 [1983]). In addition, let us remember here for instance, the claim by Douglas cited in Chapter 2: 'A gift that does nothing to enhance solidarity is a contradiction'.

10   Blood donation is not the only contemporary case of giving to strangers. As another example one can think of the internet encyclopedia Wikipedia, for instance. Besides entries,

As a gift to strangers, blood donation comes to embody some of the features of what has been associated with 'cosmopolitanism', citizenship of the world. According to Kwame Anthony Appiah (2006), the challenge we face in the age of globalisation is that while we know how to be responsible with friends and family members, we now have to find a way to be responsible for fellow citizens both of our country and of the entire planet – that is, in a world of strangers.[11] I cannot merely look after and care for those who are familiar and the closest to me, but I have to act responsibly for all the people, basically billions of people, whom I do not personally know, but to whom I exist in a virtual relationship.[12] I have to care for everybody.

So, just as cosmopolitan ethics, the gift of blood to strangers de-establishes the link between proximity and responsibility established by the giving that takes place within personal, close relationships: by donating, one takes responsibility for those distant from and unknown to oneself. The relation between the donor and the recipient could in such a case be understood in Emmanuel Levinas's (1979 [1961]: 80) terms as a 'relation without relation'. On the one hand, the blood transferred connects two people in the most material and almost intrusive manner: a bodily fluid poured out of the donor is instilled into the vessel of the donee.[13] The blood made to run from the donor to the donee is life-giving; life is in the blood. Furthermore, the blood also carries the personal mark or stain of the donor. This becomes most palpable when the blood is contaminated by HIV, for instance. In such cases, the disease the donor has is transmitted to the recipient along with the blood. Yet on the other hand, the two people connected by the blood nevertheless remain resolutely 'other' – strangers, distant and anonymous – to one another. The very possibility of personal emotional attachment and mutual solidarity is excluded between the giver and the receiver. Thereby, while there is without doubt a relation of the most concrete and bodily kind between them, the relation is simultaneously 'unrelating', as it retains the donor and the donee in a situation of mutual foreignness. The gift of blood presents thus no final synthesis between inclusion and exclusion, but it rather retains their tension in force and embodies it.

Wikipedia is dependent upon gifts in its continuing existence also in the form of money donations. In most cases, the authors and readers of Wikipedia entries remain strangers to one another, and the reader is not obliged, and not even able, to reciprocate. Gifts are given not to particular, identifiable recipients, but rather to the Wikipedia community in its entirety (see Pajunen 2012).

11   For a fascinating take on the need in a world of diversity to forge a new politics of belonging that does not exclude strangers, see Amin (2011).

12   I use the notion of the 'virtual' here in the sense specified by Deleuze (1991: 96–7).

13   The materiality and intrusiveness of the connection seems all the more heightened in the case of organ transplant. While donated blood is eventually indistinguishably dissolved in the recipient's own blood, an implanted organ remains a foreign part, a stranger, an intruder. And this is so not only in the most obvious case of being rejected by the immune system of the recipient, but also when properly functioning as part of the recipient's body.

The Dark Side of Gifts

Besides the gift of blood, another good example of the in/exclusivity of the gift is charity. Compared to blood donation, in charity the dimension of exclusion is more emphasised and intended: the other is excluded precisely by means of giving. An obvious case of this is the so-called charity gift, a service offered by such international organisations as World Vision, Oxfam and UNICEF. A charity gift means that instead of giving the other some thing, my gift to the other amounts to me donating on the other's behalf to the poor, most often of the Third or Fourth worlds. In other words, the gift in this case is a matter of giving 'giving'; what I give the other is the gift of giving. What the poor receive may be anything from clean drinking water to a sapling, a cow, a well or a school uniform for a girl. And the one on whose behalf I have made the donation receives a card telling him/her more about the gift, the difference that it makes, and so on.

The charity gift may be a very noble gesture, an act of goodness itself. There's nothing wrong as such in casting one's bread upon the waters. Thanks to the generosity of the donors, the poor communities receive some basic utensils and thus their life is made a little bit easier. What is more, the charity gift may even embody the pure, absolute gift, as the person identified and acknowledged as the giver, that is, the one on whose behalf I give, gives without knowing it. Let it be noted, though, that in most cases this is not quite true, as people tend to *ask* others to donate on their behalf instead of, say, being given a present. Nevertheless, in case the person does come to know only afterwards that s/he has given, the giving cannot involve calculation and self-interest. Or, to be more precise, the other is in fact made into a giver who has not given anything him/herself, as someone else has given in his/her place. The giver never intended to make a gift, and never made one by one's own actions. However, at the same time the charity gift is a good example that gifts are by no means neutral and without dangers. While helping the poor out of deprivation, the charity gift is also a way of keeping them at a distance, whether intentionally or unintentionally. Whereas it is usually the case that the given sets the cycle of reciprocity going, a donation or a measure of support that refuses all recompense hampers or belies reciprocity instead of promoting it. It tends to exclude rather than include, expel rather than invite. The recipient of the charity gift is excluded from the community of gifts (though this does not exclude the possibility that, *given* time, the recipients themselves can become ones who give), which is constituted in reciprocal give-and-take. As the members of the community compete with each other in generosity, they at the same time tacitly join forces to exclude others – the 'mutual enemy' – from their communion. Thereby, the pure, completely irreversible giving reveals the ambivalence of the gift: it is at once gift and poison, beneficial and harmful, a Christian virtue and an act of malice. The good easily becomes bad, and the best is turned into the worst, because the overly generous gift easily puts the recipient, as Niklas Luhmann (1977: 209; trans. Joas 2001: 136) has noted of the Christian gift, 'in a position of permanent gratefulness and permanent liability [...] from which he cannot liberate himself by his own means'. On the one hand, a recipient's incapability to repay the gift would, paradoxically, even seem to allow for giving without return, in pure loss (Marion 2002: 88–9), though on the other hand, it can be argued that the giver is not left without recompense, as s/he gains a hold over the recipient.

All in all, the gift cannot be understood properly without also paying attention to its dark side. The altruistic gift is not only a vehicle for solidarity, but it may also threaten relations and undermine feelings of solidarity (Komter 2005: 35). For example, besides being a benevolent gift given by God, to Adam and Eve the undamaged Garden of Eden was also damaging, in that it was to keep them as inferior and ignorant. As another example, the magical kiss given by the prince that succeeded in reviving Snow White also placed her in the subject position of a passive, helpless woman just lying there and waiting for the active male hero to save her.

In an article on the social psychology of the gift, Barry Schwartz (1967) acknowledged the possibility of unfriendliness as a component of gift-giving. According to Schwartz, there are gifts which express overt or covert hostility and the purpose of which is to hurt or embarrass the recipient. We have already touched upon several examples. In addition to potlatch, the poisoned apple given to Snow White by the evil stepmother presented a case of such gifts, and the famous Trojan horse could be yet another example. One can also think here of practical jokes such as the frequently appearing exploding cigars in the Warner Bros Looney Tunes cartoons. (What is more, the most famous of the claimed numerous plots by the CIA to assassinate Fidel Castro allegedly involved an exploding cigar.) Schwartz also mentions gifts that are inferior compared to gifts given to others. An obvious example is inheritance. For instance, it is told that, when Leona Helmsley, an owner of a real estate empire in New York also known as 'Queen of Mean', died in 2007, she left her dog, Trouble, a $12 million trust fund, and ordered that the majority of her estate – of more than $4 billion in worth – be used for the benefit of dogs. For two of her four grandchildren she left nothing. Additionally, one may also express unfriendliness by giving a gift that refuses reciprocity, or by repaying a gift once received with an exact return, thus expressing a desire to call it quits, that is, to end the reciprocity of gifts or at least keep the relationship on a detached, impersonal level (Schwartz 1967: 6).

However, a gift may turn out to be a failure not only due to unfriendly intentions of the giver (though for the malevolent giver the failure of the gift is of course a proof that s/he has succeeded). The gift itself may be bad. In *Social Solidarity and the Gift* (2005), Komter has divided 'bad gifts' into four categories. The categorisation draws on a survey she did in the Netherlands in the early 1990s. First, according to her there are gifts that are simply 'not appropriate'. Clothes that do not fit, a too intimate or too expensive gift received from a person one does not wish to get too involved with, or bringing champagne and cake to funerals instead of flowers are examples of such gifts. The second category of bad gifts is gifts that are 'thoughtless', 'too easy, bought in a haste, or already in the giver's possession and then passed on'. The giver hasn't really put in any effort to such gifts, which easily gives the recipient the impression that neither s/he nor their relationship is valued especially high by the giver. Third, 'pedagogical' gifts were regarded as bad gifts as well by the respondents. These are gifts that 'point to another person's weakness, criticize him or her, or communicate a form of uncalled-for advice'. One can think of here a scale, a membership to Weight Watchers, or advice books about how to bring up your children as examples. Fourth and finally, bad gifts can also just take the form of 'trash' or 'monstrosities' – anything from tasteless decorative household items to worn, damaged or just otherwise ugly pieces of clothing, for example (Komter 2005: 52–3).

In any case, besides creating and nourishing bonds, gifts may also threaten them. In some cases, a failed gift may even sever the relationship. For example, according to Caplow (1984: 1314) two out of five couples in which the recipient was unhappy with the Christmas gift given by their significant other were separated relatively shortly after, within the time of just few weeks. However, while several failed gifts are received each year,[14] Sinardet and Mortelmans (2005) found in their study that usually people nevertheless play the social game of friendliness and politeness by refraining from expressing their disappointment with the gift directly to the giver.

The Poor: Gift Versus Right

The ambiguity of the gift as well as the dialectic of in/exclusion is at play in an illustrative manner in the support given to the poor. From a sociological viewpoint, poverty is essentially defined in relation to the gift. Up to this day, the most insightful analysis of their interrelatedness is presented by Simmel in the chapter 'Der Arme' in *Soziologie*.[15] In sociological terms, the poor, according to Simmel, are not those in destitution, but people who are given aid because they are considered to be destitute: 'The poor, as a sociological category, are not those who suffer specific deficiencies and deprivations, but those who receive assistance or should receive it according to social norms' (Simmel, 1965: 138). What this implies, therefore, is that one cannot understand the poor as a sociological phenomenon separated from assistance, for the first is intrinsically tied to the latter. Instead of poverty coming first, poverty is a derivative of assistance: the poor are people who either receive or should receive help. Therefore, Simmel insists, 'poverty cannot be defined in itself as a quantitative state, but only in terms of the social reaction resulting from a specific situation' (ibid.: 138). Poverty is relational, a relative state of affairs.

---

14   According to economist Joel Waldfogel, in the 1990s annually as much as $4 billion was spent on gifts recipients did not like, which amounted to 10 percent of the estimated total of $40 billion spent on gifts each year (Waldfogel 1993; Sinardet and Mortelmans 2005: 251).

15   In what follows, all references to 'Der Arme' are made to the English translation, 'The Poor' (1965).

What Simmel means by this is, first, that as a grouping or class, the poor are defined not by themselves but from outside, by the collective attitude adopted by the surrounding 'society'. The group 'does not remain united by interaction among its members', but by the collective reaction towards poverty and the poor (ibid.: 139). The poor represent a class 'which bases its unity on a purely passive character' (ibid.: 140) – on being assisted. Indeed, consequently, although the poor is a homogeneous class as regards their position in the societal structure, at the same time the class of the poor is of the most heterogeneous kind. As Simmel writes:

> The class of the poor, especially in modern society, is a unique sociological synthesis. It possesses a great homogeneity insofar as its meaning and location in the social body is concerned; but it lacks it completely insofar as the individual qualification of its elements is concerned. It is the common end of the most diverse destinies, an ocean into which lives derived from the most diverse social strata flow together. (ibid.: 139)

Second, when he says that the poor are defined in the way others react to them with assistance, Simmel is also provocatively suggesting that the poor are given help and support not so much for their own sake as for the sake of protecting the community and maintaining the current, unequal state of affairs. As he puts it himself: 'The goal of assistance is precisely to mitigate certain extreme manifestations of social differentiation, so that the social structure may continue to be based on this differentiation' (ibid.: 122). In other words, that the poor receive assistance is 'not an end-in-itself but merely a means to an end' (ibid.: 121). Its aim is to suppress the dangers and threat the poor may potentially represent to the community and its status quo (ibid.: 122). The poor are helped just enough to keep them from revolting, but they are helped little enough to keep them as poor and retain inequality.

The poor are thus simultaneously included in and excluded from the community. They are included insofar as assistance is given to them, and yet excluded insofar as the assistance they receive degrades them, keeps them at distance, in an inferior position. Like the 'stranger', a more famous social type analysed by Simmel, the poor make visible the boundary between the inside and the outside of the community:

> The poor are approximately in the situation of the stranger to the group who finds himself, so to speak, materially outside the group in which he resides. [...] Thus the poor are located in a way outside the group; but this is no more than a peculiar mode of interaction which binds them into a unity. (ibid.: 124–5)

That is to say, the poor are at once within and outside the community, included only insofar as being excluded. The poor do not simply stand outside the group but to be poor is rather a specific form of relation. As Simmel sums it:

> … poverty is a unique sociological phenomenon: a number of individuals who, out of a purely individual fate, occupy a specific organic position within the

whole; but this position is not determined by this fate and condition, but rather by the fact that others – individuals, associations, communities – attempt to correct this condition. Thus, what makes one poor is not the lack of means. The poor person, sociologically speaking, is the individual who receives assistance because of this lack of means. (ibid.: 140)

Provided that the poor are defined above all in relation to assistance, poverty is closely tied to the gift. The English word 'alms' derives from Old English, and ultimately from the Latin *alimosina*, 'pity', 'compassion', and the Greek ἐλεήμων *(eleémón),* 'compassionate', 'merciful'. Insofar as the process of giving is not its own ultimate end, but the purpose of the gift lies also, if not primarily, in its results, what is essential in the gift is that someone receives something (ibid.: 137). In that sense, as Simmel argues, 'The sociology of the gift coincides in part with that of poverty. In the gift it is possible to discover a very extensive scale of reciprocal relationships between men [sic], differences in the content, motivation, and manner of giving as well as in that of accepting the gift' (ibid.: 137).

With regard to this, it is highly interesting that Mauss harnessed his theory of the gift to the end of underpinning social democracy (see Douglas 2008). In the last chapter of *The Gift*, he presents the moral and political implications of the work. Writing in the French tradition that strongly opposed English liberalism, Mauss is critical of the utilitarian theories of social life and action. He argues that the Western, modern society has made the human being a *homo oeconomicus*, 'economic animal'.[16] At the same time, he suggests that 'we are not yet all creatures of this genus'; 'happily we are still somewhat removed from this constant, icy, utilitarian calculation' (Mauss 2008: 98). Everything is not yet reducible to the laws of the market:

> Fortunately, everything is still not wholly categorized in terms of buying and selling. Things still have sentimental as well as venal value, assuming values merely of this kind exist. We possess more than a tradesman morality. There still remain people and classes that keep to the morality of former times, and we almost all observe it, at least at certain times of the year or on certain occasions. (ibid.: 83)

It is from the morality guiding the archaic exchange of gifts that Mauss hopes to find compensation to the commercialised morality of our times. The political

---

16   In *The Philosophy of Money*, Simmel suggests that it is precisely the mature money economy that has socialised us into calculating and cold reasoning by repeatedly forcing us to mathematical operations even in our most mundane actions. With regard to money, we don't ask what and how, but 'how much'. Due to the pervasiveness and the increasing importance of money, as argued by Simmel, the world has become an arithmetic problem: constant evaluating and calculating, numerous additions and subtractions, weighings and the reduction of qualitative values to quantitative ones have taken over the life of individuals and imposed a hue of rationality, precision and exactness over it (Simmel 2004).

agenda of *The Gift* is to justify social democracy by way of the theory of the gift. According to Mauss, 'something other than utility' circulates in the societies studied by him. Their economic life is not primarily based on utility: 'Several times we have seen how far this whole economy of the exchange-through-gift lay outside the bounds of the so-called natural economy, that of utilitarianism' (ibid.: 92). Now, Mauss argues it is exactly towards this morality that he would wish to see modern societies moving: 'we can and must return to archaic society and to elements in it. We shall find in this reasons for life and action that are still prevalent in certain societies and numerous classes: the joy of public giving; the pleasure in generous expenditure on the arts, in hospitality, and in the private and public festival' (ibid.: 88–9).

In fact, Mauss argues that the practices of reciprocity assumed long lost have not disappeared completely, but they are still functioning in our own societies, though only dormant or repressed, 'hidden, below the surface' (ibid.: 5). According to him, the morality of archaic reciprocity is already to some extent re-emerging: 'The themes of the gift, of the freedom and the obligation inherent in the gift, of generosity and self-interest that are linked in giving, are reappearing in French society, as a dominant motif too long forgotten' (ibid.: 87).[17]

In a sense, then, *The Gift* is an attempt to reverse the logic of economy from within. In the book, Mauss tries to reveal the repressed origin of economy in order to re-evaluate the value and place of the gift and solidarity in modern society (O'Neill 1999: 135, 138). He paints a very different picture of economic evolution than the one presented by economic and juristic theories. In Mauss's archaeology of economy, economic exchange and the exchange of gifts, regarded as trivial and superfluous in economic terms for long, are closely connected. He discovers the origin of economy in the gift:

> The evolution in economic law has not been from barter to sale, and from cash to credit sale. On the one hand, barter has arisen through a system of presents given and reciprocated according to a limit. This was through a process of simplification, by reductions in periods of time formerly arbitrary. On the other hand, buying and selling arose in the same way, with the latter according to a fixed time limit, or by cash, as well as lending. (Mauss 2008: 46–7)

However, I agree with Douglas (2008: xix) in her estimation that Mauss's effort to 'underpin social democracy is very weak'. Her point is that while social security and health insurance without doubt express solidarity, so do many other things as well. According to Douglas, redistributions have no immediate link to gift economies, for they do not involve any rivalry of honour. Therefore, according to her, 'Taking the theory straight from its context in full-blown gift economies to a

---

17   There are echoes of this idea of the resurgence of forgotten archaic ideals and practices in the work of more recent French theorists as well (see for instance Maffesoli 1996).

modern political issue was really jumping the gun' (ibid.: xix–xx). While this may indeed be true, I nevertheless think that the most crucial difference between social democratic policies and the system of the gift lies elsewhere. The most significant difference between them is that the social democratic policies are fundamentally based on *rights* (Godbout and Caillé 1998: 60). The recipients have a legal right to the benefits they are endowed with. The system of the gift, on the contrary, is to be sharply distinguished from any system of rights. As was mentioned earlier in Chapter 2, the gift does not acknowledge any rights to it.

What is more, it is not only that Mauss fails to see the crucial difference between social security and the system of the gift; it is also highly questionable whether it would actually be preferable for the disadvantaged to rely on charity and personal donations in their subsistence. Mauss recommends that we must return to 'habits of "aristocratic extravagance"'. By this he means that 'the rich must come back to considering themselves – freely and also by obligation – as the financial guardians of their fellow citizens' (Mauss 2008: 88). Despite the nobility of the idea – and also not underestimating the positive effects such a morality of donating may potentially have – it can nevertheless be argued against Mauss that the assistance relying on 'aristocratic extravagance' tends to reduce the rights of the poor close to negligible. If the poor are at the mercy of the more or less arbitrary generosity of the more prosperous and fortunate, they themselves, as Simmel remarks, 'disappear completely as legitimate subjects' (Simmel 1965: 121). In this sense, the poor presents a class of the 'homo sacer' (Agamben 1998). In fact, it can be speculated that as long as the assistance is dependent on generosity, goodwill and personal donations instead of rights, the poor remain poor. However, if benefits and assistance, as Simmel writes, 'were to be based on the interests of the poor person, there would, in principle, be no limit whatsoever on the transmission of property in favor of the poor, a transmission that would lead to the equality of all' (Simmel 1965: 122).

In this chapter we have discussed the dynamics of in/exclusion that the gift involves. On the one hand, the gift has the remarkable power to make strangers and even enemies into friends. By the offering, the one who was formerly excluded is included. The parasite is welcomed and invited. However, on the other hand the gift itself may also exclude the recipient. The two examples used in this chapter hopefully made this clear enough. While both blood donation and charity create a relation between the giver and the recipient, they also keep them distant to one another, with the difference, however, that the gift of blood only *sustains* the distance between the two parties in the state that it already was, while charity more or less actively *produces* that distance. Alms or charity is a gift that excludes. By exposing the recipient's inability to reciprocate, it makes them inferior vis-à-vis to the giver. In a sense, it places the recipient in the position of the parasite against one's will, of necessity.

Another significant difference between the two examples discussed above is that whereas alms and charity gifts tend to exclude the recipient from the community of gifts, in the gift of blood the exclusion pertained above all to potential givers. In blood donation, not everyone is eligible to give but, as has been stated earlier, some groups like gay men, carriers of certain diseases and drug addicts, for example, are refused the right to donate and thus excluded from the process of the gift. So, while relating, creating ties and including, the gift also unrelates, unties and excludes, and this exclusion can concern either those who are bereft of the gift, those who receive it or those who could potentially give it. The gift is a matter of *dissociative association*. Perhaps one could even see it as a way of coping with the relentless paradox of distance and proximity that pertains to social life and human existence. We are at the same time bound and out of bonds; dependent on and irrevocably distant from one another; unbearably attached to our fellow human beings and yet separated even from those who are the closest to us in a manner that makes us strangers amongst all and causes the unbearable feeling of metaphysical loneliness.[18] While both attachment and detachment, standing in relation and out of relation may be too intensive in themselves as such, the gift succeeds in reconciling them in a form that relaxes their extremity.

---

18   Simmel formulates the dialectics of proximity and distance of belonging in the essay 'Psychologie der Koketterie' (2001: 48) in the following passage, perhaps the most touching and tragic in his whole oeuvre: 'The fact that the human being is, in one's most passionate needs, dependent on the being from whom one is separated by perhaps the deepest metaphysical gap is the purest, possibly even the archetypical form of the loneliness which makes the human being ultimately a stranger not only amongst all the beings in the world, but also amongst those who are the closest to him or her'.

Chapter 6
Gendered Economies of the Gift

A gift-that-takes and giving with abandon.

It is a widely acknowledged fact in anthropological and sociological literature that gender plays a highly significant role in gift-relations. If we are to believe classical anthropological studies, in non-Western gift institutions gender relations have been strikingly unequal. There, gift-exchange appears as an activity concerning mostly only men; women take part, at most, as tokens of exchange. For example, in *The Elementary Structures of Kinship* (1969 [1949]), Lévi-Strauss famously sees the exchange of women as the most elementary form of exchange. According to him, the circulation of women as property appears as the foundation of kinship systems. The practice is guided by the incest taboo, which Lévi-Strauss regards as a universal feature of all societies: if they wish to marry and reproduce, men have to form relationships with someone outside their own family (Lévi-Strauss 1969 [1949]).

Feminist authors have contended that the practice of treating women as objects to be circulated sadly constitutes not only non-Western societies, but the Western ones, too. According to Luce Irigaray, the (re)production of patriarchal society rests on the basis of the exchange of women. As Irigaray writes in *This Sex Which Is Not One* (1985: 170):

> The society we know, our own culture, is based upon the exchange of women. Without the exchange of women, we are told, we would fall back into anarchy (?) of the natural world, the randomness (?) of the animal kingdom. The passage into the social order, into the symbolic order, into order as such, is assured by the fact that men, or groups of men, circulate women among themselves, according to a rule known as the incest taboo.

But why is it precisely the exchange of women that weaves the network of society? Irigaray takes the word of 'the anthropologist' here, the title referring scornfully to Lévi-Strauss. The reason for the exchange of women comes down to their scarcity and significance for reproduction, or so 'we are told', as Irigaray (1985: 170) sarcastically adds; note also the bracketed question marks in the quotation above as means of ridiculing what is said and emphasising ironic distance from it. In patriarchal society, women are deemed to be of most value as wives and mothers. In this light it is not the least surprising that the giving of women in marriage is the most common and elementary form of the exchange of women in our society. As Hyde (2007: 95) notes: 'Of all of the cases in which women are treated as gifts [...] the woman given in marriage [...] is primary'. One only needs to think of here the Old Testament and the suggestion: 'Let us take their daughters to us as wives and let us give them our daughters'.

However, against Lévi-Strauss, the reduction of women in gift institutions to sheer objects has been challenged in more recent anthropology and sociology alike. Drawing on materials she generated on the Trobriand Islands, anthropologist Annette Weiner (1976), for example, suggests that women are not merely objects being circulated, but they also have a more active and autonomous role. She also draws attention to the existence of gifts between genders (see also Komter 2005: 78). The active role of women is arguably much more explicit in contemporary Western societies, where the selection, buying and wrapping of presents is carried out mostly by women.[1] Overall, women are much more active givers than men.[2]

In this chapter, the interrelations of the gift and gender will be examined through the novel *Story of O* (1972 [1954]) by Anne Desclos, written under the pseudonym Pauline Réage. The novel, with a Parisian fashion photographer bearing the abbreviated name O as the main heroine, is as intriguing theoretically as it is appalling morally and emotionally. Curiously, both sentiments are derived from the same source, from the objectification of women. In the novel, women are reduced to sheer objects serving, on the one hand, the most perverted urges of the men circulating them and, on the other, the creation and nourishment of homo-social alliances. I will argue somewhat provocatively that due to its topic – women as property – that runs throughout the novel, the *Story of O* is ultimately a book on economy. With its narration of the social relations that the main heroine is tied to, the novel comes to display nothing less than the basis and law (*nomos*) of economy. Of course, the book is not about 'economy' in the conventional sense of monetary transactions and markets. However, I argue that the basis and law of the libidinal economy, if one will, of the sexual relations that the novel depicts are not dissimilar to those of a market economy. All in all, the investigation will try to show how economy and social relations are indistinct from one another. Instead of assuming a given separation between economy on the one hand, and intimate social and moral relationships on the other, the examination commences from the idea that the two are closely interwoven from the start. The reading that I am going to suggest will hopefully make clear how the figure of the circle is foundational for both gift-exchange[3] and for what I will call, by taking up a notion employed by Hélène Cixous, the *economy of propre*. Both imply the idea of return and circulation.

---

1   On the significant and active role of women in gift-giving, see for example Caplow (1982b); Di Leonardo (1987); Fischer and Arnold (1990); Goodwin, Smith and Spiggle (1990); Komter (2005).

2   In 'Christmas gifts and kin networks' (1982b), Caplow found out when examining Christmas gifts in Middletown that most gifts were given by women. Alone or jointly, they gave 84% of all gifts, while male givers without any female collaborators gave only 16%. What is more, gifts from men to men were rare, only 4% in total, whereas 17% of all gifts were given from women to women (Caplow 1982b: 387).

3   As was discussed in Chapter 2.

However, I will suggest that the *Story of O* can also be read as assigning women a more active role in the system of the gift. While they take part in the system of exchange as hardly anything but objects, the existence of the system itself nevertheless is highly dependent on the uncalculated, abundant gifts that the women give, even though they seem to give first and foremost in and by way of their passivity. These gifts do not comply with the idea of exchange and return, and cannot therefore be grasped in exchangist terms. Related to this, the novel unfolds, admittedly in an extreme manner, the question of who benefits from the gift. Occasionally, as was discussed in relation with the parasite, giving may turn out to be harmful to the giver. In the novel, the generosity of the women turns against them in the most horrible way and with the most destructive results.

Story of an Object

So, what is the *Story of O* about? Overtly, it is a story of submission, domination and degradation. In the narrative, the main heroine O is taken by her lover René to a château called Roissy, where she is mistreated and violated in all imaginable ways by her lover and several other men. Not surprisingly, the *Story of O* has been read as a book about sadomasochism. It is not unusual to regard it as a kind of female version of the books by Marquis de Sade. And it is true that Desclos did write the novel to express her affection to her lover Jean Paulhan, a French writer, literary critic and publisher, who was fond of the works of Sade. In the essay appearing in the English translation as an afterword, Paulhan (1972: 282) writes that, 'The *Story of O* is surely the most fiercely intensive love-letter a man could ever receive'. So, the book itself was initially intended as a gift, a very personal and intimate one at that. A self-authored piece of perverse erotic literature is not automatically an appropriate gift to just anyone, but to give such a gift presupposes intimate knowledge of the taste, inclination and preferences of the recipient. What is more, the gift was also bound to reveal the feelings of the giver towards the givee. Had the donor misjudged either the donee's taste or the nature of their relationship, the gift would probably not only have ended up being rejected, but also caused the relationship to rupture. One can also speculate that the gift was given in the hope of appearing as an equal in the eyes of the recipient. Paulhan was confident that no woman could ever write in the manner of Sade, and Desclos wanted to prove him wrong.

Without doubt, the *Story of O* does bear many similarities with Sade's books. First, like Sade, Desclos, aka Réage, brings explicitly to light the political nature of sexuality. In the *Story of O*, as in Sade's novels, the privacy of sexuality is shattered and inverted. As in the novels by Sade, in the *Story of O* the most intimate sexual desires and deeds become public, not only by often being performed under an audience, but also by being constantly discoursed about. A bit like the boudoir in Sade's *Philosophy in the Boudoir*, the château Roissy is a kind of theatre staging the politicisation of the physiological life of bodies through sexuality (see Agamben 1998: 134 on Sade with regard to this). The libertinage in the *Story of*

O and in the books by Sade does not pass over or spare any part of the bodies of the women brutalised. Second, just as the Sadean heroes, the men belonging as members to the society owning the château Roissy bear an analogy with sovereign power. They are in absolute control. Granted by the powers of the order and laws it seems they themselves have created, they suspend laws and transgress the norms and limits of decency. They have the liberty to use the bodies of the women in residence as they wish, to fulfil their most obscene desires. Third, even though both the novels by Sade and the *Story of O* depict cruel acts of brutalisation, those acts are not carried out in thrall of primitive drives. Quite the contrary, both the Sadean heroes and the men in the *Story of O* deliberately hold back, as it were. It is important for them that one must not succumb to one's passions. One must eschew excessive agitation. Everything happens under control, and everything is carefully organised and ordered; there is no place for uncontrolled bursts of fervour and exaltation. Much like war, as was depicted in Chapter 3, the rituals of debauchery do not involve primitive violence, but they already presuppose a social contract of some sort. In a sense, the evil that the Sadean heroes and the men of the château society do actively prevents bursts of savage violence to fluctuate.

However, the comparison to Sade obfuscates the fact that the *Story of O* has in fact barely anything to do with sadomasochism. Unlike the Sadean heroes, the men in the novel are not sadists. While torment and cruelty may give them pleasure, what they primarily seek is not pleasure. What is more, even though they may violate social rules, their actions are not primarily driven by the desire to transgression. On the contrary, they are driven by the will to appropriate; their desire is that of *appropriation*. I will elaborate the issue of appropriation in the following two sections. For the moment, I will only note that by appropriation I mean the act making something one's own, of claiming ownership. The *Story of O* is ultimately a novel about appropriative desire, and this crucially distinguishes it from the books of Sade and, importantly, also makes it ultimately a book on economy, in relation to the gift. Sade believes in the absolute freedom of human beings, men and women alike. Therefore, for him the possession of another human being would be not only unjustifiable but also unfeasible. As he writes in the pamphlet: 'Yet Another Effort, Frenchmen, If You Would Become Republicans' included in the *Philosophy in the Boudoir*:[4]

---

4   In the English edition cited the title is translated as *Philosophy in the Bedroom*. Unfortunately, the rendering of the French *boudoir* into 'bedroom' is a very unhappy and misleading one. Unlike a bedroom, a boudoir is not an entirely private space, but rather an in-between space of some sort, situated between private and public space (recall here the politicisation of sexuality in Sade). A boudoir is a sitting room or dressing room that traditionally provided a site for the sociability of gentry women and their closest friends. As such, it is a perfectly suitable site for the most intimate philosophical discussion: while a bedroom is for sleeping and sex, a boudoir is a place to talk about sex, something which would not perhaps be as appropriate for instance in a salon, more discrete and public by its nature. For Sade, the boudoir even amounts to something of his philosophical school, analogous to Plato's academy and the lyceum of Aristotle.

> Never may an act of possession be exercised upon a free being; the exclusive possession of a woman is no less unjust than the possession of slaves; all men [sic] are born free, all have equal rights: never should we lose sight of those principles; according to which never may there be granted to one sex the legitimate right to lay monopolizing hands upon the other, and never may one of those sexes, or classes, arbitrarily possess the other. (Sade 1990: 318)

Sade rejects property rights over other human beings, be they men or women, and approves only the rights of action. While a woman according to him can never refuse herself to anyone who desires her, no woman can ever be possessed by a man: 'The act of possession can only be exercised upon a chattel or an animal, never upon an individual who resembles us, and all the ties which can bind a woman to a man are quite as unjust as illusory' (ibid: 319). Thus Sade rejects the possession of other human beings not only as unacceptable but also as impossible – human beings cannot be possessed, for they are born free.

In the *Story of O*, by contrast, the main heroine O is literally an *object* belonging to her masters. This is expressed already by her concise name, O, which, quite obviously, offers itself as an acronym for Object. O is passive and submissive, and she does exactly what she is told. For most of the time, rather than acting herself freely and autonomously, she is acted upon. Accordingly, the distinction between object and person that is fundamental to modern systems of property, commodity exchange, and markets is negated in the *Story of O*. The men treat the women they pass on from one to the other as objects over which they enjoy either permanent or temporary rights of possession and use (I will return to this in the next section). The contrast to the philosophy of Sade could not be more striking. The *Philosophy in the Boudoir* is all about the education of a subject: a young virgin, Eugenie, is schooled in evil and in the pleasures of obscene sex. There are 'no limits to your pleasure save those of your strength and will', she is instructed (Sade 1990: 220). Her body and her pleasure belong to no one else than herself. As Madame de Saint-Ange instructs her: 'Fuck, Eugenie, fuck, angel mine; your body is your own, yours alone; in all the world there is but yourself who has the right to enjoy it as you see fit' (ibid.: 221). O, on the contrary, has no right to her own pleasure: 'Pleasure, we've got to move beyond that stage. We must make the tears flow' (Réage 1972 [1954]: 18). O is simply told 'to be still and to obey' (ibid.: 49). She must never look anyone of the men in the face nor speak to them.

Not surprisingly, then, the *Story of O* has been widely reproached for misogyny and for objectifying women. And it is true that disgusting things are done to the main heroine O, and that she is constantly degraded and debased. Ultimately, she is deprived of basically all human dignity and of the rights to freedom and autonomy usually considered sacred. For the men using her, she is really nothing but an object serving their needs (thereby, in reference to Chapter 3, the novel also provides a good example of how subjects and objects may occasionally exchange properties). However, I suggest that instead of just judging the way it objectifies women, we can also read the *Story of O* from another perspective. That is to say, the novel affords also a more radical reading. To me it is no defence of the objectification of women; it can be read as only displaying the objectifying gender practices prevalent and predominant in society in their lowest, in the most exaggerated, extreme form. The story forces us to encounter in fiction the traumatic Real, to phrase the matter in Lacanian terms. And one could even claim that it is precisely because the truth it reveals of social relations, of economy and of masculine desire is so unbearable that the readers may find the novel repellent. We simply cannot encounter it if we want to continue our business-as-usual.[5]

If the men of the novel are no sadists, O is definitely no masochist. She does not particularly desire to be punished or subjected, nor does she find pleasure in pain. On the contrary, she merely puts up with the violation; she does not enjoy it, only bears it. This is what is really obscene in the novel, not, as one might first think, the several depictions of brutal sex, bondage, piercing, chaining, branding, whipping and other forms of torture. In fact, the novel is not the least bit obscene in its style. For example, with its usage of words like 'sex', 'belly', 'womb' and 'buttocks' for the private parts of the human body, the text is toned down, even decent. The real obscenity of the novel lies in O's perfect compliance: she submits to her brutalising treatment without resistance. It is not the threat of violence that prevents her from leaving. She does not fear getting beaten up by René. On the contrary, the reason why she submits to the will of her lover and to being procured by him to other men is *love*. René's love for her is all the reward and all the restitution O needs. For his love, she is ready and willing to endure everything that she is put through. His love is all she cares for and all she lives for. There is no other reason, no other motive. Just as much as in her conduct, O is passive in her love, too. She wants and needs to be loved. Therefore, rather than being a subject, she is, above all, an object of love. Being loved is always passive; it is to be placed at the position of an object.

Because of René's love for her, O's giving of herself to René and to other men of his choosing is not entirely voluntary, but already a counter-gift given more or less obligatorily. She feels that she is already – and, may I add, almost irrevocably – indebted to René, that she owes to him something of which she is the beneficiary. The gift she gives is thus conditioned by a gift that supposedly precedes hers: René's love for her. O sees her submission to sufferings as a repayment for René's love. The gift she – believes she – has received from René places her completely at his mercy. If it means that, to be loved by René, she is to be chained to the wall, penetrated by other men and tortured, then so be it, she reasons: 'She did not want to die; but if torture were the price she was to have to pay for her lover's continuing love, then she only hoped he would be happy because of what she had undergone' (Réage 1972 [1954]: 40).

------

5   The idea draws from Lacan. Explicating Lacan's idea of the phantasmatic screen, Slavoj Žižek (2006: 57) suggests that reality itself can offer an escape from the traumatic Real that is too unbearable to live with: 'it is not that dreams are for those who cannot endure reality, reality itself is for those who cannot endure (the Real that announces itself in) their dreams'.

O's love for René makes her a kind of *hostess* in the brothel that her body is: it is by *receiving* other men in her belly, mouth and buttocks that O *gives* to René. There are thus two meanings to receiving: passive and active. When one receives a letter, for example, one is definitely not giving; but when the hostess receives guests at her house, she is giving (Serres 1991: 171). By receiving the sexes and secretions of men in the holes of her body, O is giving, but she is giving and active in and by way of her very passivity. However, René is not content with what she gives voluntarily. There are also gifts that must be forced out of her. She is made to give precisely what she possibly cannot give. In a sense, then, this perverts Lacan's definition of love as giving what one does not have, as O is made to give it *by force*. As René tells her:

> It's because it's so easy for you to consent that I want from you something you can't possibly consent to, even if you say yes in advance, even if you say yes now and suppose that you are actually capable of submitting to it. You won't be able to prevent yourself from saying no when the time comes. When the time comes, it won't matter what you say, you'll be made to submit, not only for the sake of the incomparable pleasure I or others will find in your submission, but so that you will be aware of what has been done to you. (Réage 1972 [1954]: 48)

Of course, one could ask why does O not simply choose to leave René and walk away. And, as the story proceeds, O is in fact offered the chance to leave. René tells her that 'she [is] free in one sense, only in one: to stop loving him and to leave him immediately' (ibid.: 76). This offer, however, is nothing but an empty gesture, for insofar as O really loves René, she is not free at all. She is not free to choose whether she loves him or not, but love rather has chosen her; she loves the man whether she chooses and wants that or not. Her love undoes her freedom. And that is why she cannot but comply: 'Since she loved him, she had no choice but to love the treatment she got from him' (ibid.: 48). This is the traumatising truth about love told by the *Story of O*.

Bonding Value

Let us come back to the issue of appropriation. As I already suggested, the *Story of O* is a narrative of appropriative desire. The men objectifying O do not primarily seek pleasure in causing pain and in transgression, but their lust is that of appropriation. While the appropriation and circulation of women undoubtedly has no explicit economic function between the men in the novel, arguably the *Story of O* nevertheless presents the very foundation and law of economy, insofar as economy is based on possession of private property and on the circulation of values. By depicting the social relations between the masters and their female slaves who appear as their property, the *Story of O* maps and brings to light this economy, which, by taking up a notion employed by Cixous (1986), I will call the economy of *propre*,[6] an economy that is driven by the will to appropriate.

O is literally *property* belonging to René. Rene's love is the love for possessing. In O, we are told, 'he loved the object he had made of her, the absolute disposition of her he enjoyed, the freedom that was his to do with her what he wished' (Réage 1972 [1954]: 113). His love for her is thus simultaneously also both self-love and, more importantly, love for what is owned, love for possessing. In French, all these aspects are conveniently expressed by the ambiguous word *propre*, which means 'proper' or 'characteristic of', 'one's own' and also 'clean'. René's *propre amour*, proper love, gives itself as *amour-propre*,[7] at once self-love and love for owning and what is owned. I would claim that what we have here is no subversion of love, for isn't the will to appropriate – albeit in a less absolute, total and thus perverted form – something that belongs to the nature of love itself? What I mean is that the difference between René's love and our most common experience of love is not one in kind but only one in degree. For isn't love always possessive, to some extent? Isn't the pursuit of love up to a certain point the same as the pursuit of possession? Doesn't love – at least when it comes to the Western idea of romantic love – always make the loved one into a property of some kind, insofar as it claims possession and exclusive rights over the object of love? At least for Nietzsche (1974: see 1, para 14, 'The things people call love'), love was the appropriating drive par excellence. As one declares one's love, one also claims exclusive ownership, as if for a plot of land. And we are also quite happy and content to belong to the other, declaring our belonging ('I belong to you', 'I'm yours') with pride, joy and enjoyment.

However, the extreme debasement and humiliation of the possession in O's case lies, of course, in the deep asymmetry of her relationship with René. There is a striking imbalance between O's total giving of herself and the recompense she receives from René. O's prestation is most personal, but René treats her with notable indifference towards her individuality. O imagines herself belonging exclusively to René, but René defies exclusivity and gives her away. Further, while O is totally possessed by René, she does not possess René. René is possessed by no one. He is totally free to do whatever he wants, with O as well as with other women. O, by contrast, is totally un-free. Or, to be more precise, as was suggested above, she is free in one sense only: she can refuse to belong to him or to anyone else. But because she ultimately only wants to be loved by someone, that is, because her will is 'the will that wills self-abandon, that says yes in advance to everything' even if her body said no (Réage 1972 [1954]: 104), she is not free at all. Accordingly, the love of O and René is not of the same kind. They are complementary, though: O's

---

6   Betsy Wing translates the French term *propre* as 'selfsame' in the English edition of Cixous's book. The translation, however, has the downside of losing the semantic link to appropriation, property and proper (in Cixous 1986).

7   The notion of *amour-propre* is from the novel itself, page 135. The concept is more famously used by Jean-Jacques Rousseau in contrast to *amour de soi*.

love is the love to be possessed, and René's to possess. René's love is the lust for ever *new possessions* (cf. Nietzsche). After he has abandoned O for good in the story, he wants to have Jacqueline, a model with whom O is working.

To be precise, O does not only will self-abandonment, but she is also asked for her consent to what would have in any case been her fate. As long as she agrees to belong to René she is not allowed to refuse anything done to her. She does not belong to herself; least of all she possesses her body. As she is told at Roissy: 'Your hands are not your own, neither are your breasts, nor, above all, is any one of the orifices of your body, which we are at liberty to explore and into which we may, whenever we so please, introduce ourselves' (Réage 1972 [1954]: 25) The men at the château have the right to use her body whenever and as they wish, O has no right to 'withhold or deny' herself (ibid.: 25). She is to let her body to be constantly at their disposal, 'constantly and immediately accessible' (ibid.: 77). She has no choice but to lend it to any use. She must remain open at all times, open her legs and never have them crossed, nor press her knees together. Thus, besides Object, O also stands for Open and Orifice:

> It occurred to her that the words *open oneself to someone*, which signify to confide oneself, had, in their application to her, but one meaning: quite literal, physical, but nevertheless absolute and essential, for the fact was that she opened her self in every part of her body which would possibly open. It also seemed that there lay her *raison d'être* [...]. (ibid.: 186)

What remains to be clarified is the sense in which O is possessed as property. To provide an answer, let us first look at what property and possession mean in more general terms. In *The Philosophy of Money*, Simmel insists that possession is an *activity*: 'Ownership that is not to some extent activity is a mere abstraction' (Simmel 2004: 304). According to Simmel, property is defined by a sum total of rights over an object. Along the same lines, Hyde (2007: 96) writes that, 'by one old definition', property is a '"right of action". To possess, to enjoy, to use, to destroy, to sell, to rent, to give or bequeath, to improve, to pollute – all these are actions, and a thing (or a person) becomes a "property" whenever someone has "in it" the right of any such action'.

Usually, property implies the *exclusiveness* of the rights. One can be said to possess something provided that others do not have (the same) rights over it. O's case is, however, somewhat different. There is no doubt that she is property, but in her case the rights of action over her are not strictly exclusive. She is property of a specific kind: *gift-property*. She is neither to be sold nor to be kept all to oneself by her owner, but to be given away. In the economy of the gift, '*to possess is to give*' (Hyde 2007: 15). René possesses and enjoys O precisely by donating her to other men. And, as long as he also enjoys her himself, the abandonment of possession is not total, but more a matter of *keeping-by-giving*. This connects to Weiner's (1992) study of the *kula* ceremonies on the Trobriand Islands and to her notion 'keeping-while-giving'. She observed that the ownership of certain kinds

of objects was inalienable in the sense that only the original owner had ultimate
rights over the object, while the subsequent owners enjoyed merely temporary and
alienable rights of possession and use, which they transferred when they passed
on the object (Weiner 1992; Komter 2005: 61). In the *Story of O*, René is such an
original owner and donor: 'she was the gift, he the donor' (ibid.: 47). On the one
hand, giving becomes only a means to assure appropriation. Réne's giving of O
is a case of *giving-for-keeping*: 'The fact [that] he gave her to others was proof
thereof, proof in his eyes, it ought to be proof also in hers, that she belonged to
him' (Réage 1972 [1954]: 47–8). On the other hand, while giving her is a way of
keeping her in possession, it also makes O 'subject to general use' (ibid.: 47). Thus
the keeping is a case of *keeping-for-giving*; she becomes an object circulating
among the men. René 'intended that from now on she be held in common by
him and by others of his choosing and still others who he didn't know who were
affiliated with the society that owned the château' (ibid.: 47).

Economy is about the creation of value, ultimately out of what is devoid of
value, the valueless. In the novel, O is without value in herself. She has value
only insofar as she, on the one hand, serves the sexual urges of the men and, on
the other, helps to solidify the relations of homo-sociality between them by being
circulated from hand to hand. Consequently, as an object, her value is divided
into two categories: she is at once an object to be used and a bearer of value. In
the materiality of her flesh, she is a utility object to serve the sexual needs of her
masters. Anyone with whom she is made acquainted are 'entitled to the free use
of her body if they ha[ve] any desire for it' (ibid.: 187). To enhance her use value,
she is also customised (by stretching her anus). This is to make her better match
the needs of Sir Stephen, to whom René ultimately donates O.

While her value as an object being used to satisfy obscenc sexual urges can
be perfectly considered – by taking up a famous notion by Marx – in terms of *use
value*, when it comes to the other type of value that O embodies, Marx's concepts
prove no longer helpful. The capacity of O's body to serve the relations between
men is not a matter of exchange value, but rather what Godbout and Caillé (1998:
174) have called '*bonding value*'. It concerns the utility of an object for the
creation and reinforcement of bonds, something which the concept of use value,
focusing on the more immediate and concrete use of objects, does not cover. And,
in contrast to exchange value, bonding value is not measured against other objects,
but it is determined first and foremost in relation to subjects who are in hold of
the object (ibid.). Coming back to O, we can see that her value as a gift-property
depends on her capacity to foster, facilitate, reinforce and stabilise ties between
men. Her bonding value is not determined in comparison to other women, but in
relation to the men enjoying her. When René gives her to Sir Stephen for good,
what matters in the disposal is more René's relation to Sir Stephen than to her.
René greatly admires Sir Stephen and wants to be like him. Therefore, if giving O
satisfies Sir Stephen, René is happy to hand her over and entrust her in his keeping.
For all his love for O, René is only pleased and grateful that Sir Stephen might
'take pleasure in something he had given him' (Réage 1972 [1954]: 141). René

says to O 'how terribly happy he was to hand her over, how terribly happy he was that she was handing herself over to Sir Stephen, to his orders and wishes' (ibid.: 104) In order to please Sir Stephen, René is willing to abandon her – along with his ultimate and inalienable rights of possession over her – to him.

With regard to her value, it is important to note that, contrary to how the bodies of and sexuality of women are typically perceived in Western culture, O's value does not decrease but increases as she is passed through the hands, sexes and mouths of men. In the novel this is stated in the most explicit terms. Desclos writes that René 'gave her so as to have her immediately back, and recovered her enrichened a hundredfold in his eyes' (ibid.: 48). Thus, ultimately, for René, O has value only insofar as she is desired by *other men*. And the more O circulates, the more she is worth. This is highly significant. For doesn't the circulation of O from man to man, refuting the distinction between object and person, exhibit nothing less than the very law of economy itself: circulation and return? The law, *nomos*, of economy, *oikonomos*, as Derrida (1994: 6) notes, always implies the idea of a 'return to the point of departure, to the origin, to the home (*oikos*)': economy consists of the circulation of goods, products, merchandise, money and capital, of the amortisation of debts and the settling of accounts, of revenues and of the substitution of exchange value for use value. In so far as gifts tend to return to their point of origin, as we have seen, gift-exchange presents the very law of economy itself. The letter O in the title *Story of O* could thereby also be understood as referring to *Oikonomos*.

However, it is crucial to acknowledge that O's value as gift-property depends not only on the number of men's hands through which she circulates, but also on the prestige of each man who has ever held her. In the possession of Sir Stephen, she becomes of more worth compared to being in the hands of René, who is of much lower rank as a man than Sir Stephen, this grey-haired English gentleman greatly admired and even imitated by René.[8]

It can be argued that, for all its monstrosity, the circulation of the women in the *Story of O* only provides a more extreme rendering of the manner in which the

---

8   An analogous phenomenon can be observed in the markets for artworks. Artists greatly benefit from the patronage of collectors, all the more so the more acknowledged and respected the buyer is. For example, a super-collector like Charles Saatchi is famous for launching the careers of relatively unknown artists: the value of the works by the artists he buys tends to increase exponentially, as other collectors quickly follow his lead. And, from the other way around, bad money tends to chase out the good. Art dealers are typically reluctant to sell works to 'speculators', who are in it for the wrong reasons: to make profit with art (Velthuis 2005: 44). Sarah Thornton (2008: 88) describes how dealers wish to place the works of their artists in the hands of the most respectable buyers: 'When gallerists are confident about demand for an artist's work, they wouldn't dream of surrendering it to the first come or the highest bidder. They compile a list of interested parties so they can place the work in the most prestigious home. It's an essential part of managing the perception of their artists. Unlike other industries, where buyers are anonymous and interchangeable, here artists' reputations are enhanced or contaminated by the people who own their work'.

constitution of women as objects to be circulated establishes patriarchal society, discussed briefly in the beginning of this chapter. However, the crucial difference to the analysis of Irigaray, for instance, is that while Irigaray suggests that it is as commodities that women circulate in patriarchal society, in the *Story of O* women are exchanged as *gifts*. Rather than appearing as commodities '*subject to a schism* that divides them into the categories of usefulness and exchange value' (Irigaray 1985: 175), in the novel women circulate more as gifts whose value is divided into use value and bonding value. In the *Story of O*, the cohesion and stability of the relations between men is achieved through the bodies of O and other women circulating in those relations. In the novel, property appears as the foundation of the collective or the community. Women are the 'things' that the members of the community, the men, have in common; the common is characterised precisely by what is proper. Or, to be more precise, the women are gift-properties, property to be given away and held in common. Therefore, paradoxically, the men have in common what is properly their own; at one point, O, for instance, is explicitly made to consent to common ownership by René and Sir Stephen. The men belonging to the community own what is common to them all, each has equal rights of usage. This, at the same time, distinguishes the women from money: their bodies do not exclude attachment, but are precisely very closely tied to a particular owner.

In sum, the *Story of O* exhibits the law (*nomos*) of economy (*oikonomos*) by depicting the relations of a homo-social collectivity based on the exchange of women. In the relations between the men, women circulate above all as gifts and not as commodities. In the economy of relations pictured by the novel, the bodies of women present a form of currency, whose value is not a matter of exchange value but that of bonding value: it is not determined in relation to other women, but with respect to how they serve to establish and maintain bonds (and in relation to the status and number of the men holding them) and the needs of the men. (With regard to the latter point, a further difference between exchange value and bonding value is that the latter is not as far removed from the object and its use: O has value for the creation and nourishment of social relations only insofar as she is also sexually attractive and desirable. It is only in his enjoyment that René possesses her. Without his enjoyment he does not *have* her (to give). He can give only as long as he enjoys himself.) Through the exchange of women-as-gifts, their owners, the men, gain more value to themselves; the value cannot be appropriated by the women themselves.

The Will to Appropriate

While exhibiting the circle as the law of economy, the *Story of O* also highlights how the economy of *propre* is masculine by its nature. In *The Newly Born Woman* (1986), Cixous argues that masculine economy is based on the 'law of appropriation'. It is driven by man's desire to appropriate what is not his: 'desire is inscribed as the desire to reappropriate for himself that which seems able to escape him' (Cixous 1986: 80). In the appropriation of the women by the men in the *Story of O*, all the three meanings of the word *propre* are at play. As the other – conveniently, in English, here we have yet another referent: O for Other – that is sought to appropriate, women simultaneously embody the opposite of *propre*: the not-mine, not-proper, not-clean (cf. ibid.: 80) In the novel, 'woman' is, originally and on her own terms, a non-*propre* that men seek to appropriate. The gap or distance that separates them from the object of their appropriative desire fundamentally constitutes the men as lacking subjects, as subjects of the lack of the proper. They lack precisely what is own, the proper, and therefore they constantly try to (re)appropriate the non-*propre*, make it their own.

Irigaray's reading of Marx's analysis of commodification in *This Sex Which Is Not One* (1985) from the perspective of the status of women in patriarchal society bears interesting similarities with the ideas of Cixous. Like Cixous, Irigaray argues that it is essential to pay attention to gender if we are to understand economy. Both thinkers connect the economy of *propre* and masculine desire to one another. Irigaray asks: 'Does pleasure, for masculine sexuality, consist in anything other than the appropriation of nature, in the desire to make it (re)produce, and in exchanges of its/these products with other members of society?' For her, masculine desire is thereby '[a]n essentially economic pleasure'. And, the other way around, the desire to appropriate is a characteristically masculine form of desire that has '*presided over the evolution of a certain social order*, from its primitive form, private property, to its developed form, capital' (Irigaray 1985: 184).

In *Malfeasance* (2011), Serres examines appropriation in relation to the problem of how to live peacefully in and with the world. According to him, pollution and our environmental problems ultimately stem from our will to appropriate (Serres 2011: 42). We inhabit by appropriating. Ecology and possession are tied to one another already via etymology, as the verbs 'to inhabit' and 'to have' have the same origin (Serres 2011).

By taking the idea of property as being always *marked* utmost literally, Serres proposes that '*appropriation takes place through dirt*' (ibid.: 3). According to him, we take possession of space and things by way of 'pollution', in the broadest sense of the term. It is by way of polluting, by soiling, by leaving a stain or some mark that one makes something one's own. Airplanes flying over the city; BoomBlasters carried around out on the street; billboards and garish illuminated signboards spreading out the name, logo, slogans and colours of companies throughout urban space; farting motorcycles shouting ego, ego; smokers with their fumes; people wearing lots of perfume; the Muzak played in shops and department stores; and the factories polluting the earth – all these are ways of invading and taking over space (Serres 2011).

For Serres, these acts of polluting all spring from the same origin: from the animal gesture of marking a territory. They have an animal origin that is bodily, physiological, organic and vital (ibid.: 12). Several mammals mark their territory, define their habitat, by filth and dirt: for example by urinating on the edge of their lair or by marking the boundaries of their niche with excrement. Our hard and soft ways of polluting alike repeat this bodily, animal gesture. Like barking dogs or dogs urinating on lamp-posts and street corners, taggers, for instance, mark their territory by spreading their name, by literally 'throwing up' (conveniently, *throwups* are a form of graffiti) their personal stain on the shared urban space. Tags mark one's territory to others and enable one to appropriate space.

The *Story of O* provides several extreme examples of how property is always marked,[9] and how the appropriation of women takes place through leaving a mark. During the rituals of brutalisation, O is soiled by the bodily discharges of the men: sweat, sperm and saliva. Her body carries their marks. Serres remarks that what is properly one's own and, paradoxically, 'clean', is one's dirt – one's aroma, stain, filth and excrement: 'One's own dung smells good'. The one who spits in the soup or in the salad bowl makes it all his/hers. No one else would ever touch it. As soon as you make something dirty and disgusting to others, it is yours (Serres 2011; 2007). What is peculiar to the appropriation of O, however, is that in her case the marks of a fellow libertine in fact do not expel and chase away others, but only make her body appear ever more desirable. In the novel, this is noted explicitly with regard to traces of whiplashes and blows of riding-crop:

> Sir Stephen readily admitted that O was infinitely more exciting when her body was covered with marks, whatever their sort, if only because these marks prevented her from resorting to subterfuges and immediately proclaimed to whomever saw them that everything was permitted in her regard. For knowing it was one thing, visual proof, proof constantly renewed, was another. (Réage, 1972 [1954]: 155–6)

Hence, the main reason for her brutalisation is not the possible enjoyment drawn out of it, but the whipping and the beating is carried out 'quite apart from the pleasure her screams and tears might afford'. Just as secretions, the whip marks, too, designate her as property. The reason for the frequent whipping is 'to keep her marked at all times', and that is why she is 'flogged as frequently as necessary' (ibid.: 156).

In addition to being marked with bodily discharges, whip marks and bruises, O is made to wear an iron ring when she is dismissed from Roissy. As if parodying and mocking marriage, the ring is placed on the ring-finger of her left hand: here, the ring is not accepted as a token of love and as evidence of the vows made, but as a sign of slavery and servitude. Nevertheless, are the two rings – and the relations made perceptible by them – ultimately that foreign to one another? After all, does not the wedding ring itself to some extent appear as a sign of ownership? As Serres provocatively writes in *Malfeasance* (2011: 32): 'Ownership in marriage is the equivalent of slavery. Here we have the mark again: the ox and the slave are marked with red iron, the automobile by the Ford logo, and *the spouse by the golden ring*'.

---

9 In *Electronic Potlach* (Rehn 2001) mentioned in Chapter 2, the gesture of appropriating can be observed in the ways cracker groups sign their 'warez'.

This is, of course, not to deny crucial differences between slavery and marriage. The fact that the ring O wears is made of iron (with a golden inner surface) is hardly insignificant. By making her wear the ring, she is, as it were, 'put in irons'; she is made submissive. In addition, her ring is identical to those worn by the other women possessed by the men affiliated to the society. Thus, unlike a wedding ring, the ring does not designate her as belonging to a particular individual, but it diminishes her singularity and uniqueness by tagging her as common property. The ring 'was the sign that she was a slave, but a common one, one held in common' (Réage 1972 [1954]: 163). Consequently, for anyone who recognises the token and is aware of what it means, it functions as an invitation to take the liberty to use her body as one may wish. As O is told at the château Roissy:

> You will then have learned to obey those who wear the same token – upon seeing it, they will know that you are constantly naked beneath your skirt, however correct or ordinary your dress and that this is on their behalf, this nudity for them. Those who find you unco-operative will bring you back here. (ibid.: 28)

Nevertheless, O's masters do not settle for marks that can be removed and that vanish in time. They also need a definitive mark of ownership. A ring can be taken off the finger and, as for flogging and beating, they too, 'no matter how often repeated', leave only 'unobtrusive and superfluous' traces (ibid.: 164). Sir Stephen wants O to wear oblong-shaped 'rings of dull stainless steel […] round, about the thickness of a pencil' (ibid.: 205). The rings, reminiscent of the links of chains, hang heavily from her pierced genitals. They are a mark that doesn't wear off: 'this iron ring which pierces flesh and weighs eternally, this mark […] will remain forever' (ibid.: 240). In addition, unlike the secretions and the ring O wears on her finger, which are incapable of distinguishing between the real owner and the guests merely paying a visit at the inn of intimacy that O's body ultimately is, the rings hanging from her pierced flesh designate her as a property of a particular master. On the blank side is engraved O's name and title, Sir Stephen's first and last names and also the devices to be used on her: a 'crossed whip and riding-crop' (ibid.: 206). And as if this would not suffice, O is also branded with a red-hot iron. 'The marks imprinted by the branding-iron were three inches high and a half that in width, were dug into her flesh as though by a gouge, were about half an inch deep' (ibid.: 217). Instead of trying to hide these marks, O carries them with disturbing pride and willingly exposes them, revealing her belonging as a form of property to a master.

Feminine Economy: Giving Without Return?

We have seen above how the *Story of O* displays the foundation and law of economy – appropriation and circle. The relations between the men in the novel, as I have argued, are economic in essence; they centre on the appropriation and circulation of women. The women circulating in and through the relations constitute and consolidate the society of the men and the solidarity among them. In their society, the gift and exchange are one and the same.

However, at the same time the novel exhibits traces of another kind of economy, one that is not based on return and revenue, but on gratuitous giving. One could fruitfully describe the two economies also by employing Bataille's (1984 [1933: 94–6) notions of 'homogeneity' and 'heterogeneity', with 'appropriation' as the basic impulse related to the first and 'excretion' as its counterpart in the latter. However, since in the *Story of O* the economies are intimately connected to gender, I follow here Cixous and take up the concepts masculine and feminine economy coined by her.

In the novel, as we have seen, the appropriating desire is presented as being masculine in essence. Cixous discusses the phallocentric foundation of the economy of *propre* with great insight in *The Newly Born Woman*. According to her, the economy of prope is organised around the masculine fear of *loss*, that is, about 'the fear of expropriation, of separation, of losing the attribute' (Cixous 1986: 80). Because of this, the economy of *propre* has an immensely problematic relation to the gift, facing insurmountable difficulties in dealing with unilateral giving and generosity. For Cixous (1986: 86–7), a masculine economy is concerned with 'return' (Fr. *rapport*). The idea of giving without a return is simply unbearable for a masculine economy. It cannot tolerate separation, detachment, expropriation and loss. One must always recover one's expenses, settle the scores and get even. Even more preferably, one should make profit, capitalise and gain more. A masculine economy therefore allows only *quid pro quo* exchanges that always guarantee a return (Schrift 1997: 11). It always makes the gift into a 'gift-that-takes': the gift must always bring in a return, come back in the form of profit (Cixous 1986: 87); René gave O away to others only to more firmly keep her in his possession and to receive her enriched. For a masculine economy, the only action worth carrying out is one that secures a profit. Therefore it cannot but regard gratuitous giving as either fake or as a form of non-reason.

In relation to the economy that she calls masculine, Cixous also asks whether another kind of economy, which she terms feminine, would be possible. She thus ascribes women a much more active and autonomous role in (gift-)economy than for example Irigaray does. Before going into the details of Cixous's depiction of feminine economy, let me just note that the terms 'masculine' and 'feminine' should not be understood here in an essentialising way. The terms do not suggest that there would be some uniquely masculine and feminine essences. In addition, masculine economy is not necessarily the same as the actions of (all) biological males, and feminine economy is not restricted solely to what females do.[10] (The character of

---

10   Cixous seems to be well aware of the possible accusations of biological essentialism implicit in the concept of feminine economy. She notes of the assumed femininity of giving without reserve in a manner that does not subscribe to the idea of any stable and consistent sexual essences: 'But is that specifically feminine? It is men who have inscribed, described,

Ann-Marie, a friend of Sir Stephen's, is a good example of this in the *Story of O*. She is possessed by no man, but she is equal to men in every possible way and also has rights of possession and use over other women.) Rather, masculinity and femininity appear as historically, culturally and materially constructed attributes. It is only because the economy is dominantly phallocentric (privileging of the phallus, the masculine) that Cixous names it masculine; and it is only because she finds signs of a prospective alternative to it in certain practices of women that she calls that economy a feminine one. It would be possible to think the relation and differences of the two economies without using notions referring to gender.

As for the practices indicating a feminine economy, according to Cixous it is above all maternal gifts, the care and loving a mother[11] gives to a child, which embody and foster a feminine economy. For feminism, motherhood is of course a sensitive and inflammable issue. However, unlike several other feminist thinkers, Cixous does not see maternity exclusively nor even primarily as a trap imposed upon women by a patriarchal society. Instead of considering how maternity makes women mere instruments of capitalist, familialist and phallocentrist reproduction, Cixous opts for a de-mater-paternalising approach. Who are other women – or men – to forbid a woman the possibility of motherhood, to deprive a 'woman of a fascinating time in the life of her body just to guard against procreation's being recuperated'? (ibid.: 89–90) To do such a thing would amount to robbing her of her life: 'Let's not repress something as simple as wanting to live life itself' (ibid.: 90).

For Cixous, feminine economy is an 'economy without reserve' (ibid.: 86). It cannot be understood in exchangist economic terms. The economic agent of the feminine economy 'doesn't try to "recover her expenses"' (ibid.: 87). She does not hold anything back, but she outpours, 'overflows' (ibid.: 91). 'She doesn't measure what she is giving' (ibid.: 100). Thus, feminine economy relates to the gift differently than the masculine one, which was based on appropriating desire. In feminine economy, the gift does not involve calculation. Therefore it allows 'for the possibility of giving without expectation of return, for giving that is truly generous' (Schrift 1997: 11). This is not to say that women's gifts would completely escape return. In comparison to masculine economy, 'all the difference lies in the why and how of the gift, in the values that the gesture of giving affirms, causes

---

theorized the paradoxical logic of an economy without reserve. This is not contradictory; it brings us back to asking about their femininity. Rare are the men able to venture onto the brink where writing, freed from law, unencumbered by moderation, exceeds phallic authority, and where the subjectivity inscribing its effects becomes feminine' (Cixous 1986: 86). What is more, a couple of pages earlier Cixous refers to the complex 'web of age old determinations' in which 'men and women are caught up'. There is thus no 'essence' or 'nature' to sex: 'One can no more speak of "woman" than of "man" without being trapped within an ideological theater where the proliferation of representations, images, reflections […] invalidate in advance any conceptualization' (ibid.: 83).

11   By 'mother' Cixous (1986: 94) means not the social role, but for her the term is a 'no-name' that designates a 'source of goods'.

to circulate' (Cixous 1986: 87). In other words, the difference is in the reason and manner of giving, and in the relation to the other, that is, to the not-mine, not-proper and not-clean. Playing on the ambiguity of the French word *rapport*, meaning both 'return', in the sense of revenue or profit, as we have seen, and 'relation', Cixous argues that it all comes down to the *rapport* involved in and produced by the gift. While in a masculine economy loss and expense are confined within the exchangist, calculative mode of valuation, in a feminine economy the fruit of the gift is the relation established – the *bonding value*. The relations weaved by the giving are more important than the possible direct profit drawn from it. As Schrift (1997: 12) sums up, a feminine economy is one 'in which direct profit can be deferred, perhaps infinitely, in exchange for the continued circulation of giving'. Therefore it is precisely the gift that appears as the basis of a feminine economy. As has been suggested throughout the previous chapters, the gift is something given without guarantee of repayment and typically in order to establish, nourish and stabilise social ties.

How does the *Story of O* display features of a feminine economy, then? To begin with, the women of the novel are not merely objects to be given, and markers of the male connection, but they also participate in the process of the gift by giving, albeit they give mostly by receiving (as hostesses),[12] by way of their passivity and consent. Like the parasite, by giving her acceptance O gives the given of the giving. Nevertheless, whereas the parasite gives only by taking, O most certainly does not hold back or try to recover her expenses. She gives without savings or reserve. Her giving, the way she gives herself, is madly extravagant, and it is so without the intention of showing off and competing with what she gives, which is predominant in potlatch, as we have seen. O abandons herself completely; instead of simply lacking a will, her will, as we were told earlier, is 'the will that wills self-abandon'. She does not return to herself but she is 'dispossessed of her own self' (Réage 1972 [1954]: 149). O does not calculate her gift, but she gives somewhat innocently or even 'naïvely': she keeps on giving even when not receiving a commensurate or equivalent return. For sure, the love of René and then Sir Stephen make up some compensation, in fact the only compensation that she ever needs for her losses, but both René and Sir Stephen dispose her in their turn.

With regard to the feminine economy, the *Story of O* affords two contrasting readings. The first is that, in the end, O's superabundant giving provides her an opportunity for 'wonderful expansion': for coming out of her self, exploring alterity, and finding out what she is and what she can be (cf. Cixous 1986: 86). On this reading, in her being, O is 'how-far-being-reaches' (cf. ibid.: 87). The most powerful and vivid picture of this becoming-other is provided in the last chapter, conveniently titled 'The Owl'. The book ends in a party assumedly hosted by a man named the Commander. At the party, O appears on a leash, wearing nothing else but an owl mask before a large audience of guests. O's becoming-owl does

---

12 More for hostessing, see Veijola and Jokinen (2008) and Jokinen and Veijola (2011).

not consist in resemblance, representation or imitation. Instead of understanding it as a mere metaphor, the becoming has to be understood in the most literal sense. Of course, it is not that she 'really' is an owl. Nevertheless, she does not merely 'play' an owl or 'act' like one, either. What the guests confront is *O-as-owl*, the becoming, taking hold of O, that is very real.[13] The owl mask is 'simultaneously transform[ing] her' and something 'the most natural on her' (Réage 1972 [1954]: 255). The becoming-owl eschews the duality between representation and being:

> O stared at them through her plumage, stared at them with wide-open eyes, eyes as round and as open as the night bird she represented, and so strong was the illusion that it struck everyone as completely natural that, when questioned, this owl prove truly what it was, deaf to human speech and mute. (ibid.: 260–261)

We are also told a couple of pages earlier that upon encountering O in her owl mask, Sir Stephen 'caressed her in a manner that was almost timid, as one does an animal one wishes to tame' (ibid.: 257–8). It is uncertain whether O is reduced to an object or whether she is a woman-becoming-owl with a cosmic libido. Somewhat earlier, Sir Stephen had told O that he thinks she desires all those men who violate her: 'You are easy, O. Wanton, one might say. You love René, but you are wanton. I wonder whether René realizes it. Is he aware that you yearn for every one of the men who desire you? Is he aware that in sending you to Roissy or in giving you to others he is simply providing you with ready-made alibis for your own wantonness?' (Réage 1972 [1954]: 117). In his afterword, Paulhan even goes as far as to maintain, provocatively, that it was O who demanded to be violated in the first place: 'From all evidence, the torturers do not find their work amusing. They have nothing of the sadistic in them. Everything happens as if from the outset it were O alone who demanded to be hurt, flushed from her retreat by punishment' (Paulhan 1972: 277). Be that as it may, her status nevertheless remains vague and ambiguous:

> But even though they did these things to O, used her thus, even taking her for an example, or for a sample, or for the object of a demonstration not once did anyone address a word to her. Was she then a thing of stone or wax, or a creature of some other world, and was it that they though it pointless to try to speak to her, or was it that they did not dare? (Réage 1972 [1954]: 262)

The other reading would be that O's giving points not to a wonderful expansion of subjectivity but, eventually, to its destruction. While cosmic, perhaps, O's libido is not unbound. Her subjectivity must never become public; it must forever remain secret; otherwise it would compromise her passivity and absolute submissiveness. Or, better, she is deprived of every possibility of an inner subjectivity. Her

---

13   Cf. Deleuze and Guattari in *A Thousand Plateaus* (1987) on 'becoming-animal' (esp. pages 232–8).

condition is that everything that was formerly secret is now made public. There is no subjective interiority she could retreat to in order to better endure what she is put through; she does not have 'any dream of any possibility of clandestine existence': 'the reality of the night and the reality of the day were going to be the same reality' (ibid.: 150). She must just keep still, lower her eyes and open herself in every part of her body.

On this reading, O's openness is not open subjectivity, but a sign of enclosed property, immediately and constantly accessible to use. Instead of being open for new possibilities and new ways of being, she is reduced to a relatively fixed form, to being an object acted upon; instead of exploring otherness, she is explored by others; and instead of visiting, she is the one who is visited. O cannot possibly win back her body and become a proper subject. The more she gives, the more firmly and definitely she is possessed as property.[14] The very end of the novel is telling in this respect. At dawn, after the party and when the guests have left, Sir Stephen and the Commander have O get up, unleash her and remove her mask. Then, 'laying her down upon the table, [they] possessed her, now that one, now the other'. Thus it all ends in appropriation. In a sense, it is the gift itself, their generosity and giving without trying to recover their expenses, that seals the miserable fate of the women in the novel; the gifts they give turn against them and prove harmful to them. To be sure, the masculine economy of *propre* depicted in the novel is possible only on the condition of the existence of a feminine economy. The men exploit and abuse the freely given. They appropriate not so much the means of production as the sources of gifts or goods. O's and her sisters' giving will be abused as long as they live. It is because of this that, taken to its logical conclusion, O's extravagant giving leads not to an expansion of the self, but to its destruction, even to death. The parasite keeps on taking to the very end, until there is no giving any more. Thus, the absolute parasite donates only death – here we have a rotten gift, a caricature of a gift that causes the disappearance of giving, puts an end to the gift, a giving that exterminates the original giving that set in motion the dynamics of give-and-take. And in fact, after The End of the *Story of O*, on the opposite page the reader is told that there was an alternative ending to the novel (just as after the first pages an alternative beginning was given). The note says: '*There existed another ending to the story of O. Seeing herself about to be left by Sir Stephen, she preferred to die. To which he gave his consent*' (ibid.: 263). This is the true conclusion of the story, the very end.[15]

---

14   For instance, afterwards her love for René appears as nothing but preparation for being able to give – and thus abandon – herself more completely: 'O told herself that she had only loved René as a means for learning of love and for finding out *how to give herself better*, as a slave, as an ecstatic slave, to Sir Stephen' (Réage 1972 [1954]: 240; italics added).

15   Paulhan as well speculates on an alternative ending: 'I too am surprised by this ending. You will not be able to get the idea out of my head that it is not the true conclusion. That in reality (so to speak) your heroine succeeds in getting Sir Stephen to bring about her death. He'll not release her from bondage until once she is dead' (Paulhan 1972: 274).

Chapter 7
Making a Gift of Death

Life-giving death, death-giving life.

Life is not a fairy tale, but occasionally it may imitate scenes from one. When the corpse of the mathematician Alan Turing was found in his bed, there was a half-eaten apple on the bedside table. A post-mortem examination stated that he had died of cyanide poisoning. Turing's is a mysterious death laden with symbolism. He was known to be haunted by a particular scene from *Snow White*, his favourite fairy tale, where the Queen, aka evil stepmother, drips an apple into a poisonous brew, letting sleeping death seep into it. Did Turing commit suicide? Was the apple discovered beside his body the suicide note of a cryptanalyst? Was his death a protest against a homophobic society, which, a few years back, had convicted him of homosexual indecency and given him the impossible choice between two bads, a prison sentence and chemical castration? Did the injections of female hormones he had been sentenced to transform Turing into his own wicked double, into a queen, an evil stepmother, who had now given him, the father of computer science, *death as the ultimate gift*? We will probably never know for sure, as the apple was never tested for cyanide. Allegedly Turing had the habit of having an apple at bedtime, and that it wasn't unusual for him to leave it half-eaten. However, how are we able to tell that, for the man fascinated by the story of the poisoned apple, this habit was not a way of preparing himself for his death, slowly and with care, a way of acting his suicide in advance, over and over again, night after night, until the actual execution of the plan?

But what does it mean to 'give' death? How does one give death as a gift? In what sense can death constitute itself as a gift? It is this that the present chapter will make an attempt in covering. In the Judeo-Christian tradition, death, the fact that the life of individuals ends in death, is regarded as an integral element of the gift of life. As Talcott Parsons, Renée C. Fox and Victor M. Lidz contend in the piece 'The "Gift of Life" and Its Reciprocation' (1978), in Judeo-Christianity the life of the individual is 'defined in the first instance as a *gift*, directly or indirectly from God'. This gift, so the authors suggest, entails an obligation to reciprocate. In relation to the gift of life received from God, dying is seen as a counter-gift, as a way of repaying the initial gift: 'the death of the individual, especially in the fullness of a complete life, [is] itself the gift which constitutes a full reciprocation of the original gift of life' (Parsons, Fox and Lidz 1978: 267). However, instead of simply being caught in the order of economy, death is surely also an event that ends all exchange. In *Symbolic Exchange and Death* (1993 [1976]), Jean Baudrillard argues that only death manages to defy the balancing of accounts. As Mark Poster (1988: 5) notes, for Baudrillard, 'only death is an act without an equivalent return, an exchange of values'. As such, it challenges the power of the simulating system that according to Baudrillard controls our lives. Ultimately, Baudrillard pictures death as a gift given to the system – a gift to which the system cannot respond. For him, death designates thus 'reversibility': it is to return to the system the life it is determined to sustain and prolong by force (Baudrillard 1993 [1976]: 4, 144–8; see also Arppe 1992: 138–9).

The movie *The Seventh Continent* (1989) directed by Michael Haneke is arguably ultimately about this kind of destruction. The very disturbing film, inspired by a news article Haneke had read, is about a middle-class family, who end up destroying all their possessions, flushing money down the toilet and ultimately committing suicide for no apparent reason and in a passionless, almost mechanical manner. However, their suicide can be seen as a way of exiting their lives wrapped up in comfort, a life that has become exceedingly repetitive, automatic and banal, a matter of forced survival instead of novelty and vital creativity. Their suicide appears as a way of refuting the symbolic order, as a sovereign act that cannot be seized by the power apparatus. As Baudrillard (1993 [1976]: 177) puts it: 'In a system which adds up living and capitalises life, the death drive is the only alternative. In a meticulously regulated universe, the only temptation is to normalise everything by destruction'.

Dying for the Other

However, instead of interpreting death, like Baudrillard does, as a form of reversibility and as a gift given to the 'system' (of simulation), in what follows I consider death in terms of *irreversibility* and a gift given to another person. In the chapter, I explore death above all in relation to the question of the possibility of a unilateral, absolute gift, a giving without recompose. In this, I draw substantially from Derrida and his book *The Gift of Death*, originally published as *Donner la mort* in 1992. Based on a close reading of the *Heretical Essays on the Philosophy of History* by the Czech philosopher Jan Patočka (1907–77),[1] the book discusses the gift in terms of the most ultimate of gifts, the gifts of life and death. In *The Gift of Death*, Derrida explores how the possibility of the gift is tied to various figures of 'putting to death' (*la mort donnée*), literally, 'giving death'. He asks: 'What is the relation between *se donner la mort* [giving oneself death] and sacrifice? Between putting oneself to death and dying for the other? What are the relations among sacrifice, suicide, and the economy of this gift?' (Derrida 1995: 10). For Derrida, the possibility of a pure gift is woven to death. The gift of death is 'a gift outside the economy' (ibid.: 96). It manages to suspend 'the strict economy of exchange', for it breaks with reciprocity and symmetry (ibid.: 102). It is a

---

1   Patočka was a student of both Husserl and Heidegger. In addition, along with Vaclav Havel and Jiri Hajek, he was one of the three spokespersons for the famous Charta 77 human rights declaration in Czechoslovakia.

unilateral, absolute gift, a giving without counting and without taking account, without expectation, even any possibility, of a repayment in kind. In the gift of death, the gift itself immediately annihilates and destroys the very possibility of reciprocity and exchange that might otherwise ensue it.

Although Derrida also mentions for instance the example of putting one's enemy to death in war, in his analysis the gift of death appears primarily under the sign of *sacrifice*. He treats death above all as something *one gives to oneself for the other*. In other words, the gift of death given to the other does not amount here to putting the other to death, but it consists of me putting myself to death, of giving myself death. My own death constitutes the gift to the other, but instead of giving death I give life. And I give life by dying myself. Thus, in this gift, the donor and the gift, the one who offers the sacrifice and its object – the sacrificial victim – become one and the same, indistinguishably. The gift of dying for the other is able to escape the economy of exchange, precisely because the giver *gives him/herself irreversibly*, that is, without recompose and return. One gives (up) one's ownmost, what is proper to oneself: one's non-repeatable, singular and unique life.

The best and, I would also say, the most beautiful depiction of the act of dying *for* the other, of giving one's own life for the other, that I've come across is provided by a children's book, *The Brothers Lionheart* (2009 [1973]) by Astrid Lindgren. In the novel, 13-year-old Jonathan Lion rescues his younger brother Karl, 10 years of age, from the fire that has set their house in flames. Taking Karl on his back, Jonathan courageously throws himself out of the window. In result, Jonathan is badly injured and dies almost immediately, but Karl, 'protected by his brother's body in the fall' (ibid.: 9), is rescued uninjured. Jonathan's act retains its full meaning only within the framework of sacrifice, of intentionally causing his own death for his brother. Only by sacrificing his own life he was able to save his little brother. Otherwise, Jonathan's death becomes a mere accident, a chance occurrence. In its depiction of Jonathan's brave act, *The Brothers Lionheart* thus reverses the conventional morality of suicide. Jonathan's suicide appears not as a desperate, selfish act, any more than as a fatal gift to the system of simulation, along which lines Baudrillard conceptualises it, not to speak of being presented as a vertiginous temptation or as an overwhelming object of great passion, as Freud saw suicide. On the contrary, the novel inscribes suicide as an acceding to responsibility, in the ethical dimension of sacrifice and the gift. Jonathan's suicide becomes a self-sacrifice and a gift of death. It is by taking a death-defying leap to his death that he assumes responsibility. This captures the ethics of the gift of death. Jonathan cares for his brother by sacrificing himself for Karl. He dies *for* Karl, gives his life for him.

Importantly, while what one gives is life, dying for the other does not mean, as Derrida reminds us, that one would be able to take the other's dying away from him or her, in the sense of dying in the place of the other, instead of the other. This, too, is something presented with great accuracy in *The Brothers Lionheart*. By sacrificing his own life for his brother, Jonathan cannot rescue his little brother

from certain death. He can only postpone Karl's death, give him a little more time
to live. He can save Karl from death only temporarily, in one particular situation,
that of the fire. What he cannot give is immortality. He cannot sacrifice his own life
for his brother's immortality; by dying himself he is not able to give Karl eternal
life. In fact, in the story, by giving his life Jonathan is able to postpone Karl's death
only a little time, for Karl's death is very much imminent. In the beginning of the
story, Karl finds out that he is sick and about to die soon:

> Jonathan knew that I was soon going to die. I think everyone knew except for
> me. They knew at school, too, because I was way most of the time, coughing
> and always being ill. For the last six months, I haven't been able to go to school
> at all. All the ladies Mother sews dresses for knew it, too, and it was one of
> them who was talking to Mother about it when I happened to hear, although I
> wasn't meant to. They thought I was asleep. But I was just lying there with my
> eyes closed. And I went on lying there like that, because I didn't want them to
> see that I had heard that terrible thing – that I was soon going to die. (Lindgren
> [1973] (2009: 1)

And indeed, Karl dies of his sickness only two months after the incident that
had led to his older brother's death. Had the two brothers calculated death, with
who-will-die-first, Karl would have sacrificed his own soon-to-be-ending life for
Jonathan instead of vice versa. And indeed, this is the way the other people in town
see Jonathan's death. Their judgment of its unfairness – why Jonathan and not
Karl? – is based on an economy of life-expectancy:

> There probably isn't a single person in town who doesn't grieve for Jonathan,
> or who doesn't think it would have been better if I had died instead. At least,
> that's what I gather from all the women who come here with their materials
> and muslins and stuff. They sigh and look at me when they go through the
> kitchen, and they say to Mother: 'Poor Mrs Lion! And Jonathan, too, who was
> so exceptional!' (ibid.: 10)

However, precisely the fact that Karl was about to die soon makes Jonathan's
death so great a gift and sacrifice. If it had been the other way around and Karl
had given his life for Jonathan, there would not have been much of a sacrifice, for
Karl was about to die soon anyway. In his case, no matter how sad and terrified of
dying he was, death might even have come as something of a relief, as he would
have finally got rid of his pain and misery. All Karl did was to cough and be ill and
lie on an old kitchen sofa-bed all day and night. The only tragedy, if one can say
so, regarding his death for him would have been the separation from his beloved
brOther and their mOther.

    To be sure, the gift of Jonathan's death is a gift that does not remain without
recognition and thus without compensation of some sort. Even if his death does
not provide him with the immortality of Homeric heroes, whose reputation lives

forever, he is not forgotten in a little while but his brave act resulting in his premature death does give him an afterlife in the minds, hearts and stories of the people who knew him. The incident of the fire and Jonathan's death was reported in a newspaper, and on another page of the same paper there was more about Jonathan, a text written by his school teacher Greta Andersson:

> Dear Jonathan Lion, shouldn't your name really have been Jonathan Lionheart? Do you remember when we read in the history book about a brave young English whose name was Richard the Lionheart; do you remember how you said: 'Just think of being so brave that they write about it in the history books afterwards; I'd never be like that!' Dear Jonathan, even if they don't write about you in the history books, you were just as brave at the critical moment and you were a hero as great as any other. Your old schoolmistress will not forget you. Your friends will also remember you for a long time. It will be empty in the classroom without our happy and beautiful Jonathan. But the gods love those who die young. Rest in Peace, Jonathan Lionheart. (ibid.: 10; italics in the original)

So, Jonathan's gift of death does not avoid return. Not only will he be remembered by his old teacher and by his friends, but the new name Lionheart suggested to him by his teacher may even be said to render him sacred. By renaming him after a king he is set apart from the rest of the people, from the profane lives of everymen, who will be forgotten. However, he did not particularly go for the profit or calculate the return that his self-sacrifice might bring. A deceased cannot know anything of any possible counter-gifts following one's own death. The reason for Jonathan's sacrifice was not to gain recognition and to be remembered, but to rescue his brother. He gave his life for his brother. And in that sense his giving is truly generous.

Let us get back to what it means to die for the other. The reason why it is utterly impossible to die in the place of the other is that death is always owned. It always remains mine, *my* death. Basing his argument on Heidegger's treatment of dying in *Being and Time*, Derrida (1995: 41) maintains that dying is something which 'nobody else can undergo or confront in my place'. As Heidegger (1962: §47 284) himself puts it, 'No one can take the Other's dying away from him'. I cannot rescue the other from certain death, as no one else's death can ever take one's death away from oneself.

Children's book as it is, it is not at all surprising that *The Brothers Lionheart* does not particularly emphasise the finality of death. We can't really blame it on Astrid. In the book, there appears an idea of a life after death. When Karl is worrying about his being dead soon, Jonathan comforts his little brother by assuring him that he'll be having 'a marvellous time' (Lindgren 2009 [1973]: 2). Like probably anyone else would, Karl finds it pretty hard to imagine there being anything particularly marvellous in lying under the ground and being dead. However, like a good Christian, Jonathan replies him: 'It's only your shell that lies there, you know? You yourself fly somewhere quite different' (ibid.). It is only his earthly remains that will be buried in the ground. The place that awaits him, Jonathan explains, is called Nangiyala. And it is 'still in the days of camp fires and sagas there', even though there is no real time in Nangiyala (in Nangiyala, the passing of 90 years of our time on earth feels like no more than two days had gone, we are told).

It is not that the novel would deny death altogether. On the contrary, in many ways reminiscent of the role it is assigned in Christian mythology, in *The Brothers Lionheart* death is an obligatory passage to afterlife: one does not get to heaven/ Nangiyala without dying first. There are also other features associated to Nangiyala that remind us of the Heaven of Christianity. First of all, like Heaven, Nangiyala is described as a transcendent place, to which people ascend. Jonathan tells Karl that Nangiyala is located 'somewhere on the other side of the stars'. Secondly, as in Heaven, in Nangiyala there is no sickness and misery. Karl finds out that not only is he healthy and well, but he also has a new body: his legs are no longer crooked at all. Nonetheless, Nangiyala is not Heaven, but a place much more exciting, as if it were designed specifically for boys: the brothers are taken to an adventure with rebellion, betrayal, dragons and fighting against the forces of evil. In addition, unlike in Heaven, in Nangiyala there is death and killing.

Nevertheless, although *The Brothers Lionheart* does not renounce death, the finality of death is missing from the novel. When one dies, one's life does not end fully. One does not go from being to non-being, but one is only transferred to another place: Nangiyala awaits the brothers after their earthly life, and after Nangiyala there lies a land named Nangilima to which they go when they die in Nangiyala. To be sure, this takes something off from Jonathan's sacrifice, doesn't it – even though the novel, so it can be argued, interestingly does not explicitly tell whether Jonathan actually is certain of being granted an afterlife in Nangiyala or only says so to comfort his little brother. Either way, it so happens that as he dies he gets to Nangiyala. By sacrificing himself for Karl, he is thus not giving or ending his finite, unique and only life, but he only leaves his earthly life and, as a result, gets into Nangiyala. Thereby the mortality of the individual is swallowed up in the story by the soul-transmigration of the self.

The idea of the transmigration of the soul surely diminishes the horridness of death. In *The Brothers Lionheart*, death is no absolute end, but Jonathan and Karl die into a new life. But what if we read *The Brothers Lionheart* side by side with *The Death of Ivan Ilyich* (2006 [1886]) by Leo Tolstoy? My suggestion is that the two books would enrich one another in their conceptions of death.

For a book written by a religious convert a few years after his conversion, *The Death of Ivan Ilyich* depicts the absolute finality and horridness of death with surprisingly gripping and realistic precision.[2] Its main character Ivan Ilyich, a member of the Court of Justice, is living a decent, secured life immersed in everydayness. One day he bumps his side on a window-frame knob when falling

---

2 Elsewhere, I have discussed the novel in these terms in relation to Simmel's and Heidegger's philosophies of death (see Pyyhtinen 2010; 2012).

from a stepladder on the occasion of hanging the draperies. He has forgotten the whole incident ever happened, but after a while he develops a strange taste in his mouth and a funny feeling in his side, a constant dragging sensation that doesn't go away but only seems to get worse day by day. Ivan is visited by many specialists, and various reasons from floating kidneys to chronic colitis and blind gut are given to his worsening state, but no cure is found. Realising that his condition has in fact nothing to do with floating kidneys or any such things, but is a matter of life and death, of living or dying, Ivan finds himself terrified: there is no way to avoid ending up dead. And what is even worse, as he becomes aware that he is going to die, he understands that he has to live the rest of his life – what is left of it – with this knowledge along with the terror of not knowing when exactly he is going to die. It is this conjoining of the existential certainty and temporal indeterminacy that is really unsettling and horrible in death:

> It's a matter of living or ... dying. Yes, I have been alive, and now my life is steadily going away, and I can't stop it. No. There is no point in fooling myself. Can't they all see – everybody but me – that I'm dying? It's only a matter of weeks, or days – maybe any minute now. (Tolstoy 2006: 56–7)

While realising the fact that he is inevitably heading towards his end and that there is nothing he or anyone else can do about it, Ivan Ilyich still has insurmountable trouble coping with all this. Even though he can see that he is dying, he cannot accept the idea or understand it:

> All his life the syllogism he had learned from Kiesewetter's logic – Julius Caesar is a man, men are mortal, therefore Caesar is mortal – had always seemed to him to be true only when it applied to Caesar, certainly not to him. There was Caesar the man, and man in general, and it was fair enough for them, but he wasn't Caesar the man and he wasn't man in general, he had always been a special being, totally different from others [...]. (Tolstoy 2006: 61)

In the mind of Ivan, death cannot apply to him; it concerns people in general, the others, and not him, because he isn't 'man in general' but a singular being. However, as his end comes closer and closer, Ivan must take his dying upon himself. 'Dying is something that every Dasein itself must take upon itself at the time', Heidegger writes in *Time and Being* (1962: §47 284). The dying that one takes upon oneself inevitably 'remains mine', as Derrida puts it in his reading of Heidegger in *The Gift of Death* (1995: 42). Death cannot be general but everywhere it appears as individually owned: 'By its very essence, death is in every case mine, insofar as it "is" at all', Heidegger (1962: §284) maintains. Each and every one has to take it upon oneself. Therefore, we can conclude by quoting Derrida: 'to have the experience of one's absolute singularity and apprehend one's own death amounts to the same thing. Death is very much that which nobody else can undergo or confront in my place' (Derrida 1995: 41).

It has hopefully come clear by now how the two texts, *The Brothers Lionheart* and *The Death of Ivan Ilyich*, complement one another in crucial respects. On the one hand, *The Brothers Lionheart* brings out the gift in one's death, which is not explicit in *The Death of Ivan Ilyich*. It is true that, as his end becomes near, Ivan Ilyich does realise that he has been hurting his family and his death will set them free. However, he does not die *for their sake*, sacrifice his life for them, but he dies anyway – he cannot help it. His death is thus a gift that is not given by anyone; it is a gift that gives itself, as it were. Therefore, by dying, Ivan Ilyich does not assume responsibility. In the depiction of Jonathan's act of self-sacrifice for his brother, by contrast, death does not appear in the first instance as impending annihilation, but as an ascending to responsibility. On the other hand, *The Death of Ivan Ilyich* depicts the passage from being to non-being involved in death, which in *The Brothers Lionheart* is smoothed away by the transmigration of the soul. Though, to be more exact, that holds true only until the very end. Having theretofore permeated the narrative, at the very end of *The Death of Ivan Ilyich* death is negated. The realisation that his death will set those close to him free at once frees Ivan from all his suffering. And, as if struck by lightning, Ivan is simultaneously rid of his fear of death: 'There was no fear whatsoever, because there was no death' (Tolstoy (2006 [1886]: 105). So, in the end religious mercy rules over the physicality of death: '"Death has gone," he told himself. "It's gone"' (ibid.: 106). There is also an allusion to God's giving of light made: 'Instead of death there was light' (ibid.: 105).

Nevertheless, it is precisely the finitude of life that places the gift of death outside the economy of exchange, for it is a gift that cannot be repaid. And indeed, because death appears in it as only a passage to a new life, in *The Brothers Lionheart* the gift of death does not break with symmetry. On the contrary, at the end of the novel, Karl returns the favour to his brother. In the midst of the final fight, Jonathan is wounded by the flame of the dragon Katla, and he is about to be paralysed. Thus Karl decides to take Jonathan on his back so that together they will jump off a precipice and get to Nangilima without having to be separated from one another ever again. Exchange of sacrifices takes place: 'You did that for me once. And now I'll do it for you. That's only fair' (Lindgren 2009 [1973]: 187). The novel ends with Karl's exultant words when jumping off the cliff with Jonathan on his back: 'Oh, Nangilima! Yes, Jonathan, yes, I can see the light! I *can see the light!*' (ibid.: 188). The life of the two brothers in Nangiyala ends in the light, as Ivan's earthly life had, finding its atonement.

Giving Death to the Other

Besides the giving of one's life for the other, which appears in the ethical dimension of self-sacrifice, there is also another kind of gift of death, which is a highly contentious issue. I am thinking of euthanasia. The right to die has been subject to great controversy in recent years in many countries. On the one hand, governmental policies on euthanasia are fairly conservative throughout the world. Involuntary euthanasia, that is, killing another person without their consent, is illegal everywhere. Active voluntary euthanasia (I will return to the concept shortly and provide a definition) is decriminalized only in Belgium, the Netherlands and Luxemburg. Furthermore, assisted suicide, which means that the patient ends their life with the assistance of a doctor, is legal in Switzerland and in the states of Washington, Oregon and Montana in the United States.

Yet on the other hand, pro-euthanasia groups (such as Dignitas, Voluntary Euthanasia Society, Dying with Dignity and Exit International) have been campaigning actively for the legalisation of voluntary euthanasia. At the same time, the opinion of the general public towards assisted dying is relatively permissive. For example, according to the 2010 British Social Attitudes survey, 82 per cent of the respondents were of the opinion that 'a doctor should probably or definitely be allowed to end the life of a patient with a painful incurable disease at the patient's request' (McAndrew 2010). However, the acceptability of assistance in dying varies considerably, depending on the nature of the patient's illness, the type of assistance provided and who would provide it. According to the study *Assisted dying and decision making at the end of life* conducted as part of the 2005 British Social Attitudes survey, while in 2005 80 per cent of the general public felt that 'the law should allow voluntary euthanasia carried by a doctor in the case of someone dying of cancer', only 60 per cent found the case of a doctor assisting a person in committing suicide acceptable. Again, less than half of the respondents, 44 per cent, thought that 'a relative should be allowed to help someone to die'. People were thus much more willing to have a doctor assist a patient in dying than a layperson, no matter how close that person would be. At the same time, however, it is interesting to observe that doctors themselves were much more reluctant in assisting people to die (Park and Clery 2008: 2).

Before we proceed to explore euthanasia as a gift, a small conceptual analysis is in place, for it is not always clear what is exactly meant when people talk about euthanasia. Some of the varying notions were already touched on above.

In philosophical and medical literature, euthanasia is typically divided into four different types along two axes: *active* versus *passive*, and *voluntary* versus *involuntary* (see for example Beauchamp 1996). (Accordingly, the types could be placed in a 2x2 matrix, which I'll nevertheless leave it to the reader to visualise, having had an OD of this triumphant sociological device – dexterous in its simplicity and, for this reason, flawed in its exclusion of the fluidity and messiness of the world – already in my student years myself.)[3] Active euthanasia is a deliberate act of accelerating the death of the other by use of drugs or poison, for instance. Active euthanasia means to purposely put to death: something is done actively with the intention to end the life of the other. Passive euthanasia, by contrast, amounts to a way of *not doing*. Whereas in active euthanasia the

---

3 For a wonderful critique of the 2x2 matrix reason along these terms, see Geoff Lightfoot's 'Nothing Beats a 2x2 Matrix' (2008).

other is actively killed, passive euthanasia is about 'letting die'. In it, death is caused by not doing what could have been done to extend the person's life. We can think of here examples such as switching off a respirator, stopping medication or abstaining from CPR, from an operation or from blood transfer.

As for the other axis, voluntary euthanasia refers to cases when a person requests, with full awareness, that action be taken to end his/her life (active voluntary euthanasia) or that treatment that would save his or her life be stopped or abstained from (passive voluntary euthanasia). In involuntary euthanasia, by contrast, the person is put to death without his or her consent or knowledge, as in the case of a brain-dead patient, for example. To be more precise, sometimes involuntary euthanasia is identified as only one of the two types of euthanasia, in which the informed consent is missing. The other one is called non-voluntary euthanasia. It means that the person is for some reason unable to make informed decisions and/or to communicate them to others because of being unconscious, unaware of what is happening, too sick or weak or too young.

Furthermore, sometimes a distinction is made between euthanasia and the aforementioned assisted suicide. In the latter, the death of the person is caused by him/herself. The assisting person only provides the patient with the means to end his/her life, without carrying out the act itself. To pick one example, in 1939 Freud asked his doctor to assist him in committing suicide, after more than 30 operations to treat mouth cancer over the years. The doctor prescribed him three doses of morphine, of which Freud died.

At first sight, it may seem completely misplaced or even erroneous to speak of the gift in the context of euthanasia, for euthanasia would appear to be not so much about the gift as about *right*. The term euthanasia is derived from Greek εὖ- *(eu-)* + θάνατος *(thanatos)*, meaning, literally, 'good death'. Pro-euthanasia associations insist that everyone should have the right to a good and happy death. Nobody should suffer from a life that is demeaning, and everybody should be granted at one's will with the possibility of being relieved from a miserable, slow and painful death. So, on the face of it, behind the defence of euthanasia is an individualist ideology pleading for the freedom of choice – and in this sense, there cannot exist any 'involuntary euthanasia'. The right to euthanasia is a matter of taking one's life in one's own hands in the ultimate decision to die.

In the Spanish film *The Sea Inside* (2004) directed by Alejandro Aménabar the dimension of right that is essential in the political dimension of euthanasia is made clear in a palpable manner. The film, based on a true story, is about a quadriplegic Ramón Sampedro (played by Javier Bardem), who fought a campaign in court to win the right to euthanasia. In the film, Ramón wishes to die because he feels that a life in his condition is unbearable. As he explains to Julia (Belén Rueda), a lawyer who, along with Gené (Clara Segura) from the organisation Death with Dignity, has offered Ramón her help in his legal case:

> I want to die because I feel that a life in this condition has no dignity. I understand
> that other quadriplegics may take offence to my saying there's no dignity in this,

but I'm not trying to judge anyone. Who am I to judge those who choose life?
So don't judge me or anyone who wants to help me die.

As he has lost practically all physical autonomy and ability, Ramón wants to have the right of death. Unable to move his legs and arms, he is completely dependent on the help of others. It is impossible for him to manage on his own, and so he lives in at the house of his brother José (Celso Bugallo) and his family, where he is taken care of by his sister-in-law Manuela (Mabel Rivera). In a way, Ramón feels isolated; his condition separates him from other people by an unbridgeable gap. As he tells Julia:

> Think about this: you're sitting there, three feet away. What's three feet? An insignificant distance for any human being. But for me, those three feet that keep me from reaching you … from touching you … are an impossible journey. Just an illusion. A fantasy. That's why I want to die.

That said, it is perhaps the separation from the sea that Ramón mourns the most. A former sailor who had sailed around the world, he is now captive of a life on land, inside a room upstairs in his brother's house, where his whole life takes place in a bed. He had the sea as his companion, mistress, love, mother and home. He inhabited the uninhabitable sea. However, the sea that gave Ramón his life also took it away. At the shore, he happened to jump to the water at the exact moment that the undertow pulled back. He hit the sea floor like a rock and snapped his neck. As if as a reminiscence from his drowned love affair with the sea, he can still smell the sea through the open window of his room from miles away, but it is impossible for him to be reunited with it. Indeed, an impossible journey, an illusion, a fantasy: he only ever visits the sea in his imagination by flying out to the seashore. The sea that used to carry him and the sea in whose arms and womb he used to eat, sleep, work and live he now only carries in himself. He only has the sea inside him now.

Coming back to the question of right and the gift, if it is in the dimension of right that euthanasia is to be placed, the right in this case is of a very peculiar kind. It seems to be completely devoid of any obligations for others, which, after all, are an inevitable correlate of rights. Even when considered as being more originary, rights nevertheless require the fulfilment of some obligations. If rights are to have any practical significance, to the rights of some persons there must correspond obligations on the part of others. In euthanasia, however, such obligations are absent. Euthanasia comes down to a right to death without an obligation for anyone to put to death the person who has the right. Even though a person may have the right to euthanasia, no one – no doctor or anyone – is or can be obliged to end his/her life. The right to death is not a matter of having control over one's life, implying that one would be authorised to end it at will. No, it is in fact more about having the right to *help* others in dying. The person whom the right concerns is not so much the one who is requesting euthanasia as the one assisting him or her: ultimately, the right to death is not after all a right to receive death, but it amounts to the *right to give* it. The right, granted by law, guarantees that the giver of the gift of death cannot be blamed or prosecuted for the death given. In euthanasia, the right to take my life and death into my own hands is a matter of authorising the other to end my life. The right authorises me to authorise the other person to put me to death. So, in a double movement, the other simultaneously assumes responsibility for me and avoids being held responsible for my death in the face of law.

Importantly, it is also because of the absence of an obligation to give death, which would derive from the right to receive death, that euthanasia is a *gift*. From the right to authorise the other to give me death without him/her having to face any legal consequences for the act it does not automatically follow that the other will act upon it. The giving always remains voluntary and a surprise, an event. It 'depends on the powers that be', as Ramón says in the movie with a smile on his face when confronted by Julia about whether he thinks someone will help him in his pursuit. Even though he chooses to die, and even though he *expects* and *asks for* the gift, he is still at the mercy of others and their willingness to give. Consequently, from the viewpoint of the gift (of death), the distinction between active and passive euthanasia as well as that between euthanasia and assisted suicide becomes irrelevant. In each case, one has to rely on the others and their willingness to give death. Accordingly, both the doing and the not-doing comprise acts of giving.

In *The Sea Inside*, the death given to the other appears simultaneously as a criminal act and as an act of love. Because Ramón loses his case in court, death must be given to him in secrecy. The gift must erase all traces of the giver; the given must appear without a confirmed giver. The giver must not be made visible, but rendered uncertain, anonymous and unidentifiable. In this sense, then, when illegal, euthanasia is a gift whose giver should not be acknowledged and recognised. It is as if the gift was not given at all, but only received.

Euthanasia is able to remain a gift only outside market exchange. In some countries, with the legalisation of euthanasia there have emerged organisations offering their services for people who have chosen to end their lives. While they are typically non-profit organisations, monetary transactions may nevertheless intervene, for it is not uncommon that the organisations require a transfer of money from the customer. And in that case, death is no longer given and received as a gift, but sold and bought as merchandise or service. In the novel *The Map and the Territory* (2012) by Michel Houellebecq, there's a troubling and remarkable satiric passage that depicts the morally dubious situation resulting from the exchange of money for death. In the novel, the architect father of the main character Jed Martin has rectal cancer. Finding the idea of being inserted an artificial rectum as rather unpleasant, Jed's father chooses euthanasia. When Jed follows his father's tracks to Zurich, he finds out that the house of the euthanasia organisation called Koestler that his father had contacted is located next to a brothel, Babylon FKK Relax-Oase. Thus, the novel draws a very gloomy parallel between euthanasia and prostitution. The euthanasia centre and the brothel are depicted as businesses trying to satisfy their customers' basic human needs: *while the eros centre charges for sex, the thanatos centre charges for death*.[4] What is more, while the business of the latter is booming, the first does not seem to be doing particularly well:

> The Koestler association boasted, in peak periods, of satisfying the demands of one hundred clients every day. It was in no way certain that the Babylon FKK Relax-Oase could boast of a comparable attendance, despite the fact that its opening hours were longer – Koestler was essentially open in office hours, with a late opening until nine on Wednesday – and the considerable efforts at decoration – of dubious taste, that's sure [with the entrance being adorned with very kitsch erotic frescos, a threadbare red carpet and potted palm trees], – which had been put aside for the brothel [...]

> Just as he was about to ring the bell, two men dressed in cotton jackets and trousers came out carrying a pale-coloured wooden coffin – a light, bottom-of-the-range, model, probably made of chipboard – which they placed in a Peugeot Partner van parked in front of the building. Without paying any attention to Jed they went back in immediately, leaving the doors of the van wide open, and came out a minute later, carrying a second coffin, identical to the previous one, which they in turn put in the van. They had blocked the shutting mechanism of the doors to facilitate their work. That confirmed it: the Babylon FKK Relax-Oase hardly buzzed with such activity. The market value of suffering and death had become superior to that of pleasure and sex, Jed thought, and it was probably for this reason that Damien Hirst had, a few years earlier, replaced Jeff Koons at the top of the art market. (Houellebecq 2012: 251–2)

In *The Map and the Territory*, it is suggested that the profits to be drawn in the thanatos business can be considerable. The members of the Koestler association are rumoured not only to be making a living as euthanisers, but to be doing so well that they actually 'make a killing': 'A euthanasia was charged at an average rate of five thousand euros, when the lethal dose of sodium pentobartial came to twenty euros, and a bottom-of-the-range cremation doubtless not much more. In a booming market, where Switzerland had a virtual monopoly, they were, indeed going to *make a killing*' (ibid.: 255).

In *The Sea Inside*, by contrast, no monetary transactions intervene, and thus the offering of death, so one can argue, is able to present itself as a gift and as a token

---

4   The formulation appearing in italics is a modified, liberal quotation from Baudrillard (1993 [1976: 175–6). All in all, it is interesting to note that the narrator of the novel disdains euthanasia in a manner that brings to mind the criticism Baudrillard puts forth in *Symbolic Exchange and Death*. In addition to juxtaposing 'thanatos' and 'eros', Baudrillard also mentions 'the story of "motel-suicides" in the USA, where, for a comfortable sum, one can purchase one's death under the most agreeable conditions (like any consumer good)' (ibid.: 175).

of love. Ramón is cared for affectionately by two women: by Julia and by Rosa (Lola Dueñas). Julia and Rosa are very different: one is a complex and intelligent lawyer, while the other is a down-to-earth and plain-spoken factory worker. All in all, the two women appear almost as two antagonistic forces, those of death and life, if you will: whereas Julia is willing to give Ramón a hand in his endeavour to die, Rosa tries every which way to keep him away from death and persuade him that life is worth living. This is not to say that they would actually have any power over Ramón to give him a nudge one way or the other, for he is as adamant in his decision as he is bodily immobile: he has already chosen to die. It is rather the case that each cares for Ramón in her own way: Julia wishes to free Ramón from his care by helping him die, and Rosa aspires to do the same by sustaining his life. It is, however, only the first offer that is accepted by Ramón. The latter one he regards as a poisoned, unwelcome gift. As he explains it to Rosa who has just tried to make him change his mind about euthanasia: 'You call that love? Holding me against my will? Look. The person who really loves me will be the one who helps me die. That's love, Rosa. That's love'.

There is a strong magnetism operative in Ramón's relationships to the two women. At first, it appears to be of a very strange kind: instead of opposite poles attracting each other and like poles repelling each other, it rather works the other way around. Firstly, the more Rosa, who says Ramón gives her more strength to live, tries to convince Ramón, who has lost his will to live, of the joy and beauty of life, the more they repel each other, which leads their relationship to the verge of a break-up. Secondly, death seems to be pulling Julia and Ramón unavoidably together and, at the same time, tearing Julia and her husband apart from one another. Julia was diagnosed with CADASIL (Cerebral Autosomal Dominant Arteriopathy with Subcortical Infarcts and Leukoencephalopathy) a couple of years earlier, and back then she considered euthanasia, but gave up the idea. However, now she is drawn not only to Ramón but also to death again. After having a stroke while visiting Ramón which puts her permanently in a wheelchair, she realises that there may not be anything left of her if and when she is to have another stroke. Julia's husband remains hopeful about her condition, but Julia herself has given up hope: she cannot see the point in getting out of bed, going to work and chasing one's dreams when a stroke which is just waiting to happen will destroy her again. And so she tells Gené that she wishes to join Death with Dignity.

Ramón and Julia make a pact. They start working together on a book that would record Ramón's life story, and Julia promises him that when the book is completed and printed, then it will be time. She will come to visit him with the first copy of the book with her and rid him of his misery. Ramón fantasises about the occasion rendering their relationship like of the romance of Romeo and Juliet: 'you'll appear, Julia, my Juliet. It will be the sweetest death imaginable. Love shared in its purest form. And balance will be restored. Finally, balance'. In a life in which far-from-equilibrium is the law and equilibrium is the exception, death will bring balance. It will be the end of Ramón being a parasite, living off and by others against his will.

However, just like the love of Romeo and Juliet, the love of Ramón and Julia eventually remains impossible, an illusion, nothing but a fantasy, just as the aforementioned prospect of Ramón reuniting himself with the sea ever again. One day, Ramón finds out that the book has arrived by mail. He is devastated; Julia had betrayed her promise. However, it turns out that he is not left bereft of the gift of death. For in the meanwhile Rosa has decided that she wants to help him die. Or, to be precise, it is not so much that she wants him to die as wanting to be identified herself as a person who loves Ramón. As Rosa tells Ramon: 'I finally understood, you see? I understood. What you said in Coruña. "The person who really loves me will be the one who helps me die." I'm sure about my feelings, Ramón. I love you. Do you want my help?' So it's like a practical syllogism, a logical deduction: the person who really loves Ramón will help him die; Rosa is certain that she loves Ramón, and thus she feels that she must help him die to become that person. Accordingly, she cannot not give him death, for if she puts him to death, her love for Ramón cannot possibly be denied; such a thing would be a logical impossibility. Putting him to death is to confirm her love indisputably.

Indeed, as Rosa promises to assist Ramón, their love reaches its fulfilment. Paradoxically, here love conquers death by purposely causing death. While death is a third that in a definite manner intervenes between the two and ultimately abolishes their relation,[5] the abolition or extermination at the same time designates here the fulfilment of Rosa's and Ramón's love, the only manner it can possibly actualise. In consequence, contrary to what first seemed, the laws of magnetism have been in place after all: opposite ends attract and like ends repel.

Even though Rosa makes Ramón an offer to put him to death, in the film the giver of the gift interestingly remains unidentified. Of the others helping him in dying, the camera shows only a close-up of hands, with the task of each added to that of the previous one in a sequential manner as if on an ad hoc assembly line. What can be seen on the screen is first a pair of hands preparing Ramón for his death by washing him with a sponge, then several pairs of hands toasting with sparkling wine by Ramón's bedside and, among them, a hand holding a cigarette and offering him a smoke. After that, in the next shot we see a pair of hands measuring out the exact right amount of poison by using a scale; then a hand passing on the poison in a brown bag to another mystery hand; then a hand pouring the crystalline powder into a glass of water with a spoon and mixing the liquid; another hand clothed in a sweater and placing a straw in the glass; a pair of gloved hands installing a rack on Ramón's bed; and finally, a hand in a rubber glove placing on the rack the drinking glass containing the poison. What a division of labour – yet one not implemented in order to speed up the process, but above all to lower the veil of secrecy, to render the ultimate giver, the executive, unidentifiable by alienating the finished product from each particular participant. A sequential handicraft of assisted suicide. What is more, doesn't the visual technique of

---

5   I have discussed death as an interrupting third also in my *Simmel and 'the Social'* (2010; see pages 105–7).

displaying only the hands of the persons helping Ramón at the same time also address the viewer, and in a very direct, disturbing way? Even though the sequence of hands is not presented from the first-person perspective (as it is characteristic of combat computer and video games, for example), that is, through the eyes of each character, the scene almost forces the viewer to become involved. It invites the viewer to ask him/herself, would I, if faced by a similar situation, be ready to do the same for someone I love and care about? How far would I be willing to go in giving? Would I be ready to give the most unbearable thing, put my loved one or friend to death? Would I be ready to kill in the name of love or friendship, kill the other because of loving the other; care by means of killing?

The movie ends with a scene showing Ramón lying alone in his bed in a room. Reminiscent of Socrates standing before a jury, Ramón is talking to a recording video camera, addressing his last words to the judges, political figures and religious authorities who have sentenced him not to death, but to suffering a life without dignity:

> Distinguished judges, political figures and religious authorities … What is the meaning of dignity? Regardless of how your conscience replies, I have determined that mine is a life without dignity. I would have at least wanted to die with dignity. Today, weary of all the institutional apathy, I'm obliged to do this in secret, like a criminal. You should know that the process leading to my death was scrupulously divided into tiny actions that constitute no crime in themselves, carried out by several friends of mine. If you should choose to punish my collaborators, I'd advise you to cut off their hands. Because that is all they contributed. The head, or shall I say the conscience, was mine. As you can see, beside me there is a glass of water containing a dose of potassium cyanide. When I drink it, I will cease to exist, renouncing my most precious asset: my body. I consider life to be a right, not an obligation, as has been in my case, obliged to bear this horrible situation for 28 years, 4 months and a few days. Looking back, my evaluation of the time elapsed is not a happy one. It was just time, passing against my will, for almost my whole life. From now on, time will be my ally. Only time and the evolution of the human conscience will decide some day if my request was reasonable … or not.

Even though Ramón regrets the fact that he has to act in secret like a criminal, paradoxically the illegal status of his assisted suicide ultimately allows him to have control over his life and death. Legalised euthanasia, by contrast, as Baudrillard puts it in *Symbolic Exchange and Death* (1993 [1976]: 175), is a 'semi-official doctrine or practice', which is subject to exact measures of social control. According to Baudrillard, euthanasia only ensures an increase in social control. 'From birth control to death control […] the essential thing is that the decision is withdrawn from [the people]'. They 'live or die according to a social visa'. People are either denied the right to die, or they shall die only if the law and medicine allow them to do so (ibid.: 175).

In Ramón's view, his life and death are finally entirely his. In his closing plea, he presents himself as if as a puppeteer, pulling the strings of his puppets. What the hand contributes does not match the share of the mind for him. However, no matter what Ramón says, the sequence leading to his death cannot be grasped adequately in terms of a mind making a decision. In his dying, Ramón is as much – if not even more – dependent on others as in his living. He can bring an end to his involuntary state of parasitism only by parasiting others, those close to him. He desperately needs their hands to come together to be able to die. To use a term with which Heidegger (2002) conceptualised thinking, dying in Ramón's case is literally *Hand-werk*.

After pledging his drink to his absent jury with the words quoted above, Ramón, the quadriplegic Socrates, reaches out for the glass of water prepared for him, drinks the liquid and then waits for the cyanide to kick in. 'Okay'. He takes a deep breath. 'Heat'. He clears his throat a couple of times. Then: 'Here goes'. Ramón croaks, his eyes turn upside down and then – sleeping death.

To conclude, what the two gifts of death – self-sacrifice and euthanasia – discussed mainly through *The Brothers Lionheart* and *The Sea Inside* in this chapter have in common is that both were ultimately about *care*.[6] In the case of self-sacrifice this is of course quite easily thinkable, but maybe not so in the case of euthanasia. Unlike in dying for the other, in euthanasia the gift given to the other is not that the other acquires more time to live, but the exact opposite: the life of the other is ended. Instead of trying to temporarily save the other from death, as in self-sacrifice, death is in fact hastened. How can one possibly care for the other by putting the other to death? We must turn to Heidegger in hope of an answer. In *Being and Time* (1962: §26), Heidegger discusses two forms of caring for the other: first, freeing the other *from* one's care and, second, freeing the other *to* one's care. While dying for the other could be said to fall within the latter type, euthanasia can be identified with the first. By giving the other death, I free the other from his/her responsibility and (need to) care for him/herself. Instead of the death given to oneself (as was the case in the gift of my dying for the other), it is the death given to the other that constitutes the gift in euthanasia. Therefore, euthanasia is not only a manifestation of the gift of death, but also a manifestation of death *as* gift. Whereas in self-sacrifice what is given as a gift is *life* (one gives the other more time to live by giving one's own life away), in euthanasia, by contrast, one gives the other by putting him/her to death.

Both self-sacrifice and euthanasia – as discussed above – managed to suspend the strict economy of exchange. This is because one of the parties of potential exchange departs from the relation, and they do so precisely *because of* the gift: while self-sacrifice wipes the giver off the face of the earth, therefore leaving the ensuing counter-gift without a recipient, euthanasia leaves no one to return the gift received. However, doesn't the act of putting the other to death accomplish the irreversible, irrecoverable gift in a much more absolute, total sense than one

---

6   For the ethic of care, see for example Tronto (1993).

can ever achieve when dying for the other? While self-sacrifice makes the other in principal eternally grateful to me because of what I have done, euthanasia exterminates the circulation of the gift and ends all exchange in a much more decisive manner. Instead of receiving a symbolic reward or recompense for my act (by being rendered sacred, for example, as was what happened to Jonathan due to dying for his little brother in *The Brothers Lionheart*), in the act of deliberately killing another person, giving – insofar as life is valuable and good – cannot but always remain also a most horrible and morally problematic act. It is stripped off of all heroism. In most countries, to put another person to death, even at their request, is still murder.

Chapter 8
The Gift is Not One

The gift of paradoxes.

The Black Sheep (1996) by Italo Calvino tells a story of a country where all the inhabitants were thieves. Every night, everyone would leave home and break into a neighbour's house. And at dawn, they'd get back home with their loot only to find out that their own house had been robbed too. Since they all stole from each other, nobody got rich at the expense of others and nobody was poor either. Life went on smoothly and each lived happily together. Things remained so until one day an honest man came and moved into town. At night, instead of going out robbing, he'd just stay at home to read novels and have a smoke. So, when the thieves came they didn't dare to go in as they saw that the lights were on. The others explained him that even if he did not want to do anything himself, he should not prevent the others from stealing, for every night he stayed at home a family would have nothing to eat the following day. Honest as he was, the man did not object but to please the others he developed the habit of going out in the evening. However, instead of going robbing he only went to a bridge and watched the river flow below. And, as expected, when he returned home at dawn he found out that he had been robbed.

So, at the arrival of the honest man, everything changed. The internal balance of the community was shaken. As the honest man let the others steal everything he had without stealing from anybody, there was always someone who came home at dawn to find their house untouched – the house the honest man should have robbed. Because of this, after a while the ones who weren't being robbed became richer, while the ones who came to steal from the honest man's house found it was always already empty. And so they were left empty-handed. The ones who had become rich realised they did not want to steal anymore, but they started going to the bridge just like the honest man had and watch the water flow beneath. However, as they realised that they would probably be robbed while they stayed on the bridge, they paid some of the poor to go and rob for them and the poorest of the poor to defend their property from the others. This meant not only signing contracts, fixing salaries and percentages, but also setting up a police force and building prisons. Of course, they were still thieves the whole lot of them, apart from the honest man who had died of hunger very shortly after his move.

Isn't the system of relations depicted in *The Black Sheep* that of the gift itself? Isn't each person in the short story a parasite living off one's neighbour, and each also a donor or (absent) host? Of course, the primary conduct in the community is not conspicuous giving but stealing. Instead of expressing Christian virtues, the inhabitants are thieves. They raid their neighbour instead of loving them. However, what is interesting is that the internal equilibrium of the community is achieved in the story through action that one would at first sight expect to be destructive. In the story, stealing appears as the progenitor of order: the life of the community remains in equilibrium as long as each steals from the next person. In a country of thieves, stealing becomes one's duty, the communal *munus*. Thou shalt steal, for while thou are raiding thy neighbour thou leave thy home unoccupied for others to raid it. A full circle is accomplished when each parasites his/her neighbour, who in his/her turn parasites the next one, so that eventually we get to the last person who parasites the first. In fact, the perversity of the *kula* ring depicted by *The Black Sheep* is that each inhabitant is a giver only insofar as one is also a thief; one loves one's neighbour by raiding one's neighbour, another neighbour. Apart from the honest man, who is the true black sheep of the story, for he exempts himself from the communal duty, everyone is at once a donor and a thief; everyone both gives and takes. It is only when someone refuses to take that the equilibrium produced by the chain of gifts is broken. Indeed, in a system where everyone else is a parasite, the ultimate parasite is someone who does not parasite the others, for s/he simultaneously stops giving. To be sure, the honest man is not a parasite in the anthropological sense of the word, as the others are, but he is a parasite in the sense that the term is used in information theory: he interrupts the system and does not let it function.

The story of the country of thieves elucidates my main line of argument that runs throughout the book: that the gift is more original and principal than exchange. Even though the system is stable (until the arrival of the honest man, that is), there is no exchange in the parasitic cascade depicted by *The Black Sheep*. No one ever receives (steals) from the same neighbour who receives (steals) from oneself, which also means that no one ever gives to the same neighbour who gives to oneself, and therefore it is not possible to keep one's eye on one's property and act like a tradesperson. There is no reversal of direction in the system, but things always go in the same direction.

However, to be exact, not only is the gift more fundamental than exchange but, as I have argued in the preceding chapters, it is ultimately also incompatible with exchange. While exchange may be based on the gift, the gift itself must abhor exchange. Gratuitousness is absolutely necessary for the gift. Whenever what is given is given only 'in exchange', so to speak, the gift in and of the giving is annulled by definition. Nevertheless, it is not that the gift is completely separate from exchange. Gratuitousness and exchange are, rather, two dimensions of the gift that, as I have argued, at once presuppose and exclude each other. The gift of gift-exchange needs to be guided by the ideal of the pure, absolute gift (even if the latter can never be actualised in reality) and, from the other way around, even the gratuitous giving in pure loss seems to presuppose some selectivity, certain rights and duties, and at least some minimum amount of reciprocity (insofar as the givee has an effect upon the giver already by having been given the gift), if it is not to remain illusory, utopian and abstract. Thus, while I have stressed the primacy of giving over exchange throughout the book, this does not mean that the dimension of exchange would be irrelevant. It is an important dimension of the gift, but it makes up only one dimension; it is important not to reduce the gift to it.

It is not enough to focus on the giving alone to understand the gift also because of the fact that the actualisation of the gift depends not on giving alone, but on the given thing and on receiving alike. As noted earlier, I regard the compound structure of someone giving some-thing to someone else as vital and essential to the gift. Chapters 2–4 examined this structure most explicitly, with Chapter 2 focusing on giving ('someone gives …), Chapter 3 on the thing given (… some-thing …) and Chapter 4 on receiving and taking (… to someone other'). The following Chapters 5–7 explored further the im/possibility of the gift, each centring on a specific aspect. Chapter 5 tied the possibility of the gift with mutual foreignness of the donor and the donee (in terms of the gift of blood as a gift between strangers), and also examined how the pure gift may in fact exclude the recipient, despite the good intensions of the giver. Chapter 6, in turn, addressed the relation of the gift to gender, economy and value, and examined the articulation of the economy of the gift in terms of masculine and feminine. Like *The Beach* discussed in Chapter 4, the *Story of O* traced the trajectory of the gift in the passage into a certain social order. While in *The Beach* the gift was tied to the founding of a paradisiac community that at once excludes violence and is only made possible by violence, in the *Story of O* the uncalculated and innocent gift was exploited, appropriated and abused by the libertines, and resulted in a monstrous society exhibiting misogyny and gendered violence. Finally, Chapter 7 wove the possibility of the gift to death by examining the giving of death as a gift placed outside the economy of exchange.

Because in the book I have been interested in the gift above all as a philosophical concept, I have felt compelled to try to some extent to eliminate the empirical, since due to its messiness the empirical even presents an obstacle of some kind to recognising the abstract idea. Accordingly, when I have said 'the gift' in the singular, I haven't been referring to any empirically realised gifts in particular. On the contrary, I have above all evoked the abstract philosophical idea of the gift. (And in that sense, notwithstanding all the emphasis put on the gift-object, I have to admit that the book presents a dematerialised reasoning of some kind.) However, the paradox, of course, lies here in the fact that the abstract idea can be recognised only through the concrete, empirical occurrences of gifts – in this case through the imaginings, ideas, narratives and impressions about what the gift is in the stories, myths and fairy tales I have made use of. And indeed, empirically, as an everyday concept the gift should be understood in the plural, for there exist not only one but multiple kinds of things given as gifts. The gift is not one.[1] On the contrary, gifts may take several forms; the gift is indeed any object and no object. What is more, occasionally one and the same physical object may appear as different kinds of gifts in different relations. The apple discussed in the very beginning of the book is an example of this. It appeared, first, as a token of simultaneous love and rebellion (you and me against the world); second, as a

---

1　With regard to this, Aafke Komter (2007: 104) too has suggested that '*the* gift does not exist, in the sense that there is not one general, unequivocal and non-ambiguous sense in which to understand the gift'.

token of submission and gratitude to an authority; and, third, as a poisoned gift given with the purpose of harming the recipient. The bodies of women in the *Story of O* discussed in Chapter 6 provide another example. The bodies were offered as uncalculated, gratuitous gifts when the women gave themselves. However, when they circulated in the homo-social relations between the men, the women appeared as tokens of exchange bringing back profit.

As a very rough synthesis of the previous chapters, one could say that in general there are three basic types of gifts (which by no means exhaust all the heterogeneous gifts given and received out there in complex and diffuse relations between people): First, I spoke about gifts that are exchanged. Probably most gift-relationships are governed by the reciprocity rule, *quid pro quo*. The purpose of such gifts is to establish, stabilise, or nourish a relationship and express communality. While there is no explicit monetary price set on a gift, more often than not the recipient is nevertheless expected to repay in some way or another the gift once received. These gifts are not voluntary and spontaneous, but obligatory – they are captured by the term *munus*. The things circulating in the archaic tribes studied by anthropologists are a classical example of gifts of this type. For Mauss, the gifts exchanged in archaic societies presented themselves even as a kind of money: he ultimately regards gifts as means of discharging debts.

The paradox of these gifts, as I have tried to stress throughout the book, is that while most gifts assumedly do indeed appear within relations of exchange, it is highly questionable whether according to its concept there can be any gifts in exchange, that is, whether it is at all possible for gifts to be exchanged and remain gifts.[2] In other words, while it may be true that in gifts reciprocity is the rule, reciprocity nevertheless does not suffice to define what a gift is, but it rather tends to disqualify what makes an act of giving a gift. This is because there has to be something in the giving that does not return to the giving subject; otherwise there is no giving up and thus no gift involved. In the absence of a loss or sacrifice, the gift gets negated. Therefore, to be exact, the gifts appearing as tokens of more or less ceremonial exchange are more about *counter-gifts* than about gifts *per se*. They should be considered in terms of reciprocal recognition instead of giving (see Hénaff 2010).

Second, besides gifts that are exchanged (if there can be any in the strict sense of the term), in the preceding chapters I also – or rather primarily – spoke about gifts that are not exchanged, but given (up). Instead of returning to the giver some day either as such or in the form of symbolic recognition, gifts of this second type are abandoned and discharged. The etymological origin of these gifts

---

2   Or we might just need an altogether different concept to designate these offerings, although gift and present are the only ones we've got. Mauss makes the following remark in his essay *The Gift*: 'The terms that we have used – present and gift – are not themselves entirely exact. We shall, however, find no others' (Mauss 2008: 93).

is *donum*, not *munus*. The map Richard received from Daffy in the movie *The Beach* discussed in Chapter 4 is one example of the gifts of this kind, but they were exemplified also and more significantly by human blood (in Chapter 5), human body (in Chapter 6) and life (in Chapter 7). When given as gifts, human blood, human bodies and its parts, as well as life, are elevated above the economic sphere of equivalences, and in this sense they are rendered *sacred*. There's an absolute prohibition that forbids their commerce. They can be neither bought nor sold without degrading them (accordingly, the abuse and circulation of the bodies of women among the men in the *Story of O* easily feels like a sacrilege). Sacred objects escape the economy of gift and repayment, and they are alien to exchange. In giving them, the giver disposes and abandons something essentially of him/herself. What is given away is one's *propre*: one's own, something proper to or characteristic of oneself, something clean not to be dirtied by buying and selling (we find one exemplification of this in the hostility of many art world insiders toward the commodification or commercialisation of art). What is more, the sacred objects given tend to be irrecoverable and devoid of return. One does not, nay, cannot give for example one's life for the other by assuming that some day when one's own life needs to be saved the other will return the favour and act alike. Dying for the other is a gift that can be repaid in kind only in stories fabulating of an afterlife.

Whereas the paradox of *munus* gifts was that while most gifts probably appear as tokens of exchange and are therefore annulled as gifts, the paradox of *donum* gifts is that they present the absolute, pure form of the gift, but can hardly ever appear as gifts in reality. It is part of the paradoxical nature of the gift that while gratuitousness is the essence of the gift, whenever gratuitous giving appears, its essence is negated (Derrida 1994: 23). Derrida argued that, at the most extreme, the gift cannot be present as a gift, neither to the giver nor to the recipient. For when it is, the very moment the gift is per-ceived and re-ceived, it gets nullified as a gift, because already the very identification of the gift as a gift throws it back to the economy of exchange: the donee cannot help feeling obliged to pay back with gratitude, at the very least, and the donor makes a symbolic return payment to him/herself. So, not only does exchange deny the gift of its essence, but the very intention to give gratuitously suffices to do that. According to Derrida (1994: 23), this is because of the economic structure of consciousness: 'The simple consciousness of the gift right away sends itself back the gratifying image of goodness or generosity, of the giving-being who, knowing itself to be such, recognizes itself in a circular, specular fashion, in a sort of auto-recognition, self-approval, and narcissistic gratitude'.[3] For Derrida, as we have seen, it is only when one gives without knowing (thus tying the gift closely to secrecy), or when one gives one's life for the other that the gift may be possible.

---

3   For more on the 'economic logic of subjectivity' and the attempts to overcome it, see Moore (2011).

The third type of gift-objects was met above all in the potlatch, a gift-giving festival or a 'war of property', where the gift becomes a *weapon* and a stake in a game. While the potlatch is a culmination of the logic of exchange, it simultaneously points and aims towards the extermination of the system of exchange. Each giver in one's turn tries to end exchange by becoming the only one distributing and giving out anything anymore and by so doing humiliate and flatten one's rivals. In the potlatch, each giver aspires to be placed in the penultimate position, that is, of the one who is not obligated to give any more, but who only receives – the position of the parasite. The one in the penultimate position receives regard and is made permanently superior, since no one is able to repay him/her in kind. While from a material point of view the final offer makes apparent the inferiority and insufficiency of the word in relation to the thing, subjectively the word may in fact become of more worth than the thing for the last donor, as s/he was willing to dispense all one's riches for the sake of status and symbolic recognition. The potlatch is an enlightening example of the fact that, by giving, as Godelier (1999: 7) remarks, one not only shares what one has but also fights with what one has. 'To give is to show one's superiority, to be more, to be higher in rank, *magister*' (Mauss 2008: 95). Thereby, gifts may express not only solidarity but also superiority, even hostility. The gift may be both good and bad at the same time, they may both nourish and threaten relations – this ambiguity was expressed by the diversion of the gift into present and poison. The uncertainty about the goodness or badness of the gift was the most evident in the apple offered to Snow White by her evil stepmother, but ultimately no gift is able to cast it off entirely.

To me, each one of the aforementioned kinds of gifts – all of which have to be understood as ideal types of some sort: in reality things often appear muddled and more numerous – represents one of the 'social universals' specified by Serres as discussed in Chapter 3: exchange, the sacred and war. In other words, what I am suggesting is that the gift itself can assume the form of each of the three objects corresponding to the three universals depicted by Serres: it may appear as *merchandise, sacred object* and *weapon*. In this sense, the gift is truly any object and no object in particular.[4]

---

4   By drawing on Alan Page Fiske's (1991) model of four basic types of human relationships, Komter (2007), for example, has categorised the types of gifts into four in a manner that is in certain respects overlapping with the one just sketched. As the first category Komter mentions gifts that are given to enhance connectedness with other people. She specifies such gifts as 'markers of "community"'. The second category of gifts depicted by her is gifts that mark 'superiority in power relations'. As the third type she specifies gifts that serve 'equality matching'. They are gifts given in relationships where *quid pro quo* is the guiding principle and motivation for giving. In such relationships, gifts appear as 'tokens of balance'. Fourthly and finally, Komter draws attention to gifts given in the hope of profit. According to her, in relationships where people respond to others instrumentally, people give only to those they may expect immediate or future benefit. This last category of gifts Komter defines as 'tokens of utility or material (economic) value'. To some extent, the third type of gifts specified by me – gift as a weapon – arguably covers both the second and fourth types

As a final remark, I would like to emphasise that, while in the book I have explored the possibility and impossibility of the gift and argued for its ubiquity in relationships between human beings, I have done my best to keep faithful to a demand of neutrality as far as possible. This means that I have tried to avoid making any judgments of the gift as either good or bad, either desirable or unpleasant. The main reason for the bid for neutrality is the ambiguity of the gift itself. While gift-giving is widely and self-evidently celebrated as a virtue in our culture, with a whole array of positively valued characteristics from generosity to goodwill, altruism love, care and solidarity associated with it, the gift may also be harmful. In fact, it is not uncommon that we are uncertain, just as Snow White was when being offered the apple, about the goodness or badness of the gift. It is not always (or perhaps ever) possible to tell for sure, whether the gift is a present or poison, and this makes it dangerous. It is dangerous for the recipient and the giver alike. The gift is dangerous for the recipient, because it may degrade, humiliate, exclude and place in a position of permanent liability, or bring the donor annoyingly close, even create a bond that is so tight that it becomes suffocating (therefore it may occasionally be more tempting to refuse a gift than to accept it). And, from the other way around, because of the loss (by giving, one may lose everything) and of the possibility of parasitism and abuse involved, the gift is dangerous for the giver as well. What is more, the offering gesture always risks being turned down.

All in all, due to its ambiguity, there is no unequivocal sense in which to grasp the gift.[5] On the contrary, the gift can be understood only through *paradoxes*. They include, as we have seen throughout the book, the following:

- gifts are at once alienable and inalienable, expropriative and appropriative: they necessitate the giving up of something, and yet they remain symbolically inseparable from the giver (gift-giving thus simultaneously involves the loss of self and the expansion of self);
- while any gift tends to create a bond of some sort (with four elements involved in the elementary gift-relation), the gift must also be out of bonds;
- insofar as the rule is that gifts involve an expectation of reciprocity, exchange is the truth of the gift, but insofar as reciprocity and exchange annul the gift, it is a truth that the gift must escape and not make explicit;
- gifts involve obligations which are devoid of any corresponding rights;

– gift as a marker of superiority and gift as a means to draw profit – by Komter. Yet the first type – gift as merchandise or means of exchange – is even more comprehensive: in fact, it ultimately covers all of the categories of gifts sketched by Komter. Each and every type of gifts depicted by her is inscribed within exchange. And in a sense, this is perfectly understandable, for Komter seems to be interested not so much in the philosophical concept of the gift as in the actual gifts given by people within social relations. Nevertheless, her perspective tends to downplay conceptually any incompatibility between the gift and exchange.

5   See also Komter (2007: 104).

- the gift, as gratuitous and unconditional giving, is impossible, and yet there exist gifts, though without them having dissipated the impossibility;
- the gift is possible, but only insofar as it does not appear as a gift;
- in the absence of a sacrifice the gift negates itself, but insofar as one cannot sacrifice without knowing it, the gift seems to get annulled itself as soon as the subject becomes conscious of the sacrifice made;
- for there to be a gift, the given needs to be accepted by the other, and yet, as soon as acceptance is *given*, the gift is already within the order of reciprocity, and thus gets annulled;
- the gift is any object and no object;
- gift-giving is responsible only inasmuch as it is irresponsible, inclusive only inasmuch as exclusive;
- the gift is both good and bad, present and poison (the very best of gifts easily turn into the worst and the most dangerous).

The absolute gift is paradoxical in that it exhibits contradiction with what is possible. The pure gift is the impossible occurrence of gratuitous giving, the event of the impossible itself. It is what it cannot be. The pure gift may perhaps never be realised in reality, but even the gifts that actually take place in reality need to be given aspiration by it. One ought not to think ill of this paradoxical nature of the gift. That the gift cannot be captured unambiguously, as if in a flash of insight, is not a sign of a blind alley for thought, but I would claim that to a great extent the generosity of the gift as an object of study, its gift for thought, lies precisely there. As Kierkegaard (1985 [1844]: 37) put it in one of his best-known quotes: 'the paradox is the passion of thought, and the thinker without the paradox is like the lover without passion: a mediocre fellow'. At best, paradoxes invite to a leap of imagination and unfold the unseen and unimagined potential of concepts.

Bibliography

Abbas, Niran (2005) Introduction. In Abbas Niran (ed.) *Mapping Michel Serres*. Ann Arbor: University of Michigan Press.

Adorno, Theodor (2000) The Essay as Form. In Brian O'Connor (ed.) *The Adorno Reader*. Oxford: Blackwell.

Agamben, Giorgio (1998) *Homo Sacer. Sovereign Power and Bare Life*. Translated by Daniel Heller-Roazen. Stanford: Stanford University Press.

Amin, Ash (2011) *Land of Strangers*. Cambridge: Polity.

Appiah, Kwame Anthony (2006) *Cosmopolitanism: Ethics in a World of Strangers*. London and New York: W.W. Norton & Company.

Arppe, Tiina (1992) *Pyhän jäännökset – Ranskalaisia rajanylityksiä: Mauss, Bataille, Baudrillard* [*Sacred Remains – French Transgressions: Mauss, Bataille, Baudrillard*]. Helsinki: Tutkijaliitto.

Barad, Karen (2007) *Meeting the Universe Halfway: Quantum Physics and the Entanglement of Matter and Meaning*. Durham: Duke University Press.

Bataille, Georges (1984 [1933]) *Visions of Excess: Selected Writings 1927–1939*. Edited and translated by Allan Stoekl with Carl R. Lovitt and Donald M. Leslie, Jr. Minneapolis: University of Minnesota Press.

Baudrillard, Jean (1993 [1976]) *Symbolic Exchange and Death*. Translated by Iain Hamilton Grant. London: Sage.

Beauchamp, Tom (ed.) (1996) *Intending Death: The Ethics of Assisted Suicide and Euthanasia*. Englewood Cliffs, NJ: Prentice-Hall.

Beer, C.S. de (2010) Pragmatogony: The Impact of Things on Humans. *Phronimon* 11(2): 5–17.

Bennett, Jane (2010) *Vibrant Matter: A Political Ecology of Things*. Durham and London: Duke University Press.

Benveniste, Émile (1997 [1948–49]) Gift and Exchange in the Indo-European Vocabulary. Translated by Mary Elisabeth Meek. In Alan D. Schrift (ed.) *The Logic of the Gift. Toward an Ethic of Generosity*. New York and London: Routledge.

Blanchot, Maurice (1988) *The Unavowable Community*. Translated by Pierre Joris. Barrytown: Station Hill Press.

Blau, Peter (1964) *Exchange and Power in Social Life*. New York: Wiley.

Bourdieu, Pierre (1977) *Outline of a Theory of Practice*. Translated by Richard Nice. Cambridge: Cambridge University Press.

Bourdieu, Pierre (1990) *The Logic of Practice*. Translated by Richard Nice. Cambridge: Polity.

Bourdieu, Pierre (1997) Marginalia – Some Additional Notes on the Gift. In Alan D. Schrift (ed.) *The Logic of the Gift. Toward an Ethic of Generosity*. New York and London: Routledge.

Caillé, Alain (2005) Anti-utilitarianism, economics and the gift-paradigm. www. revuedumauss.com.fr/media/ACstake.pdf (Checked May 13 2013).

Calvino, Italo (1996) The Black Sheep. In Italo Calvino, *Numbers in the Dark and Other Stories*. Translated by Tim Parks. New York: Vintage Books.

Caplow, Theodore (1982a) *Middletown Families*. Minneapolis: University of Minnesota Press.

Caplow, Theodore (1982b) Christmas gifts and kin networks. *American Sociological Review* 47: 383–92.

Caplow, Theodore (1984) Rule Enforcement without Visible Means: Christmas Gift Giving in Middletown. *American Journal of Sociology* 89(6): 1306–23.

Cheal, David (1988) *The Gift Economy*. London and New York: Routledge.

Cixous, Hélène (1986) *The Newly Born Woman*. Translated by Betsy Wing. Minneapolis: University of Minnesota Press.

Coole, Diana and Frost, Samantha (eds) (2010) *New Materialisms. Ontology, Agency, and Politics*. Durham and London: Duke University Press.

Davis, John (1996) An anthropologist's view of exchange. *Social Anthropology* 4(3): 213–26.

Deleuze, Gilles (1991) *Bergsonism*. Translated by Hugh Tomlinson and Barbara Habberjam. New York: Zone Books.

Deleuze, Gilles and Guattari, Félix (1987) *A Thousand Plateaus: Capitalism and Schizophrenia*. Translated by Brian Massumi. Minneapolis and London: University of Minnesota Press.

Deleuze, Gilles and Guattari, Félix (1994) *What Is Philosophy?* Translated by Hugh Tomlinson and Graham Burchell. New York: Columbia University Press.

Derrida, Jacques (1994) *Given Time: I. Counterfeit Money*. Translated by Peggy Kamuf. Chicago and London: The University of Chicago Press.

Derrida, Jacques (1995) *The Gift of Death*. Translated by David Wills. Chicago and London: Chicago University Press.

Derrida, Jacques (2000) *Of Hospitality*. Translated by Rachel Bowlbry. Stanford, CA: Stanford University Press.

Derrida, Jacques and Marion, Jean-Luc (1999) On the Gift: A Discussion between Jacques Derrida and Jean-Luc Marion. Moderated by Richard Kearney. In John D. Caputo Michael J. Scanlon (eds) *God, The Gift, and Postmodernism*. Bloomington, IN: Indiana University Press.

Descartes, René (1983 [1644]) *Principia philosophiae (Principles of Philosophy)*. Translated by Valentine Rodger and Reese P. Miller. Dordrecht: Reidel.

Donati Pierpaolo (2003) Giving and Social Relations: The Culture of Free Giving and its Differentiation Today. *International Review of Sociology* 13(2): 243–72.

Douglas, Mary (1978) *The World of Goods*. London: Basic Books and Penguin Books.

Douglas, Mary (2008) Foreword: No free Gifts. In Marcel Mauss *The Gift. The form and reason for exchange in archaic societies*. London and New York: Routledge.

Elder-Vass, Dave (2013) The Moral Economy of Digital Gifts. Unpublished paper.

Esposito, Roberto (2010) *Communitas: The Origin and Destiny of Community*. Translated by Timothy Campbell. Stanford, CA: Stanford University Press.

Esposito, Roberto (2011) *Immunitas: The Protection and Negation of Life*. Cambridge: Polity.

Esposito, Roberto and Paparcone, Anna (2006) Interview. *Diacritics* 36(2): 49–56.

Feifer, Maxine (1985) *Going Places*. London: Macmillan.

Firth, Raymond (1959) *Economics in the New Zealand Maori*. Wellington: R.E. Owen.

Fischer E. and Arnold S.J. (1990) More than a labour of love: Gender roles and Christmas gift shopping. *Journal of Consumer Research* 17: 333–45.

Fiske, Alan Page (1991) *Structures of Social Life: The Four Elementary Forms of Human Relations*. New York: The Free Press.

Foucault, Michel (2000) Different Spaces. In Foucault, *Aesthetics, Method, and Epistemology*. Edited by James Faubion. Penguin Books: London.

Frazer, Sir James (1976 [1890]) *The Golden Bough: A Study in Magic and Religion*. New York: Macmillan.

Frow, John (1997) *Time and Commodity Culture: Essays in Cultural Theory and Postmodernity*. Oxford: Clarendon.

Gasché, Rodolphe (1997) Heliocentric Exchange. In Alan D. Schrift (ed.) *The Logic of the Gift. Toward an Ethic of Generosity*. New York and London: Routledge.

Girard, René (1979) *Violence and the Sacred*. Translated by Patrick Gregory. Baltimore and London: The John Hopkins University Press.

Godbout, Jacques T. (1992) *L'espirit du don*. Paris: Éditions La Découverte.

Godbout, Jacques T. and Caillé, Alain (1998) *The World of the Gift*. Translated by Donald Winkler. Montreal and Kingston: McGill-Queen's University Press.

Godelier, Maurice (1999) *The Enigma of the Gift*. Translated by Nora Scott. Cambridge: Polity.

Goodwin, Cathy, Smith, Kelly L. and Spiggle, Susan (1990) Gift giving: Consumer motivation and the gift purchase process. *Advances in Consumer Research* 17: 690–698.

Gouldner, Alvin (1960) The Norm of Reciprocity. *American Sociological Review* 25(2): 161–78.

Graeber, David (2012) *Debt: The First 5,000 Years*. Brooklyn, New York: Melville House.

Gregory, Chris A. (1982) *Gifts and Commodities*. London: Academic Press.

Hacking, Ian (2002) *Historical Ontology*. Cambridge, MA: Harvard University Press.

Healy, Kieran (2006) *Last Best Gifts. Altruism and the Market for Human Blood and Organs*. Chicago and London: University of Chicago Press.

Heidegger, Martin (1962) *Being and Time*. Translated by John Macquarrie and Edward Robinson. Oxford: Blackwell.

Heidegger, Martin (1971) The Thing. Translated by Alfred Hofstader. In *Poetry, Language, Thought*. New York: Harper & Row.

Heidegger, Martin (1972) *On Time and Being*. New York: Harper & Row.

Heidegger, Martin (2002) The Origin of the Work of Art. In *Off the Beaten Track*. Edited and translated by Julian Young and Kenneth Haynes. Cambridge: Cambridge University Press.

Hénaff, Marcel (20109 *The Price of Truth: Gift, Money, and Philosophy*. Translated by Jean-Luc Morhange. Stanford: Stanford University Press.

Houellebecq, Michel (2012) *The Map and the Territory*. Translated by Gavin Bowd. New York: Knopf.

Hubert, Henri and Mauss, Marcel (1964 [1899] *Sacrifice: its Nature and Function*. Translated by W.D. Halls. London: Routledge.

Hyde, Lewis (2007 [1983]) *The Gift: How the Creative Spirit Transforms the World*. Edinburgh: Canongate.

Ingold, Tim (2011) *Being Alive. Essays on Movement, Knowledge and Description*. London and New York: Routledge.

Irigaray, Luce (1985) *This Sex Which Is Not One*. Translated by Catherine Porter with Carolyn Burke. Ithaca: Cornell University Press.

Joas, Hans (2001) The Gift of Life. The Sociology of Religion in Talcott Parsons' Late Work. *Journal of Classical Sociology* 1(1): 127–41.

Johnson, Vida T. and Petrie, Graham (1994) *The Films of Andrei Tarkovsky: A Visual Fugue*. Bloomington: Indiana University Press.

Jokinen, Eeva and Veijola, Soile (2011) Time to hostess. Reflections on borderless care. In Claudio Minca and Tim Oakes (eds) *Real Tourism: Practice, Care, and Politics in Contemporary Travel Culture*. London and New York: Routledge.

Karpik, Lucien (2010) *Valuing the Unique: The Economics of Singularities*. Translatd by Nora Scott. Princeton, NJ: Princeton University Press.

Kierkegaard, Søren (1985 [1844]) *Philosophical Fragments*. Edited and translated by Howard V. Hong and Edna H. Hong. Princeton, NJ: Princeton University Press.

Komter Aafke E. (2005) *Social Solidarity and the Gift*. Cambridge: Cambridge University Press.

Komter Aafke E. (2007) Gifts and Social Relations: The Mechanisms of Reciprocity. *International Sociology* 22(1): 93–107.

Latour, Bruno (1986) The powers of association. In John Law (ed) *Power, Action and Belief: A New Sociology of Knowledge?* London: Routledge & Kegan Paul.

Latour, Bruno (1993) *We Have Never Been Modern*. Cambridge, MA: Harvard University Press.

Latour, Bruno (1996) *Aramis or the love of technology*. Cambridge, MA: Harvard University Press.

Latour, Bruno (1999a) *Pandora's Hope. Essays on the Reality of Science Studies*. Cambridge, MA: Harvard University Press.

Latour, Bruno (1999b) On Recalling ANT. In John Law and John Hassard (eds) *Actor Network Theory and After*. Oxford and Keele: Blackwell and the Sociological Review.

Latour, Bruno (2005) *Reassembling the Social. An Introduction to Actor-Network-Theory*. Oxford and New York: Oxford University Press.

Latour, Bruno (2010a) *On the Modern Cult of the Factish Gods*. Durham and London: Duke University Press.

Latour, Bruno (2010b) *Cogitamus. Six letters sur les humanités scientifiques*. Paris: La Découverte.

Latour, Bruno (2013) *An Inquiry into Modes of Existence: An Anthropology of the Moderns*. Translated by Catherine Porter. Cambridge, MA: Harvard University Press.

Lehtonen, Turo-Kimmo (2008) *Aineellinen yhteisö* [*Material Community*]. Helsinki: Tutkijaliitto.

Lehtonen, Turo-Kimmo (2012) Latourin disipliini [Latour's discipline]. *Tiede & edistys* 37(2): 180–3.

Levinas, Emmanuel (1979 [1961]) *Totality and Infinity: An Essay on Exteriority*. Translated by Alphonso Lingis. Hague, Boston and London: Martinus Nijhoff.

Lévi-Strauss, Claude (1969 [1949]) *The Elementary Structures of Kinship*. Translated by James Harle Bell, John Richard von Sturmer and Rodney Needham. Revised edition. Boston: Beacon.

Lévi-Strauss, Claude (1987 [1950]) *Introduction to the Work of Marcel Mauss*. Translated by Felicity Baker. London: Routledge & Kegan Paul.

Lightfoot, Geoff (2008) Nothing Beats a 2x2 Matrix: a Short Commentary on George Ritzer's 'Globalization of Nothing'. *Ephemera* 8(4): 371–83.

Lindgren, Astrid (2009 [1973]) *The Brothers Lionheart*. Translated by Joan Tate. Oxford: Oxford University Press.

Locke, John (1979 [1689]) *An Essay Concerning Human Understanding*. Oxford: Clarendon Press.

Luhmann, Niklas (1977) *Funktion der Religion*. Frankfurt am Main: Suhrkamp.

MacCannell, Dean (1989) *The Tourist. A New Theory of the Leisured Class*. New York: Schocken Books.

Maffesoli, Michel (1996) *The Contemplration of the World: Figures of Community Style*. Translated by Susan Manuel. Minneapolis: University of Minnesota Press.

Malinowski, Bronislaw (1961 [1922]) *Argonauts of the Western Pacific*. New York: Dutton.

Marion, Jean-Luc (2002) *Being Given. Toward a Phenomenology of Givenness*. Translated by Jeffrey L. Kosky. Stanford, CA: Stanford University Press.

Marion, Jean-Luc (2011) *The Reason of the Gift*. Translated by Stephen E. Lewis. Charlottesville and London: University of Virginia Press.

Marshall, Lorna (1961) Sharing, Talking, and Giving: Relief of Social Tensions Among Kung Busmen. *Africa* 31(3): 231–249.

Marx, Karl (1975 [1867]) *Capital: Critique of Political Economy. Vol. 1*. In Karl Marx and Friedrich Engels *Collected Works*. New York: International Publishers.

Mauss, Marcel (1973) The Techniques of the body. *Economy and Society* 2(1): 70–88.

Mauss, Marcel (1997 [1924]) Gift, Gift. Translated by Koen Decoster. In Alan D. Schrift (ed) *The Logic of the Gift. Toward an Ethic of Generosity*. New York and London: Routledge.

Mauss, Marcel (2008 [1924]) *The Gift. The form and reason for exchange in archaic societies*. Translated by W.D. Walls. London and New York: Routledge.

McAndrew, Siobhan (*2010) Religious faith and contemporary attitudes*. In Allison Park, John Curtice, Katarina Thomson, Miranda Phillips, Elizabeth Clery and Sarah Butt (eds) *British Social Attitudes: 2009–2010*. The 26th Report. London: Sage.

Miller, Daniel (1995a) *Acknowledging Consumption: A Review of New Studies*. London: Routledge.

Miller, Daniel (1995b) Consumption and commodities. *Annual Review of Anthropology* 24: 141–61.

Molière (2008) *Don Juan and Other Plays*. Oxford World Classics. Translated by George Graveley and Ian Maclean. Oxford: Oxford University Press.

Moliterno, Gino (2001) Zarathustra's gift in Tarkovsky's The Sacrifice. In *Screening the Past*, Issue 12.

Moore, Gerald (2011) *Politics of the Gift: Exchanges in Poststructuralism*. Edinburgh: Edinburgh University Press.

Mortelmans, Dimitri and Sinardet, Dave (2004) Reflecting Culture and Society? Norms and Rules Governing Gift-Giving Practices. *The Netherlands Journal of Social Sciences* 40(2): 176–201.

Nietzsche, Friedrich (1968) *The Will to Power*. Translated by Walter Kaufman and R.J. Hollingdale. New York: Vintage.

Nietzsche, Friedrich (1974) *The Gay Science*. Translated by Walter Kaufman. New York: Vintage.

Nietzsche, Friedrich (1999) *Thus Spoke Zarathustra. A Book for All and None*. Translated by Thomas Common. Mineola, New York: Dover Publications.

Offer, Avner (1997) Between the gift and the market: the economy of regard. *Economic History Review* L(3): 450–476.

Olsson, Gunnar (2007) *Abysmal. A Critique of Catrographic Reason*. Chicago and London: Chicago University Press.

O'Neill, John (1999) What Gives (with Derrida)? *European Journal of Social Theory* 2(2): 131–45.

Otnes, Cele and Beltrami, Richard Francis (eds) (1996) *Gift Giving: A Research Anthology*. Bowling Green, Ohio: Bowling Green State University Press.

Pajunen, Tero (2012) Wikipedia altruismin välineenä? [Wikipedia as a means of altruism?] The Department of Social Research/Sociology, The University of Turku (Unpublished Bachelor's thesis).

Park, Alison and Clery, Elizabeth (2008) *Assisted dying and decision making at the end of life*. London: NATCEN, National Centre for Social Research.

Parsons, Talcott; Fox, Renée C. and Lidz Victor M. (1978) The 'Gift of Life' and Its Reciprocation. In Talcott Parsons *Action Theory and the Human Condition*. New York and London: The Free Press.

Paulhan, Jean (1972) A Slave's Revolt. An Essay on *The Story of O*. In Pauline Réage *Story of O*. London: Corgi Books.

Poster, Mark (1988) Introduction. In Jean Baudrillard *Selected Writings*. Edited by Mark Poster. Stanford, CA: Stanford University Press.

Pyyhtinen, Olli (2010) *Simmel and the Social*. Basingstoke and New York: Palgrave.

Pyyhtinen, Olli (2012) Life, Death and Individuation: Simmel on the Problem of Life Itself. *Theory, Culture & Society* 29(7/8): 78–100.

Pyyhtinen, Olli and Tamminen, Sakari (2007) Inhimillistä, aivan liian inhimillistä? Foucault, Latour ja ihmistieteiden antropologinen uni' [Human, All Too Human? Foucault, Latour and the Anthropological Sleep of the Human Sciences] *Tiede & edistys* 3(32): 229–51.

Pyyhtinen, Olli and Tamminen, Sakari (2011) We have never been only human: Foucault and Latour on the question of the *anthropos*. *Anthropological Theory* 11(2): 135–52.

Réage, Pauline (1972 [1954]) *Story of O*. London: Corgi Books.

Rehn, Alf (2001) *Electronic Potlatch – a study on new technologies and primitive economic behaviours*. Stockholm: Kungliga Tekniska Högskolan.

Sade, Marquise de (1990) *Justine, Philosophy in the Bedroom, and Other Writings*. Translated by Richard Seaver and Austryn Wainhouse. New York: Grove Press.

Sahlins ([1974] 2004) *Stone Age Economics*. London and New York: Routledge.

Schrift, Alan D. (1997) Introduction: Why Gift? In Alan D. Schrift (ed.) *The Logic of the Gift. Toward an Ethic of Generosity*. New York and London: Routledge.

Schwartz, Barry (1967) The Social Psychology of the Gift. *American Journal of Sociology* 73(1): 1–11.

Serres, Michel (1982) *Hermes: Literature, Science, Philosophy*. Edited by Josué V. Harari and David F. Bell. Baltimore and London: John Hopkins University Press.

Serres, Michel (1991) *Rome: The Book of Foundations*. Translated by Felicia McCarren. Stanford, CA: Stanford University Press.

Serres, Michel (1994) *Atlas*. Paris: Juliard.

Serres, Michel (1995a) *Angels: A Modern Myth*. Translated by Francis Cowper. Paris: Flammarion.

Serres, Michel (1995b) *Genesis*. Translated by Geneviève James and James Nielson. Michigan: The University of Michigan Press.

Serres, Michel (1995c) *The Natural Contract*. Translated by Elizabeth MacArthur and William Paulson. Ann Arbor: University of Michigan Press.

Serres, Michel (1997) *The Troubadour of Knowledge*. Edited by Sheila Faria Glaser and William Paulson. Michigan: University of Michigan Press.

Serres, Michel (2007) *The Parasite*. Translated by Lawrence R. Schehr. Minneapolis: University of Minnesota Press.

Serres, Michel (2008) *The Five Senses. A Philosophy of Mingled Bodies*. Translated by Margaret Sankey and Peter Cowley. London and New York: Continuum.

Serres, Michel (2011) *Malfeasance. Appropriation through Pollution?* Translated by Anne-Marie Feenberg-Dibon. Stanford, CA: Stanford University Press.

Serres, Michel with Latour, Bruno (1995) *Conversations on Science, Culture, and Time*. Translated by R. Lapidus. Michigan: University of Michigan Press.

Shaviro, Steven (2010) *Post-Cinematic Affect*. Winchester and Washington: zero books.

Simmel, Georg (1950) Faithfulness and Gratitude. In Kurt Wolff (ed.) *The Sociology of Georg Simmel*. New York: Free Press.

Simmel, Georg (1965) The Poor. Translated by Claire Jacobsen. *Social Problems* 13(2): 118–40.

Simmel, Georg (1992 [1908]) *Soziologie*. Georg Simmel Gesamtausgabe Band 11. Frankfurt am Main: Suhrkamp.

Simmel, Georg (2001 [1909]) Psychologie der Koketterie. In *Georg Simmel Gesamtausgabe Band 12: Aufsätze und Abhandlungen 1909–1918, Band I*. Frankfurt am Main: Suhrkamp.

Simmel, Georg (2004) *The Philosophy of Money*. Third enlarged edition. Translated by D. Frisby and T. Bottomore. London and New York: Routledge.

Sinardet, Dave and Mortelmans, Dimitri (2005) Preserving the Front Stage: Causes, Consequences and the Symbolic Meaning of Failed Gift Exchanges. *International Review of Modern Sociology* 31(2): 251–75.

Stiegler, Bernard (1998) *Technics and Time, Vol. 1: The Fault of Epimetheus*. Translated by Richard Beardsworth and George Collins. Stanford, CA: Stanford University Press.

Strathern, Marilyn (1988) *The Gender of the Gift*. Berkeley: University of California Press.

Strathern, Marilyn (1996) Cutting the Network. *The Journal of the Royal Anthropological Institute* 2(3): 517–55.

Strick, Philip (1987) Offret (The Sacrifice). *Monthly film bulletin* 54(636): 7–8.

Thornton, Sarah (2008) *Seven Days in the Art World*. London: Granta.

Titmuss, Richard (1970) *The Gift Relationship. From Human Blood to Social Policy*. London: George Allen & Unwin.

Tolstoy, Leo (2006) *The Death of Ivan Ilyich*. Translated by A. Briggs. London: Penguin Books.

Tronto, Joan C. (1993) *Moral Boundaries. A Political Argument for an Ethic of Care*. London: Routledge.

Tylor, Edward Burnett (1871) *Primitive Culture: Researches into the Development of Mythology, Philosophy, Religion, Art, and Custom*. London: Bradbury, Evans and Co.

Veijola, Soile and Jokinen, Eeva (1994) The Body in Tourism. *Theory, Culture & Society* 11(3): 125–51.

Veijola, Soile and Jokinen, Eeva (2008) Towards a Hostessing Society? Mobile Arrangements of Gender and Labour. *NORA – Nordic Journal of Feminist and Gender Research* 16(3): 166–81.

Velthuis, Olav (2005) *Talking Prices. Symbolic Meanings of Prices on the Market for Contemporary Art*. Princeton, NJ: Princeton University Press.

Waldfogel, Joel (1993) The Deadweight Loss of Christmas. *American Economic Review* 83(5): 1328–36.

Weiner, Annette (1976) *Women of Value, Men of Renown: New Perspectives in Trobriand Exchange*. Austin: University of Texas Press.

Weiner, Annette (1992) *Inalienable Possessions: The Paradox of Keeping-while-Giving*. Berkeley: University of California Press.

Whitehead, Alfred North (1933) *Adventures of Ideas*. Cambridge: Cambridge University Press.

Whitehead, Alfred North (1964 [1920]) *The Concept of Nature*. Cambridge: Cambridge University Press.

Whitehead, Alfred North (1978 [1929]) *Process and Reality*. Corrected edition. New York: Free Press.

Zelizer, Viviana (1994) *The Social Meaning of Money. Pin Money, Paychecks, Poor Relief & Other Currencies*. New York: Basic Books.

Žižek, Slavoj (2009) The Reality of the Virtual (Part 1 of 7). YouTube. <http://www.youtube.com/watch?v=NXi46W51104>. Checked 13 June 2013.

Žižek, Slavoj (2006) *How to Read Lacan*. London: Granta Books.

Index